Numenéra™
BREAK THE HORIZON

CREDITS

Designer	Bruce R. Cordell
Additional Writing	Monte Cook and Sean K. Reynolds
Creative Director	Monte Cook
Managing Editor	Teri Litorco
Editor	Charlotte Irrgang, Irrgardless
Proofreader	Ray Vallese
Art Director	Bear Weiter
Layout	Vee Hendro
Cover Artist	Bruce Brenneise

Cartographer

Hugo Solis

Artists

Jacob Atienza, Bruce Brenneise, Vincent Coviello, Biagio D'Alessandro, Michele Giorgi, Alexander Gustafson, Raph Herrera Lomotan, Anton Kagounkin Magdalina, Federico Musetti, Mirco Paganessi, Angelo Peluso, Roberto Pitturru, Scott Purdy, Riccardo Rullo, Nick Russell, Martin de Diego Sádaba, Sam Santala, Audre "Charamath" Schutte, Joe Slucher, Lee Smith, Ben Wootten, Kieran Yanner

MonteCook
Games

TABLE OF CONTENTS

Navigating This Book   4

PART 1: ROAMING THE WORLD   5
Chapter 1: Why Travel?   6
Chapter 2: Equipment for Travel   11
Chapter 3: Mounts & Commonplace Vehicles   19
Chapter 4: Vehicles & Travel Devices of the Prior Worlds   26
Chapter 5: Comprehensive Travel Option Listing   40

PART 2: STRANGERS ON THE PATH   55
Chapter 6: Creatures   56
Chapter 7: NPCs   72

PART 3: WHERE THE SYNTH MEETS THE ROAD   77
Chapter 8: Encounters and Hazards Along the Way   78
Chapter 9: Travel-themed GM Intrusions   110

PART 4: ADVENTURE BECKONS   113
Chapter 10: The Roughest Day   114
Chapter 11: Travelers Never Did Lie   132

2. The main body...

NAVIGATING THIS BOOK

Corridors, page 53

Bezdel, page 21

You fly high above everything, mounted on a red-eyed biomechanical beast with transdimensional and telepathic senses (perhaps a bezdel). Your privileged perch provides a wide overview of *Break the Horizon*.

This book is all about travel in the Steadfast, Beyond, and much farther, including distant galaxies and other dimensions. It adds greater levels of mobility to your Numenera campaign, with options and equipment that let you travel longer and explore more—including all the weirdness and prior-world wonder you might expect from travel options in the Ninth World.

Intrigued, you unfold a colorful map scribed by Aeon Priests purporting to be a guide. And indeed, the document describes many strange things you might find as you venture forward.

Encounters and Hazards Along the Way, page 78

Part 1: Roaming the World contains several chapters, beginning with Why Travel?, detailing potential travel seeds for player characters (PCs) and nonplayer characters (NPCs) alike. The next few chapters introduce new travel equipment, mounts and commonplace vehicles, and vehicles and travel devices from prior worlds. Some of these, the PCs might be able to purchase if they find the right purveyor. Others are things characters might find or salvage (or craft, for Wright characters).

Why Travel?, page 6

Be on the lookout for in-world advice sections from The Safe Wayfarer Travel Guide. Consider reading them to your players (or provide pieces here and there as printed documents, such as a broadsheet or pamphlet created by the Amber Gleaners). Some of this advice could make all the difference when going someplace strange. At minimum, each one provides the seeds for an encounter or two. In fact, most have ties to specific options presented in other parts of the book.

Finally, Part 1 concludes with a comprehensive listing of all the travel options presented in every Numenera title to date.

Amber Gleaners, page 245

For example, you can easily look up the invisible corridors that lace the Ninth World's vast ocean, and much, much more.

Part 2: Strangers on the Path includes a bestiary of new creatures you might encounter during your Ninth World travels. Plus, a chapter detailing several NPCs who also get around the Steadfast and the Beyond, one or two of whom characters might meet.

Part 3: Where the Synth Meets the Road includes a lexicon of travel-themed GM intrusions plus the expansive chapter called Encounters and Hazards Along the Way, containing multiple single encounters and hazards to sprinkle into the game that PCs might experience along the way to someplace else.

Part 4: Adventure Beckons contains two full adventures, either of which could stand alone, but both are designed to be layered into a campaign where PCs are already on the road for something else when something interesting happens . . .

Numenera Discovery   *Numenera Destiny*

Throughout this book, you'll see page references to various items accompanied by these two symbols. These are page references to *Numenera Discovery* and *Numenera Destiny*, respectively, where you can find additional details about that rule, ability, creature, or concept. Often, it will be necessary to look up the reference to find information you need. Other times, it's not necessary, but looking it up can deepen your experience and understanding of the game and the setting.

PART 1: ROAMING THE WORLD

Chapter 1: Why Travel?   6

Chapter 2: Equipment for Travel   11

Chapter 3: Mounts & Commonplace Vehicles   19

Chapter 4: Vehicles & Travel Devices of the Prior Worlds   26

Chapter 5: Comprehensive Travel Option Listing   40

WHY TRAVEL?

Most people of the Ninth World don't have a grasp of its expanse. They are isolated, never traveling more than a few miles from where they were born. This gives them a narrow view of existence and how the world works. They don't want or need to learn any differently because the dangers that separate communities are significant enough that attempting to bridge that isolation often leads to death.

Consequently, many communities are insular. Most individuals have a wide knowledge base—or at least a trove of hearsay and gossip—regarding other people in the community: who's up to what, where one might go to get a particular kind of service, what those in power are planning, the nature of upcoming events or threats, and so on.

On the other hand, knowledge of anything beyond the community drops quickly to unreliable rumor. Residents are more likely to call the nearest tribe of abhumans "demons" than their actual name. There are likely tall tales about the dangers and legendary locations suspected to lie just beyond the community's farms and hunting grounds (though some such tales likely have a grain of truth to them). Similarly, lots of communities are cut off and may not even know of any others—or if they do, it's only as funny stories told by the rare traveler moving through. That said, many people have heard of the Aeon Priests and the Amber Pope, but where exactly such people are based is a much fuzzier concept.

REASONS TO TRAVEL

Despite the dangers, there are always people willing to risk breaking the horizon by taking a trip. They may be driven to do so by hunger, war, trade, or—as in the case of many PCs— a desire to explore the unknown.

Besides a yearning to see distant shores, PCs are often motivated to travel for more utilitarian reasons, especially if they have ties to family or other NPCs or are motivated by the needs of others. The following section provides several such travel inspirations that can either motivate the PCs directly or motivate NPCs, who then ask the PCs to help them successfully complete their own particular trips.

The following section is an overview of many reasons for PCs to travel. At the most basic level, you can treat the various reasons for travel as adventure seeds.

In addition, any of these reasons to travel could be treated as a component of long-term play. To aid in using these as long-term tasks, each travel opportunity is presented as a task with a time component. In addition, each travel opportunity provides an example reward that the PCs might gain if they complete the trip.

Sometimes long-term play is an activity that just a few of the PCs do while other PCs are involved in other time-consuming tasks like crafting. However, there's no reason all the characters can't take on the same long-term task. Doing so certainly increases the chance of success since travel to distant locations is usually dangerous.

Long-Term Play, page 324

Long-Term Tasks, page 324

Aeon Priest, page 264

Amber Pope, page 133

A PC can generally engage in up to two long-term tasks simultaneously, assuming they are not physically impossible to accomplish at the same time.

ADVENTURE LIKELY ALONG THE WAY

As is usual for long-term tasks, a trip might well be interrupted so PCs can deal with an unexpected encounter or hazard along the way or because some other opportunity demands the PCs' immediate attention. Interrupting long-term tasks does not usually affect the overall goal of the trip unless PCs choose not to continue after the interruption, or are prevented from doing so.

Hunt Animals for Food (1 month): During specific seasons of the year, especially valuable game animals—such as hulking but slow-moving gniwaks, silver-winged cappiarads, or the swift but delicious yioran—are known to move through an area several days' travel away from a camp or established community. If characters wish to take advantage of this special hunting season, they must travel to that distant location, set up a base camp, and spend a couple of weeks hunting, dressing, and preserving the game they bag, then return. During that time (in addition to any other chance encounters they may face along the way), they may have to deal with other, more dangerous predators seeking the same game.

If PCs complete this task, they can increase food stores for a small community by 1 day per PC who participated. Most people value this food highly for its taste and somewhat scarce nature. PCs seeking payment for their contribution may be paid about 60 shins each or rewarded with a couple of cyphers for the group.

Pilgrimage (1+ month): Even those who rarely or never travel abroad might be willing to pick up and go to a relatively distant location. They may wish to witness an important spiritual event, location, person, or structure, or go in search of an expanded understanding of themselves or a higher good. Almost every region offers residents the opportunity to make such a journey at least once in their lifetimes, including the following examples.

- A pilgrimage to the Temple of the Wellspring in Cheloh, the City of the Sacred Veil, in Lostrei.
- The Wandering Walk is a pilgrimage route through the Ninth World. No one knows the exact length of the Wander, nor can anyone seem to point to its exact beginning or end.
- A pilgrimage to a distant city called Nevoluin to undergo gradual transformation by nests of dried reeds and plants (called kodestri) built by "invisible spirits."
- A religious pilgrimage to the island of Meaqos to surf the sacred whirlpool that appears regularly. Celebrants throw in offerings, allow pilgrims to throw themselves into the swirling water (they say they are following an ancient text to enter the "Hollow World"), and, on occasion, welcome "avatars" of the Great God Below who sometimes emerge from the bay.

Encounters and Hazards Along the Way, page 78

Interrupting Long-Term Tasks, page 325

Gniwak: *level 2; health 20*

Cappiarad: *level 1; flies a short distance each round*

Yioran: *level 3; moves a long distance each round*

Titanothaur: *level 10*

Edge of the Sun is a Numenera supplement that includes an adventure called "The Sun Doth Move" that features the PCs' delivery of a vital message to the Amber Pope.

There are many who speculate that the Wander is actually a circle that encloses the whole of the Ninth World and that some, especially those with enhancements or otherworldly attributes, have been trekking its eternal loop since before recorded time.

Long-Term Tasks, page 324

Encounters and Hazards Along the Way, page 78

• A pilgrimage of the sick and suffering to a quiet village called Sleeping Rock. The village sometimes experiences moments of temporal instability, called skips, that can cure those suffering from an illness.

If PCs complete a pilgrimage, whether for their own sakes or as guardians/guides of the actual pilgrims, each character gains 1 XP (more if it was especially fraught or long-lasting) from the increased self-knowledge also gained.

OTHER LONG-TERM TASKS REQUIRING TRAVEL

Numenera Destiny introduces several long-term tasks. Many of them have a travel component, including the following.

• Discover a New Area of Interest (1 month)
• Establish Satellite Settlement (time varies)
• Scavenge Iotum (1 month)
• Treat With a Neighbor Community (1 month)
• Prospect for Iotum (1 month)
• Find Specific Iotum (1 month)
• Develop External Networks (1 month)
• Find or Develop a Specific Plan (1 month)

Deliver a Message (1+ months): Whether accompanying other couriers or serving in that role themselves, important messages to distant locations are common reasons to travel. Specific kinds of messages include:

• Valuable intelligence must be delivered to a distant group of defenders regarding enemy movements that are not widely known but which could make the difference in an upcoming decisive battle.
• An NPC crafter needs a valuable iotum component delivered to a distant compatriot so they can repair an important installation vital to that community's survival. For example, it filters out radiation or poison in the atmosphere or water, keeps a dimensional rift safely shut, allows a particular type of crop to grow, etc.
• In a distant clave somewhere in the Beyond, an Aeon Priest has made a momentous discovery with ramifications that could envelop the entire world

(i.e., a plague of titanothaurs is arising, dangerous felons of a prior world were accidentally released, a mysterious artifact at the edge of the sun is malfunctioning, and so on). They want the message delivered to the Amber Pope in Qi.

If PCs either successfully guard a messenger or deliver an important message themselves, they might be paid with an artifact and a few cyphers, and/or unlock an opportunity for an even grander adventure with more extreme travel opportunities.

Attend an Official Function (2 weeks): Sometimes nobles of the Ninth World claim perquisites of their station that require people in surrounding lands to journey to their manor for a specific reason: either a singular event or once every so often. Reasons for such an imposition include the following.

• The noble or their child is to be wed and demands attendance and gifts.
• Yearly taxes must be paid in person to avoid later reprisals.
• Attendance at the noble's court, compulsory for all nearby persons once each year.
• The noble publicly claims they are giving out gifts to attendees, but secretly plans on exposing all who show up to a device that will give the noble some measure of control over them.
• A yearly celebration that people all over the region look forward to attending.

If the PCs successfully attend an official function (or guard/guide those who are required to do so), their rewards may not be immediately apparent. Though, perhaps some payment, gift, or a new piece of information is granted.

Merchant Voyage (3+ months): The reckless breed of shin-chasing Ninth Worlders known as merchants are willing to travel to distant lands to pursue trade. Signing on to a merchant's overland caravan or sea-going ship is a travel opportunity PCs encounter while visiting cities and other large communities, though coming across a merchant in mid-journey is also possible. All sorts of encounters and hazards can potentially endanger a merchant and their goods. Signing on people with abilities like the PCs is just smart business.

If PCs successfully keep a merchant caravan or ship safe during the course of their contract, their rewards include food and board for the entire period of their stint, plus a share of the trade goods (or payment for the same of about 60 shins each).

Traveling Entertainers (2+ months): A few bands of traveling entertainers—such as minstrels, prostitutes, salvationists (who claim to minister for some higher being), thespians, and more—ply the Steadfast and the Beyond, seeking to entertain others whose daily existence usually contains few spectacles—especially ones designed to delight onlookers. Like any other travelers, such entertainers are always on the lookout for additional guards, but they also seek other entertainers who might provide an act or entertainment of their own. One such band of entertainers includes Ossam's Traveling Menagerie and Soaring Circus. Ossam's is a caravan of wooden wagons that house creatures and performers, as well as a floating numenera platform that serves as both transport for equipment and a hovering stage during shows.

If PCs successfully complete a contract with a group of traveling entertainers, they can't help but gain training in one entertainment-related skill of their choice.

Off to War (4+ months): If two regions come into conflict, people are required to fill out an army's ranks. Such fighters can be gathered from nearby population centers through conscription, by hiring them, or both. If whatever noble who is waging war can afford it, the services of a mercenary company are usually preferred over forcing unwilling farmers and hunters to fight. Player characters are a cut above the common person and are unlikely to be conscripted, but rather hired as a small mercenary company or as part of a larger organization. Current large-scale conflicts that might draw PCs into a war, prompting them to travel to distant locations to battle strangers for what is hopefully a just cause, include the following.

- By decree of the Amber Pope, the Steadfast and the Order of Truth wage war with the lands to the north (believed by many to be enthralled by a secretive and mysterious cult called the Gaians).

- The Pytharon Empire seeks to require control over the region of Milave by force of arms.
- The Jagged Dream successfully instigates a war between two large kingdoms of the Steadfast.

Though interruptions in long-term play are likely for other travel tasks, it is certain for characters who head off to war. Examples include: small-scale skirmishes that occur if characters are sent to scout ahead; opportunities to explore something strange, when asked to check out something weird off the main route; and having it fall to PCs to intercede and negotiate when tensions in their company reach a boiling point.

And finally, PCs must face the war itself. One way to manage a large war with hundreds or even thousands of combatants mechanically is by using the community stats system for ranking the relative power of opposing hordes, armies, and rampaging beasts as described in *Numenera Destiny*.

If the PCs successfully survive their time at war, they are each due 4 XP for their service.

Road to Otherwhere (1+ months): Roads are rare, but some do exist. Work crews are contracted by some of the larger kingdoms in the Steadfast to build a new road or repair an existing one. Kingdoms and some large communities build roads to enhance both trade and the ability of rulers to rapidly deploy defensive forces. Road-building is hard work,

Ossam's Traveling Menagerie and Soaring Circus, page 159

Jagged Dream, page 218

Community Stats, page 297

Hordes, Armies, and Rampaging Beasts, page 312

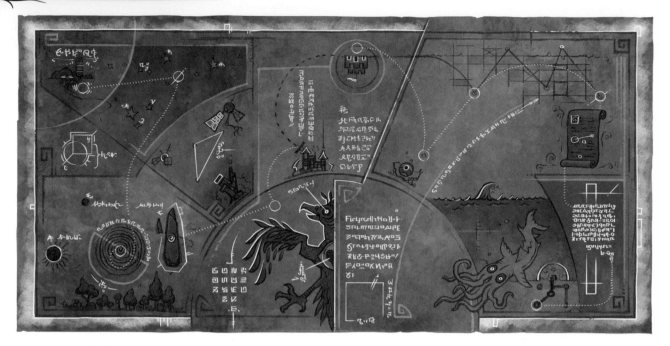

Contemporary Ninth World roads vary from simple dirt tracks used by farmers all the way up to stone-paved highways with drainage ditches and other sophisticated design elements to prolong their usefulness.

but PCs could also be contracted as guards, as route surveyors, or to oversee other workers. Roads are constantly falling into disrepair, and, at least in the Steadfast, any given kingdom is likely looking to either fix up a stretch of road on their border or to build a new one.

If PCs complete their contract related to building or repairing a new stretch of road, rewards include food and board during the entire period of their stint, plus 100 shins to the whole group for their effort.

Croxton, page 73

Iron wind, page 90

Tornado, page 309

Amber Gleaners, page 245

Thieves in the Night, page 105

THE SAFE WAYFARER TRAVEL GUIDE TO TRIP PLANNING

The most important part of any trip is the planning you do ahead of time. Figuring out exactly where you're going, the route you'll use, mounts or vehicles that might be available, and something about the regions through which you'll be passing is essential to any trip.

If an unexpected trip is thrust upon you, trip planning may not be something you're able to do. But if you have a few days or longer, taking the time to follow some of these tips could make a real difference.

Get a Map. Have you heard of the Amber Gleaners? They're explorers. And they like to make maps. If you offer them some of your own knowledge, they might be able to make a copy of one of their maps for you. The organization is establishing field stations here and there about the Steadfast and the Beyond. Look for a symbol of a sphere with a single symmetrical continent stamped upon it.

Avoid the Iron Wind. Sometimes severe storms, including tornados, can rip across the landscape. While even severe storms are usually impossible to predict (and that includes tornados), a traveling Aeon Priest named Croxton is rumored to have an "iron wind almanac" said to predict every major infestation of the event for the next several years.

Make Arrangements for While You Are Gone. If you're someone of means, you may have obligations, a property, possibly a spouse or partner, children, or other regular duties that could suffer while you are gone. Don't stint on making arrangements for an agent to take over in your absence. Moreover, don't widely advertise your absence. Otherwise, unscrupulous thieves could take advantage, and, upon your return, you might find your home has been looted of valuables, or some similar situation where others have illicitly exploited your absence.

CHAPTER 2

EQUIPMENT FOR TRAVEL

When possible, characters rely on cyphers or artifacts to help them on their way as they travel the Ninth World and beyond. Experienced travelers also rely on equipment that isn't scavenged from the numenera. Using gleaned bits of knowledge or observations of how prior-world magic operates, crafters, Wrights, Aeon Priests, and others who are just extremely motivated have developed ways to fashion clever and useful items out of the materials at hand. In the right situation, such contemporary equipment can be just as useful as a cypher or artifact.

For purposes of the entries on the next pages, "Equipment" items are fairly common, and "Special Equipment" items are much rarer—the products of particularly astute tinkerers and Wrights, most likely. Most special items follow the guidelines for the availability of special equipment as described in *Numenera Discovery*.

Some equipment (and all special equipment) is local to only certain locations. That is to say, just because one can find a particular item in one place doesn't mean it can be found for sale elsewhere.

OVERLAND EQUIPMENT

The equipment described on the following tables supplements the equipment presented in *Numenera Discovery*, including the Items for Exploring table that lists such basic fare as explorer's packs, matchsticks, rope, and so on.

Special equipment, page 98

Items for Exploring, page 97

Sometimes travel is uncomfortable, even dangerous. But every trip teaches a lesson—especially the tough ones.

EQUIPMENT FOR OVERLAND TRAVEL

Beastlure	10 shins	Various forms, but often takes the form of a device that is hung from a tree or planted on a spike. It uses wind to spin or otherwise move with a motion that entices various predatory beasts. Eases tasks to hunt or track beasts in some circumstances.
Cold-weather clothing	5 shins	Heavy, insulated, long coat; includes insulated gloves and boots.
Medicinal	10 shins	A small bottle of 10 pills that provide pain relief and some defense against standard diseases. Eases Might defense tasks against disease if taken within 28 hours of exposure.
Mirror	5 shins	Hand-size, ideal for looking around corners or using a grooming kit's contents.
Ringlock	10 shins	A sturdy metallic ring (level 5) about 6 inches (15 cm) in diameter that can be locked shut; good for securing latches, chests, doors, and similar barriers.
Scent-eraser soap	8 shins	A small bottle of liquid, soapy material. If used to fully wash with in a bath or standing bath, your natural odor is neutralized. Creatures that use scent as a component of their perception (and almost all do) are hindered when attempting to find or track you. (Six doses per bottle.)
Scent-proof bag	2 shins	Fits over an explorer's pack (or items of equivalent size) and safely contains any scents of food or other odors that might draw a predator in the wilderness.
Shin belt	3 shins	Appears as a normal, if somewhat thick, belt; contains hidden compartments that can be filled with shins (up to 200). Hinders pickpocketing attempts by two steps.
Sleepleaf	2 shins	Sheaf of dried leaves that smells faintly of mint. Crumbling 1 leaf into hot water and consuming before sleep adds +1 to your next ten-hour recovery roll. (Each sheaf contains about 10 dried leaves.)

Medicinals can help prevent or treat glowing mortification (page 89).

Travel papers are demanded by the riders making up the Border Patrol encounter (page 82).

Attracted by Smell, page 81

THE SAFE WAYFARER TRAVEL GUIDE TO PACKING

The most important part of any trip is the packing you do ahead of time. Take a moment to gather a few needful items now before you head off, and you'll save yourself all kinds of trouble later on. As they say, by failing to prepare, you are preparing to fail.

Travel Papers. If you're traveling in the Steadfast among the large kingdoms, investing in some official travel papers (or at least official-*looking* ones) may help speed you through entanglements sometimes encountered on the road, especially when two or more kingdoms are bickering. Travel papers usually take the form of a letter of safe conduct or some other document written by a high-ranking authority in one kingdom that explains your presence in that kingdom or a different one.

Costs range from complimentary (if actually working on behalf of a particular authority) to a few hundred shins if paying for something that provides more than just a semblance of propriety.

Preventative Medicines. Certain areas are known to host specific diseases. It's often possible to acquire a few doses of specifically targeted medicinals that can help ward off or treat various diseases of the Ninth World.

Packing Smart. Take the time to plan out what and where everything will go—in your packs, on your mounts, or within the vehicle you plan on using. An impressive amount of trouble can be saved later if a little thought beforehand is applied. That includes packing provisions in scent-proof wrappings; some predators are attracted by smell.

MINOR QUALITY OF LIFE EQUIPMENT FOR TRAVEL

Items on this table do not always have a direct game effect unless the particular corner case that requires their use comes up. Still, many travelers find these items essential for arriving at their destination more rested and in better spirits than otherwise.

Bandana	1 shin	If worn reversed, keeps the sun off the back of your neck as you travel. When journeying in windy or dusty conditions, pull it over your mouth and nose to keep out the drit.
Bite repellent	2 shins	Repels biting insect swarms (level 1) for 10 hours. 1 dose.
Bowl/mug/utensils	2 shins	Each traveler should have some method of easily eating while on the road.
Camp pillow	1 shin	Comfort shouldn't suffer while traveling.
Cookware	2 shins	Rations get old quickly on a long trip; most travelers eventually get a heavy metal pot and/or grill rack or griddle for cooking, frying, or otherwise preparing food while traveling; includes a spoon for serving.
Earplugs	1 shin	Could be used to ease defense tasks against sonic attacks but will mostly be used to mute the sounds of snoring from fellow travelers.
Flotation device	3 shins	Useless unless planning travel by boat or ship, in which case wearing this bulky vest-like garment could keep you afloat for days without excess strain, in the event your craft sinks.
Foldable camp chair	3 shins	Folds up for easy packing, unfolds for camp seating.
Gamebox	5 shins	Box containing dice and pack of cards, designed for play while riding or mounted; passes the time during long stretches of travel.
Grooming kit	3 shins	Comb, clippers, soap, and similar products. May also contain cosmetics, cologne, and perfume. If the latter options are correctly applied, you could ease an initial positive interaction check with a stranger.
Hammock	2 shins	Useful in locations where bedrolls or tents can't be deployed.
Hatchet	2 shins	Ideal for cutting firewood (can also be used as a light weapon).
Journal	5 shins	Bound book with blank pages perfect for recording the progress of your journey and new creatures and locations discovered, and for mapping ruins.
Rainwear	3 shins	Hooded poncho and lined pants; includes waterproof boots.
Sunhat	1 shin	Shades your head and face during a long, hot day of travel.
Toiletry kit	2 shins	Various needful things for maintaining health and hygiene; includes a toothbrush, a container of toothpaste, and a bog roll.
Travelcloth	1 shin	A 3-foot (1 m) square cloth with a multitude of uses, including: rolling up to use as a pillow; unfolding for a small blanket (or big bandana); bundling up loose objects to easily carry them; waving as a signaling device; and a hundred other needs a traveler might have, including drying off when wet.

Every trip finished is another story for your quiver of anecdotes to surprise and delight others.

SPECIAL EQUIPMENT FOR OVERLAND TRAVEL

Caterpillar slippers	10 shins	This pair of soft shoes resembles two fat green caterpillars the size of human feet. When worn, the shoes carefully grip with dozens of tiny hooklike feet. This eases climbing tasks, walking on slippery surfaces, and other tasks where the hooks can engage with a solid surface. The slippers are at least partly alive and die after about a year. Less, if they aren't exposed to sunlight for a few minutes each week.
Eye shades	10 shins	Darkened lenses fitted to a frame; protects eyes from sun glare and bright light. In such situations, it reduces hindrances to visual perception tasks that might have otherwise been present.
Feather tool	5 shins	This is a tool with a handle that has been hollowed out and plugged with a precise amount of floatstone—just enough to almost completely cancel its weight. This doesn't affect the item's usefulness or other properties, but it is less of a burden to carry or pack for traveling. Plus, it won't hurt if you drop it on your foot, and it floats on water.
Fireproof rope	5 shins	This rope is made of flexible synth fibers tied together with incredibly dense and complex knots. Works like normal rope, but efforts to burn or melt it fail. (Usually, the supplier of this item also has fireproof thread and fireproof twine, which are just thinner ropes of the same material.)
Fishing hand	5 shins	This looks like the hollowed-out claw or forelimb of some kind of sea creature. When worn on the hand, it can project a strong filament with a synth fob on the end. The fob emits pheromones that attract fish. When it touches flesh, it extends barbed spikes to hook whatever touched it and attempts to reel in the filament. The wearer can also retract the filament at will. It is strong enough to hold about 30 pounds (13.6 kg) off the ground. The hand eases fishing tasks.
Food patch	10 shins	If this approximately 1-foot (30 cm) greenish membrane is slapped onto exposed skin, it adheres. If the patch is exposed to sunlight a couple of hours each day, you gain enough energy to go without food for that day. A food patch slowly grows since it is partly alive. It must be removed within about six months; otherwise, it will completely cover you. Luckily, removing the patch is as easy as scraping it off.
Image catcher	30 shins	Box with a slot that will accept a specially coated plate (10 shins per plate). If the box is motionless, a plate is inserted in the slot, and the aperture is opened for several rounds, an image of whatever is visible in front of the aperture appears permanently on the plate. Reusable.

Floatstone, page 98

Night-sky identifier	10 shins	Star chart useful for navigation; eases navigation tasks if used at night under non-cloudy conditions.
Pure water bottle	20 shins	Water left in this bottle for at least ten minutes is rendered suitable for drinking, free of dangerous substances or disease.
Ringlock, Aeon-grade	120 shins	As ringlock, but level 8.
Rope, contracting	25 shins	Use as normal 50-foot (15 m) rope, but the user can cause it to contract (from either end) to one-tenth its length with enough vigor to lift about 300 pounds (130 kg).
Rope, superlative	35 shins	This 200-foot (60 m) length of thin rope is hard to cut or break (level 8).
Scream cable	30 shins	This stiff but flexible cable is about 30 feet (10 m) long and has a small device attached to one end. It takes about one minute to set it up, usually by placing it on the ground to define an area with no large objects or creatures nearby. The activated cable constantly creates an ultrasound tone, too high-pitched for most humans to hear, that repels most tiny insects and annoys creatures who can hear it. If anything comes within about 1 foot (30 cm) of the cable, it emits a rapid pulse of sounds in the human range, loud enough to wake anyone sleeping within a long distance of it.
Shell tent	15 shins	In its collapsed form, this looks like an oddly shaped flat piece of faceted synth as big as a large book. When the correct spot is pressed, it unlocks and can be unfolded over two rounds into a small rigid shelter (level 2) the size of a one-person tent. Most of these items create a shelter that is a simple dome or other rounded geometric shape, but some look more like the shell of a giant animal, such as a turtle, beetle, or crab. The unfolded tent is strong enough to repel hail, small falling branches, and other casual damage that would tear or flatten a canvas tent. Folding the tent back into its collapsed form takes about one minute.
Sleep cocoon	20 shins	This bedroll resembles a large, woven spiderweb pressed into a flat blanket shape. It slowly releases regenerative substances into anyone wrapped in it, promoting rest and healing. A creature who makes a ten-hour recovery roll while wrapped in the cocoon adds +2 to their roll.
Spyglass	30 shins	Enables viewing of distant objects without hindrance; in some circumstances, it may ease perception tasks. Not quite as effective as binoculars, but takes up less space for purposes of traveling.
Sting repellent	5 shins	As bite repellent, but more potent; repels biting and stinging insect swarms (up to level 2) for 10 hours. 1 dose.
Synth burner	20 shins	When assembled, this looks like a metal bowl surrounded by inward-pointing metal spikes in a large synth frame. It takes two rounds to assemble and set it up, and an action to activate it. The burner uses any kind of synth as fuel, which is placed in the bowl and creates a cold, brilliant light that is brighter than a bonfire and can be seen for miles. Different kinds of synth create different colors of flame. A hand-sized chunk of synth burns for about one hour, leaving behind tarry ash. Removing or covering the synth in the bowl immediately extinguishes it. Looking directly at the light within short range requires a creature to make a Might defense roll or be blinded for one minute.
Travel papers	0–200 shins	Not always available or heeded, but can ease persuasion or deception tasks by up to two steps if you are attempting to justify your presence in a particular location.
Universal anchor	5–20 shins	This ovoid made of rubbery synth has a hole through the middle and hundreds of flexible tendrils covering the exterior edge. The tendrils automatically extend outward and hold themselves rigid against any firm surface, making the item useful for holding things in place, for wedging into crevices to use as anchors for climbing, or even as wheel coatings for terrestrial vehicles. Pressing on the right spot along the edge makes the ring retract nearby tendrils. These items are available in many sizes, from a handspan across (often used as a children's toy) to as wide as a human's arm. The universal anchor eases tasks where gripping and stability are useful (on a vehicle, this includes moving over rubble, navigating steep inclines, and making sharp turns).

AERIAL EQUIPMENT

SPECIAL EQUIPMENT FOR AIR TRAVEL

Altimeter	15 shins	Disc-like device that indicates approximate height via a dial.
Goggles	10 shins	Lenses fitted to eyecups strapped around the head; useful for protecting your eyes while traveling quickly, as is often the case while flying in a vehicle with a seat exposed to the environment or on a flying mount.
Hypoxia pill	20 shins	A small bottle of yellow pills; prevents altitude sickness if a pill is taken while flying too high, or up to 28 hours before doing so. (About 20 pills per bottle.)
Safe descender	50 shins	A body harness secured to a backpack. If a cord is pulled while falling from a great height, a chute (sometimes made of sewn cloth, other times composed of something much weirder) emerges from the pack, catches the wind, and allows you to land in a mostly safe manner instead of plunging to your death. Reusable with a successful difficulty 3 Intellect task to repack the chute.

EFFECTS OF HYPOXIA

If humans fly too high, or otherwise face situations with too little air, they risk suffering from hypoxia (sometimes called altitude sickness). Effects include shortness of breath, wheezing, bluing of the skin, coughing, and confusion. (The complete lack of air—vacuum—is a different situation entirely.) All tasks by someone suffering from hypoxia are hindered by one or more steps, depending on the severity. This lasts until you are treated (such as with a hypoxia pill) or return to a normal altitude and stay there for about an hour if suffering from light hypoxia; long-term effects may linger for months before clearing up if you suffered severe hypoxia.

The more you travel, the more you realize your own sense of self-importance is inflated. You're a mote of being in a wide world in an even-wider universe of space and time. Cultivate gratitude that you have a moment to reflect on your place in it.

UNDERWATER EQUIPMENT

EQUIPMENT FOR UNDERWATER TRAVEL

Aerobullosis pills	20 shins	A small bottle of greenish pills; prevents divers' disease if three or more are taken immediately after arising too deeply from deeper underwater, or up to 28 hours before doing so. (About 20 pills per bottle.)
Dry storage, rental	1 shin/day	For those traveling underwater, coastal communities may offer a space for explorers to store equipment, usually enough to fit two explorer's packs, two large weapons, and one or two other items.
Fingerwebbing	8 shins	A small bottle of material sprayed between your fingers to create webbing. Lasts for one hour and doubles swim speed.
Float-up	20 shins	Harness-like straps with tiny sacs on the back. When the cord is pulled while submerged, it quickly floats you up to the water's surface. (Users are advised to have a handful of aerobullosis pills on hand.)
Saltfilter	12 shins	A membrane bag that filters salt from seawater, filling the interior with perfectly potable water.
Sinkers	2 shins	Boots with leaded soles; good for walking around on solid ground beneath the water rather than flailing about in open water, but slows movement by half. (Users are advised to have some kind of water-breathing method at hand.)
Waterbag	2 shins	Fits over an explorer's pack (or items of equivalent size) and makes it waterproof (and slightly more hydrodynamic if the character goes swimming).

EFFECTS OF DIVERS' DISEASE

If a human or similar creature descends deep underwater, becomes acclimated to the increased pressure there, then too quickly returns to the surface, they face a host of unpleasant effects that range from fatigue and pain to paralysis and unconsciousness. Unless treated with aerobullosis pills or something similar, all tasks attempted by the character are hindered by three steps.

SPECIAL EQUIPMENT FOR UNDERWATER TRAVEL

Diving bubble	100 shins	This small round bubble converts water into breathable air for up to five people who connect to it via their own 50-foot-long (15 m) retractable tube and ventilator. Up to five sets of breathing equipment may come with the diving bubble.
Spraybreather	150 shins	This tiny canister sprays a transparent gelatin that forms around your head, creating a permeable oxygen barrier that filters breathable air from the water. Doesn't work above water. Lasts for 28 hours.
Vocal focus	20 shins	Allows you to speak and be heard and understood at up to long range underwater.
Watermask	50 shins	Creates a seal over your mouth and filters the oxygen out of water to make it breathable for 10 hours.
Watervent (internal)	100 shins	An injection that shoots a rice-sized bit of numenera into your neck. On the following round, the numenera opens, creating an internal filtration system that allows you to breathe water. Lasts for five hours.

UNDERWATER WEAPONS

Cawold	5 shins	Heavy weapon. Similar to a greataxe, designed for great hydrodynamics and swifter movement in water. (Attacks made out of the water with a cawold are hindered.)
Elbow harpoon	8 shins	Medium weapon. Designed as a short-distance propelled harpoon for underwater combat; returns to you through a cable-retrieval system.
Fin piercer	1 shin	Light weapon. Dual-edged piercing weapon made of metal, 1.5 feet (.5 m) long. Designed for speed underwater but feels off-balanced when used on land.
Narbos	5 shins	Light weapon. Bottle of liquid metal that you paint onto at least three nails of one hand; the material hardens into pointed claws that inflict 2 points of slashing damage (or 3 points if you paint and use both hands). One bottle is enough to paint twelve nails, which stay on until clipped or broken off.

SPECIAL UNDERWATER WEAPONS

Sonar stream	50 shins	Medium weapon. Projectile weapon that shoots a long-range sonar pulse that inflicts Intellect damage. The stream is pinpointed, so you must be able to see your target to aim and hit it. Works only when immersed in liquid. Shoots ten times; takes one hour to recharge.
Supercavitation bubbler	10 shins	Medium weapon. Shoots high-velocity liquid projectiles that use cavitation bubbles to aim true and reach long distance. Requires liquid projectiles (1 shin each).

UNDERWATER ARMOR

Bubblewrap	20 shins	Offers buoyancy and pressure control, as well as heat and cold protection, for five hours. Does not provide Armor but can be worn over light armor.
Dive suit	50 shins	Offers buoyancy and pressure control, as well as heat and cold protection, for five hours. Treated as heavy armor in all respects, including granting 3 Armor (and thus cannot be worn with other armor).
Fish eyes	20 shins	Pair of anti-fog, pressure-sensitive goggles to enhance underwater vision (treat darkness conditions as dim light conditions) and protect eyes. Requires ambient light to operate.
Scaled skin	50 shins	Light armor that provides protection from pressure dangers and doubles swim speed.
Warm skin	25 shins	Provides +3 to Armor against cold. Disintegrates after about a week.

CHAPTER 3

MOUNTS & COMMONPLACE VEHICLES

When people of the Ninth World travel, most prefer to arrive at their destinations as quickly and comfortably as possible. Those without extraordinary means rely on trained creatures and commonplace vehicles whenever possible.

MOUNTS

Domesticated beasts—and, in some cases, intelligent creatures with whom a deal has been struck—serve as mounts in every community, on every farm and freehold, and along every road and travel route of the Ninth World. Many of these mounts either are seen commonly enough or are impressive enough that they have been chronicled in the pages of travel guides and other writings (see Comprehensive Travel Option Listing). Hundreds of others have yet to be presented, a handful of which are described in this chapter.

On average, a healthy, living mount can travel anywhere from 25 to 35 miles (40 to 55 km) each day, regardless of whether it can move faster for short periods (such as a long distance each round instead of a short distance each round). This is because most mounts need to take breaks for rest, water, and food. Even so, several consecutive days at a mount's maximum rate requires a couple of days of rest (or at most, moving at only a quarter of their maximum rate) before it can pick up that same pace again.

The people of a few villages located in the Black Riage build wagons out of the wood of the ravioth tree, as they have for generations. These wagons don't need wheels because ravioth trees resist the pull of gravity and float.

UNDERSTANDING MOUNT LISTINGS

Each mount is presented with its level (and target number in parentheses), its price (if the characters can find a seller, which isn't guaranteed), and a short description.

GM INTRUSIONS FOR MOUNTS AND COMMONPLACE VEHICLES
In addition to general travel-themed GM intrusions provided in Chapter 9, several GM intrusions specific to land, water, air, and void vehicles, respectively, can be found in Chapter 4. Most can be adapted as GM intrusions for mounts and commonplace vehicles. Choose which works best, or roll.

Chapter 9: Travel-themed GM Intrusions, page 110

Chapter 4: Vehicles & Travel Devices of the Prior Worlds, page 26

Comprehensive Travel Option Listing, page 40

Bodrov, page 138

Rambu level 2 (6) 30 shins

The broad back of the many-legged, sturdy rambu can hold up to four riders either mounted or in a small howdah. A rambu can move a short distance each round.

Zennit level 2 (6) 90 shins

This 12-foot (4 m) tall furred bipedal creature is somewhat humanoid, although its head is not human in any way; its long snout, tusks, and piercing, rage-filled eyes suggest a predator. However, like a parent that gives rides to their child on their back, a domesticated zennit can serve as a normal-sized human's mount. A zennit can move a long distance each round with a rider, though only for about an hour unless it has a special saddle. Such a saddle can sometimes be obtained from a dealer in exotic mounts for 10 additional shins.

Morwen level 3 (9) 120 shins

A 21-foot (7 m) long slug-like creature to which a large coach-like compartment (a howdah) is usually attached. The howdah can hold up to ten passengers, or as is often the case, serve as a mobile shop for whatever the owner is selling. A morwen can bear its howdah a short distance each round, or an immediate distance each round on steep slopes and walls.

Ollivant level 3 (9) 250 shins

This translucent blob about 10 feet (3 m) in diameter can travel a short distance each round across most terrain, including up cliffs and walls, and even on ceilings. Several vacuoles are visible within the creature's see-through flesh. With domesticated ollivants, a large one often holds a "rider" that is apparently asleep. In fact, the "rider" directs the ollivant through a biofeedback connection, while being supplied air and even a little nutrition, for up to 10 hours at a time. Someone "riding" an ollivant is completely enclosed, and thus can't engage in normal combat until they wake up and emerge as an action.

The people of Bodrov have learned the trick of quickly descending from their 500-foot (150 m) tall plateau by jumping off when standing in proximity to a hive of buzzing whittle-wasps. Almost always, a swarm of wasps emerges to catch the falling Bodrovian, then settle them safely on the ground below.

| **Saquin** | level 3 (9) | 120 shins |

This strange creature can move on several spider-like legs, but its preferred method of travel is to swing from point to point. The saquin enables each swing by explosively extending a long strand of web-like substance that adheres to a distant point, even while still swinging from a previous strand. A domesticated saquin can carry one rider, moving up to a very long distance every other round when it can swing (and a short distance each round it can't swing). Such circumstances include canyons or areas with a reasonable density of spires, forests with a branch conformation that allows space to swing, or a similar environment.

| **Verx** | level 3 (9) | 120 shins |

An 18-foot (6 m) long walrus-like swimming creature that breathes both air and water. A verx can be used as a swimming mount when domesticated. Verx can generate bubbles of breathable air—which they normally use as part of their strategy for capturing tiny rays and finned creatures for food—to sustain an air-breathing rider for several hours at a time.

| **Firestrider** | level 4 (12) | 50 shins |

Red-glowing tendrils trail behind these six-legged lizard-like creatures. A firestrider is able to bear one or two riders on its back and still move a long distance each round for up to two hours at a stretch, or a short distance each round across mountainous terrain that would be a barrier to normal creatures. However, for every hour after the first two a firestrider is pressed to continue, the rider must succeed at a riding task (hindered by one additional step for each hour ridden beyond the first two), or the mount throws the rider and does its best to trample them for several rounds. Any firestriders who see this attack must also be controlled by their riders, or they will join in the mayhem.

If not for the firestrider's temperament, steed merchants would charge double or even triple.

| **Nacious** | level 4 (12) | 160 shins |

Somewhat spider-like with their multiple long, skinny legs, but large enough to carry a rider on their abdomen. Riders usually use a special underslung saddle, or, if they have an especially good relationship with their mount, can induce the nacious to spin a web-like sling that works just as well. A nacious with a rider can move a long distance each round on regular terrain, or a short distance each round when climbing or even clinging to a ceiling.

The Westwood, long considered impenetrable and dangerous, is lately yielding to the people of Navarene and their desire to tame it for their own ends. Daring the ghosts and ravenous beasts, settlers discovered a spider-like creature that could be trained as a mount. The creature was named a "nacious" because of the sound it mutters over and over as it bears a rider beneath its abdomen.

Westwood, page 137

| **Tharink** | level 4 (12) | 150 shins |

This four-footed creature moves and runs like an animal, but its skin is tough as bark (Armor 1) because it's actually a plant. A tharink's head mimics the exterior appearance of a living creature, but it can split bilaterally to reveal a wide, flower-like mouth with petals as hard as any animal's teeth. A tharink can either move on the character's turn, or make a separate biting attack of its own.

| **Bezdel** | level 5 (15) | 300 shins |

This flying creature has a series of red-glowing eyes that stretch along its long, worm-like body. The eyes at one end are somewhat larger and perhaps serve as a head. Great insect-like wings keep the bezdel and one human-sized rider aloft. It can travel a long distance each round, or an average of 30 mph (50 km/h) during long-distance travel, though it can only fly for about four hours each day (requiring rest and feeding during the other hours). The bezdel has the ability to sense transdimensional energy sources and, if given its head, might fly towards the nearest it can sense (if any) and seek to make a nest there. Probably apocryphal stories report that under severe threat or in other extraordinary circumstances, the mount and rider can slip into an alternate dimension.

Steed Merchants Having
A Sale, page 103

Aneen, page 225

Get a Map, page 10

Firestrider, page 21

Vehicular Movement,
page 404

Vehicular Combat,
page 405

Commonplace Objects,
Crafting, page 132

Io, page 111

An expensive item, if
shins were hypothetically
being used to conduct
the transaction, could
cost up to 500 shins.
A very expensive item
up to 10,000 shins.
And an exorbitant item
would cost even more.

THE SAFE WAYFARER TRAVEL GUIDE TO SELECTING THE PROPER MOUNT

It can be an exciting time when you select a mount, if you find the right one! Sometimes, it may simply be a creature you need only to get you from one place to another, and that's that. On the other hand, you might form a connection with your mount—in which case it could be the beginning of a relationship that will last for years. That's why it's important to choose the right mount for you and your needs, if given the opportunity.

Choose the Right Size Mount. The primary thing to keep in mind is that you aren't too heavy or large for your mount so that you don't hurt them during a trip. Some riders don't like to be overshadowed by their mounts, but with everything being equal and an adequately trained mount, usually bigger is better. Be wary of steed merchants selling undersized mounts for their type (or that are otherwise unacceptable), which might be signaled by the merchant being willing to sell the creature at less than half the shins a quality specimen would otherwise go for. Undersized mounts might be sickly, deformed, or too immature to carry a rider for long.

Choose the Right Mount for Your Needs. An all-purpose mount that can travel overland for long distances without tiring is ideal. But if you're traveling through weird terrain, a swampy area, canyonlands, or the wreckage of a broken ruin, something like an aneen may not serve. If you're surprised by a sudden change in the landscape through which you want to travel, getting the best mount probably isn't possible. However, if you make an effort to get a map, you can plan ahead for which mount you will need too.

Choose a Mount that Suits Your Personality. If you think a mount will be with you for a long time, you can increase the odds of the relationship being a good one by assessing the personality of your mount ahead of time. Sure, it can be difficult to tell a creature's personality after only spending a few minutes with it, but you can often get a better idea of its temperament if you speak with several people who have been around the mount in order to increase the odds that someone will provide their honest assessment. For example, it may seem like riding firestriders is a grand idea because of their speed, but learning about their biological instincts may change the average rider's mind.

COMMONPLACE VEHICLES

All kinds of vehicles are in daily use in the Ninth World, and PCs likely see and use some themselves. Characters may begin their career traveling by way of a wagon, some kind of water vessel, or by riding a mount. Later, of course, they could find something touched by the prior worlds, allowing them to rocket through the air, the void, or into another dimension. Until then, the following vehicles are available for PCs to rent, purchase, or even craft.

FIGHTING IN A VEHICLE

If PCs are involved in combat in which they are only partly or lightly enclosed (or not at all enclosed, as in the case of carts, rowboats, and so on), use the normal combat rules, as modified by vehicular movement. However, if PCs are involved in a combat where they are completely enclosed in a vehicle with no possibility of openness to the environment through which they can fire weapons (so that

it's not really the characters fighting, but the vehicles), use the vehicular combat rules from *Numenera Destiny*.

UNDERSTANDING VEHICLE LISTINGS

Each vehicle is presented with its name, level (and target number in parentheses), price, and a short description. Since prices in shins rarely exceed a few hundred in average transactions, prices above that level are provided as price categories. Wealthy merchants, individuals, nobles, organizations, and others with lots of resources can meet these higher non-shin costs through a combination of barter, obligation exchange, and trade of valuable cyphers and artifacts, or in some cosmopolitan areas, io.

An **expensive** item is something that would strain a common person's finances.

A **very expensive** item is probably out of the reach of most people except in very special circumstances.

An **exorbitant** item is something only the very rich or nobles can afford.

Nothing is as potentially dangerous as traveling to an unknown place. Except for never stirring from your life's daily routines and slowly dying inside from boredom.

LAND

Commonplace land vehicles require something (usually a trained mount) to pull them.

Cart, hand-pulled   level 2 (6)   25 shins
Enables task of carrying small amounts of cargo, debris, riders, and so on.

Chariot   level 2 (6)   80 shins
Carries one or two passengers in a small cab up to a long distance each round, if hitched to a beast trained to pull.

> There's a place in the Beyond where geysers burst up from the ground with such frequency and predictability that the locals have devised craft that "ride" from one burst to the next across a valley.

Wagon   level 2 (6)   70 shins
Carries about 1,000 pounds (450 kg) of cargo if hitched to a beast trained to pull.

Coach   level 3 (9)   Expensive
Carries six people inside and two on the driver's seat outside if hitched to a beast trained to pull.

WATER

Commonplace watercraft require paddling, rowing, and/or sails to move against the current or direction of a river's flow. If moving with the direction of the water, watercraft can exceed the movement noted for the craft if the water bearing it is moving faster.

Raft   level 1 (3)   10 shins
Carries up to five people on water (minimum crew 1); intrinsically poor quality hinders tasks related to piloting, repairing, and using the raft by two steps. Usually only moves an immediate distance each round.

Canoe   level 2 (6)   30 shins
Carries one or two people on water. Tasks related to piloting the canoe are hindered by two steps in rough water. Moves up to a short distance each round in calm water or an average of 3 miles per hour (5 km/h).

Kayak   level 3 (9)   50 shins
Carries one person on water; eases tasks to avoid capsizing by two steps. Moves up to a short distance each round in calm water or an average of 3 miles per hour (5 km/h).

Rowboat   level 2 (6)   100 shins
Carries up to six people on water (minimum crew 1). Moves up to a short distance each round in calm water or an average of 6 miles per hour (10 km/h).

Subsurfacer   level 4 (12)   Expensive
One-person wooden craft that can submerge and move underwater by using a hand-operated mechanism. Moves an immediate distance each round.

> There's a rumor that if you know the right secret, you could allow yourself to be drawn up with a volume of water taken from the Tithe River by the Obelisk of the Water God. Then, instead of being flung high into the air followed by a fall to your death, you would be safely transferred to one of several other hidden locations within the Steadfast and the Beyond.

Obelisk of the Water God, page 140

Sailboat   level 3 (12)   Very Expensive

Carries up to ten people on water (minimum crew 2) plus a moderate amount of cargo; enables overwater movement of a short distance each round in calm water or an average of 8 miles per hour (13 km/h) as long as the wind is right.

In the Caecilian Jungle, there's a plant that grows such massive, wide leaves that the people who live there use them as one-person boats.

Coaster   level 3 (9)   Exorbitant

Two-masted vessel not suited to long trips away from land, but able to carry several dozen people (minimum crew 10) and some cargo. Enables overwater movement of a short distance each round in calm water or an average of 8 miles per hour (13 km/h) as long as the wind is right.

Longship   level 4 (15)   Exorbitant

Carries up to forty people (minimum crew 20) on water plus a moderate amount of cargo; enables overwater movement of about 8 miles per hour (13 km/h) as long as the wind is right, and half that against the wind with rowing.

Cog   level 4 (12)   Exorbitant

Single-masted vessel with a flat bottom; able to carry more cargo than a longship of similar size (but otherwise moves and crewed as a longship). The flat bottoms give them an advantage in shallow harbors, while their high, steep sides hinder tasks to board by enemy crews.

Caravel   level 5 (15)   Exorbitant

Similar to a coaster, but its stronger, sturdier hull (thanks to improved construction techniques) gives the caravel more rigging and size options. This means most caravels are at least three-masted, allowing them to move much faster than most other craft on the water. It carries up to 50 people (minimum crew 30, mostly engaged with adjusting the rigging and repairing leaks). A caravel moves a long distance each round in calm water or an average of 10 miles per hour (16 km/h) as long as the wind is right. Able to carry several tons of cargo and attempt long ocean voyages.

Carrack   level 5 (15)   Exorbitant

Carracks are the largest ships built by the humans of the Ninth World, and often lead large fleets of smaller ships. These craft usually mass at least 700 tons. They are larger than a caravel, with a complicated array of sails and advanced architectural features, including a bowsprit and one or more interior levels above the hold. A carrack can carry over 150 people (minimum crew 80).

Fengali Forest, page 165

The shipwrights in Ghan coat the hulls of their caravels with a special sap—expensive and hard to obtain—from trees in the Westwood. This sap makes the ship's hull twice as strong but gives it a stark red color. It's said that in the far southern reaches of the Sere Marica, there are caravels built to incorporate strange stones that sing when the sea is calm and glow warmly when the waves are rough.

A type of tree grows in the Fengali Forest that creates intricate spinner-like vanes to help broadcast its seeds far and wide. Those willing to brave the poisonous flowers rife in the forest can harvest these before they launch themselves and use them as single-person aerial transports. Each spinner seed is only good for a couple of trips.

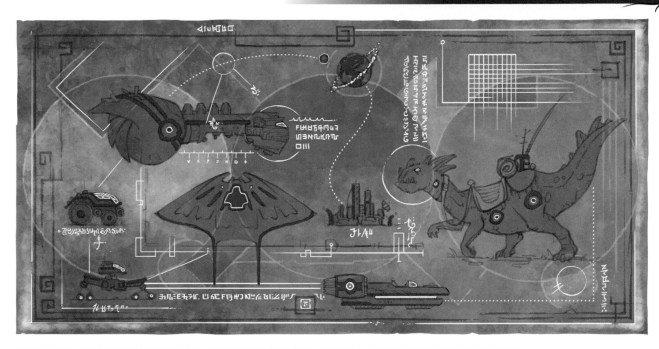

AIR

Glider   level 2 (6)   Expensive

Fabric fixed between a rigid frame into which a single pilot can strap themself. Best suited for terrain with high locations from which to leap, especially areas that feature thermals. When attempting to launch into flight, rise higher on a thermal, or land, the rider must succeed on a difficulty 4 Speed task or suffer a mishap. Moves up to a very long distance each round when conditions are just right or up to 8 miles per hour (13 km/h) under similar perfect conditions.

> A species of porpoise living under the City of Bridges will come to you if you offer it a salty-sweet treat. For the promise of more, it'll pull you through the water to another location in the city. Of course, getting into and out of the water is on you.

City of Bridges, page 141

Balloon   level 3 (9)   Expensive

Comes in a variety of colors and customizations, but the general principle is that a bag of hot air (heated at need by an engine or a numenera item) lifts a gondola with room for six passengers, including the operator. Not great for long-distance travel without some type of control over the wind, or another customization by a numenera device. Moves up to a short distance each round or up to 5 miles per hour (8 km/h) in the direction of the wind. Steering is accomplished by changing altitudes to catch winds blowing in other directions.

Customization by Numenera Device, page 32

Dirigible   level 4 (12)   Exorbitant

More sophisticated than a balloon, a dirigible is a cigar-shaped craft that mixes the technology of a commonplace vehicle and one of the prior worlds, given that the lighter-than-air gas that fills it, and the engines that drive it through the air, are certainly provided by little-understood devices. Typically, one or more gondolas are suspended below the much larger envelope filled with lifting gas. Moves a minimum of a short distance each round or up to 5 miles per hour (8 km/h) under perfect conditions. A dirigible can carry about 100 people (minimum crew 50).

> Cire captained a unique living ship. It was a sort of hybrid of whale and nautilus, but also had elements that were clearly built by hand (with the ship's permission).

Cire and her living ship appeared in the novel Tomorrow's Bones *by Shanna Germain.*

CHAPTER 4

VEHICLES & TRAVEL DEVICES OF THE PRIOR WORLDS

People who often travel across the Ninth World (and beyond it) prefer to use more extraordinary options, if available. Such devices and vehicles can be salvaged from ancient ruins, crafted by Wrights, or, in some limited locations, purchased.

Many instances of travel-enhancing devices and numenera vehicles have been previously described; refer to the Comprehensive Travel Option Listing. Hundreds of others have yet to be presented; a relative handful of those are described in this chapter.

Chapter 3: Mounts & Commonplace Vehicles, page 19

Comprehensive Travel Option Listing, page 40

COMMONPLACE VEHICLES VS. THOSE OF THE PRIOR WORLDS

PCs may become embroiled in vehicle combat in which one side rides in a commonplace vehicle, and the opposed group rides in a vehicle enhanced by, or entirely of, the numenera. When that happens, increase the effective level of the vehicle built with the numenera by two steps.

For instance, if NPCs in a level 2 commonplace chariot face off against a PC-piloted level 4 speedster, the mismatch in advancement works in the speedster driver's favor. Treat the speedster as a level 6 vehicle in comparison to the level 2 chariot.

Vehicles, The Stars Are Fire, page 92

Chariot, page 23

Speedster, page 28

Repairing Damaged Objects and Structures, page 122

Crafting, page 117

Artifact Plans, page 145

UNDERSTANDING TRAVEL DEVICES AND VEHICLE LISTINGS

Items in this chapter are often priceless because those who own them won't give them up for a mere exchange of shins. Instead, these devices are usually found, crafted, or, in some cases, traded for in return for some other numenera device characters are willing to part with. Alternatively, characters might be given or lent a vehicle by someone who asks them to use it to complete a task.

All of which is to say that unlike in Chapter 3: Mounts & Commonplace Vehicles, the devices and vehicles presented here do not list a sale price. Each vehicle is presented with its name, level (and target number in parentheses), depletion, and a short description.

Why not use the standard artifact format for vehicles in this chapter? Two reasons: one, as we've established, vehicles of the numenera are a subset of artifacts, and the format used for vehicle presentation hereafter helps make that distinction. And, two, the format is very similar to that used in the previous chapter detailing commonplace vehicles and mounts, as well as entries in *The Stars Are Fire*, which further drives the point home (so to speak).

Vehicle Depletion: If a vehicle becomes depleted, it can potentially be repaired by the right cypher or artifact, or by someone trained in crafting numenera who attempts to repair the damaged object.

Crafting Travel Devices and Vehicles: If a character wishes to attempt crafting one of the artifacts or vehicles presented in this chapter, they must first obtain the correct plan. Use an Artifact Plan template with the same level as the item to be crafted as the basis for the plan provided to the PC. You can customize the plan or just use it as is. For example, if a character wishes to craft a level 2 drit wheel (described hereafter), provide the artifact template for a level 2 artifact.

The best times in life are those when you are anticipating an upcoming trip to someplace completely new and unknown.

VEHICLES OF THE PRIOR WORLDS

LAND

Drit wheel level 2 (6) **Depletion:** 1 in 1d20 (check per week of use)
Knobby two- or three-wheeled vehicle with a roaring power source that supports a basic frame with an exposed seat for one rider (and sometimes a passenger); ideal for wild terrain and off-road travel. Moves a short distance each round in rough terrain or an average of 30 mph (48 km/h) during long-distance travel.

Runner level 2 (6) **Depletion:** 1 in 1d20 (check per week of use)
Two 12-foot (4 m) tall articulated biomechanical legs support an exposed cab with room for a pilot and one passenger; moves a long distance each round (even in rough terrain), or an average of 50 mph (80 km/h) during long-distance travel.

Skim flitter level 3 (9) **Depletion:** 1 in 1d20 (check per week of use)
A sweptback frame with an exposed seat for one pilot that hovers up to 1 m (3 feet) over any terrain (including water and other liquids); ideal for utterly wild terrain and over-water excursions. Moves a long distance each round or an average of 60 mph (95 km/h) during long-distance travel.

Omni wheel level 3 (9) **Depletion:** 1 in 1d20 (check per week of use)
Two-wheeled vehicle with telescoping spokes capable of adapting to nearly any terrain (except water or other liquids), supporting a basic frame with a seat for one rider (and sometimes a passenger) open to the environment; ideal for utterly wild terrain and off-road travel; able to "climb" natural steep and near-vertical surfaces. Auto-stabilization eases all tasks related to piloting and riding it. Moves a long distance each round in any terrain or an average of 70 mph (112 km/h) during long-distance travel.

Some residents of Far Brohn have secured several sathosh to use as a power source for a massive vehicle of the prior worlds. They are repairing and customizing it in order to make it into a war vehicle.

Far Brohn, page 157

Sathosh, page 251

GM intrusion:
The vehicle doesn't deplete, but it does slowly power down, and remains so for about ten hours as it recharges its reserves.

GM intrusion:
*Extreme weather
conditions threaten
to make the vehicle
spin out of control.*

Portwalker level 3 (9) **Depletion:** 1 in 1d20 (check per week of use)

An enclosed cabin holds up to six people, including the operator. The cab is supported by several extendable stilt-like metallic legs whose heights can be increased or decreased at need. Despite its massive size and somewhat recalcitrant control mechanism (all tasks to drive the portwalker are hindered), these vehicles see some use in seaside ports, where the walker can head out and meet a ship in the bay, then pull it into dock. A portwalker can also be used on dry land, where those willing to risk falling over can accelerate a portwalker to move at a very long distance each round over the course of five rounds; however, they must succeed on a difficulty 5 Speed task each round when moving at that pace, or the whole thing tumbles and crashes.

Two-legged Wayfarer level 3 (9) **Depletion:** 1 in 1d20 (check per week of use)

Two 15-foot (5 m) tall articulated biomechanical legs support an enclosed cab with room for a pilot and four passengers; moves a long distance each round (even in rough terrain), or an average of 50 mph (80 km/h) during long-distance travel.

Crab-like creatures living in the Wyr River are sometimes trained by locals living along the banks to pull their craft upriver. They use their oversized pincers to grab onto the craft above them and use their spike-like legs to dig into the river bottom to gain a surprising amount of purchase—even in rough water. Watching from afar, observers might not even notice them as they stay mostly underwater—though they might spot a pincer tip tightly clutching the hull from time to time. Such an observer may wonder what the motive source of power is for craft as simple as rafts to be pulled against the river's flow.

Speedster level 4 (12) **Depletion:** 1 in 1d20 (check per week of use)

A sweptback frame with a seat for one rider (and often a passenger) open to the environment. Hovers up to 2 m (6 feet) over any terrain (including water and other liquids); ideal for utterly wild terrain and over-water excursions. Auto-stabilization eases all tasks related to riding by two steps. Moves a very long distance each round in any terrain or an average of 150 mph (240 km/h) during long-distance travel.

Strider level 4 (12) **Depletion:** 1 in 1d20 (check per week of use)

Two 21-foot (7 m) tall articulated biomechanical legs support an enclosed cab with room for a pilot and six passengers. Moves a short distance each round in rough terrain, or an average of 30 mph (48 km/h) during long-distance travel. Striders almost always come with at least one ranged weapon customization, such as a deployable, swiveling, long-range energy weapon that inflicts 8 points of damage.

Wyr River, page 154

GM intrusion: *Pilot
error threatens to cause
the vehicle to crash.*

Domed wheeler level 4 (12) **Depletion:** 1 in 1d20 (check per week of use)

Six-wheeled vehicle supporting an enclosed cabin that protects a pilot and up to four additional passengers. Its cabin always has breathable air, even in dangerous or airless environments. Auto-stabilization eases all tasks related to driving. Moves a long distance each round on paved and broken surfaces or an average of 40 mph (64 km/h) during long-distance travel.

Speedster, battle level 5 (15) **Depletion:** 1 in 1d20 (check per week of use)

As speedster, with the addition of reinforced cowling providing the exposed rider with 2 Armor. Built-in weapons include deployable, swiveling, long-range energy weapons that inflict 9 points of damage.

Light wheel level 6 (18) **Depletion:** 1 in 1d20 (check per week of use)

Two-wheeled vehicle composed of solid light that is capable of adapting to most terrain. Supports a sleek, reinforced, armored frame with a partly exposed seat for one rider (and sometimes a passenger), providing the rider with 1 Armor. Suitable for crossing above any surface via a self-deploying hard-light bridge (a thin strand of constantly extending force creating a surface that persists for about 1 minute). The bridge can reach nearly any height, though its maximum gradient shouldn't exceed 30 degrees. Auto-stabilization eases all tasks related to piloting and riding by two steps. Moves a long distance each round on a self-deploying bridge or an average of 120 mph (190 km/h) during long-distance travel.

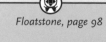

Floatstone, page 98

Orrila, page 158

The floatstone quarries east of Orrila are a treasured resource for craftspeople and Wrights who want to make flying craft, since the proper quantity of floatstone can turn even a commonplace cart into something able to take to the air, or at least hover over the roadless landscape.

LAND VEHICLE GM INTRUSIONS

In addition to general travel-themed GM intrusions provided in chapter 9, several GM intrusions specific to land vehicles (many of which could be adapted to commonplace vehicles) are provided here. Choose which works best, or roll.

d10	Intrusion
01	Vehicle runs out of fuel or power, or some other motive force gives out.
02	Unexpected obstacle threatens to cause a crash.
03	Unexpected gap requires the rider to "jump" between stable surfaces by launching off a suitable ramp-like incline.
04	Another vehicle swerves into PC's vehicle.
05	Loose sand/gravel/particles/ice on the surface threaten to cause a wipeout.
06	Too much velocity while going around a corner threatens to cause a wipeout or crash.
07	Vehicle takes damage and threatens to detonate its power source.
08	Stowaway discovered.
09	Vehicle's brakes freeze.
10	Vehicle's wheel, track, or similar device unexpectedly blows out.

Chapter 9: Travel-themed
GM Intrusions, page 110

THE SAFE WAYFARER TRAVEL GUIDE TO DRIVING A VEHICLE OF THE PRIOR WORLDS

Some of you will be lucky enough to one day pilot a numenera vehicle. The experience in and of itself is likely to be illuminating. More amazing will be the speed at which you reach your destination. And, perhaps only with such a vehicle will you be able to reach previously inaccessible and strange locations!

However, many issues face pilots and passengers of a conveyance that was built by non-human hands or crafted from iotum first forged by the same. Here are a few things to keep in mind as you climb aboard your strange new vessel.

Will It Go Where You Want? Many vehicles have relatively straightforward piloting options. Others have complicated control surfaces, require some sort of psychic control, or need you to request a destination from an onboard device or entity. It's always possible that when you direct your vehicle to take you to destination X, you might end up at location Y instead, making you a lost traveler. If at all possible when using a vehicle of the prior worlds, keep an alternate method of finding your way back home in reserve.

Lost Traveler, page 92

What Else Is Inside? Even small vehicles salvaged from a ruin might have a compartment containing something unsettling or dangerous. Larger vehicles, of course, may have entire chambers that aren't immediately obvious or might provide access to interstitial extradimensional spaces—either of which could contain surprise occupants or other disruptions that, if sprung upon someone using a vehicle at just the wrong time, could lead to disaster. This is why before the first time you operate your new vehicle, you should take the time to do an exacting search and inventory of it. Better to learn an unpleasant truth when you're ready for it than have it spring out when you're least expecting it!

Surprise Occupants,
page 103

Others Want Your Vehicle. Congratulations! You've somehow gained ownership of a weird device that allows you to go far and fast, courtesy of the prior worlds. Of course, this means you've also just become the target of anyone jealous of your good fortune who has an outsize sense of entitlement. So, be on your guard against the threat of vehicle jacking. And, if possible, customize your new conveyance with some kind of thief deterrent.

Vehicle Jacking, page 29
Thief deterrent module,
page 36

WATER

The warriors of Aras commonly modify their bodies with animalistic surgery (including grafting, genetic manipulation, and implantation). Some prefer modifications that give them the ability to swim faster and farther than unmodified people. A small unit of such warriors can quickly pull captured or stolen ships through the waves to where they can later be broken down and refashioned into "Jaekships," further enhancing the effectiveness of their water army.

Aras Island, page 164

Roarboat   level 2 (6)   **Depletion:** 1 in 1d20 (check per day of use)
Seaworthy hull with exposed seats for a pilot and up to eight passengers (minimum crew 1). Moves a long distance each round or up to 50 mph (80 km/h) on calm water (half movement rates in choppy water). The mechanism is named for the roaring sound it emits when operating. Also a bit tippy; GM intrusions related to the roarboat occur on a d20 die roll of 1 or 2.

Sea voyager   level 4 (12)   **Depletion:** 1 in 1d20 (check per month of use)
60-foot (18 m) long, seaworthy hull with an exposed upper deck plus several completely enclosed interior chambers suitable for living, leisure, crafting, exploration, spying, and other purposes. Supports a team of about twelve human-sized occupants (minimum crew 4). Moves a long distance each round or up to 50 mph (80 km/h) on calm water (half movement rates in choppy water).

WATERCRAFT GM INTRUSIONS

In addition to the general travel-themed GM intrusions provided in chapter 9, several GM intrusions specific to water-capable vehicles are provided here. Choose which works best, or roll.

d10	Intrusion
01	Vehicle begins taking on water due to minor leak.
02	Vehicle capsizes.
03	Vehicle begins to sink due to major leak caused by structural flaw.
04	Vehicle collides with marine life/debris on water that impacts the vehicle, damaging it.
05	Power source unexpectedly dies.
06	Unmapped underwater terrain feature threatens/causes imminent collision.
07	Vehicle takes damage and threatens to detonate its power source.
08	Storm blows up and threatens to capsize vehicle.
09	Character(s) fall overboard.
10	Pirates! (Or, at least, people with bad intentions pull up in another watercraft.)

AIR AND VOID

GM intrusion:
Unexpected floating debris impacts the vehicle, damaging it.

Surveyor   level 2 (6)   **Depletion:** 1 in 1d20 (check per week of use)
Hovering 15-foot (5 m) diameter disc floats up to 30 feet (9 m) above the ground. Very stable, but moves a maximum of an immediate distance each round and, as such, isn't ideal for long-distance travel unless towed by another vehicle or creature. In fact, surveyors are often used in this way, but these discs also make ideal points to watch what goes on below them and even mobile shop fronts for merchants.

Lithe wing   level 3 (9)   **Depletion:** 1 in 1d20 (check per day of use)
A sweptback frame with an exposed seat for one pilot; flies a long distance each round or an average of 120 mph (190 km/h) during long-distance travel.

Blast wing   level 4 (12)   **Depletion:** 1 in 1d20 (check per week of use)
As lithe wing, with the addition of reinforced cowling that provides the exposed rider 2 Armor. Built-in weapon is a deployable, swiveling, long-range energy weapon that inflicts 9 points of damage.

Flit disc   level 5 (15)   **Depletion:** 1 in 1d20 (check per week of use)

A 30-foot (9 m) diameter open-air crystalline disc with room for several people plus a load of cargo (minimum crew 1). Sometimes, secondary structures are built on top. Everything is enclosed in an invisible field that shields passengers from excessive airflow but otherwise doesn't interfere with movement onto or off of the vehicle. A control surface allows the vehicle to hover or travel up to a very long distance each round, or an average of 150 mph (240 km/h) during long-distance travel.

Lance wing   level 5 (15)   **Depletion:** 1 in 1d20 (check per day of use)

Sweptback, dart-like flying vehicle with bilateral wings; enclosed cabin seats a pilot and one passenger. Provides about a day of air and pressure at a time before it must be recharged by spending at least an hour in a breathable atmosphere. Built-in weapons include very long-range cannons that spew tiny metal flechettes. Flies a very long distance each round or an average of over 700 mph (1,125 km/h) during extended trips.

> **GM Intrusion (group):** *The flit disc loses navigation and delivers its passengers to a random location.*

> According to a journal that apparently fell, burning, from the sky, a group of explorers managed to get inside one of the scarred monoliths floating above Ghan. More surprisingly, they were able to make the entire thing move like a massive dirigible. However, that's where the journal, badly burned and stained with what is probably blood, leaves off.

FLYING VEHICLE GM INTRUSIONS

In addition to the general travel-themed GM intrusions provided in chapter 9, several GM intrusions specific to flying vehicles are provided here. Choose which works best, or roll.

d10	Intrusion
01	Vehicle runs out of fuel or power (thankfully, not while in flight, but preventing flight).
02	Extreme turbulence threatens to cause a loss of control in flight.
03	A glitch in the flight control—or pilot error—causes vehicle to bank too sharply, threatening a crash.
04	Unexpected debris/birds/flying creatures impact the vehicle, damaging it.
05	Damage to the vehicle means that without repair, landing attempts will potentially result in a crash.
06	Unexpectedly tall terrain feature threatens imminent collision.
07	Vehicle takes damage and threatens to detonate its power source.
08	Another flying vehicle hits the PC's vehicle from above.
09	Vehicle runs out of fuel or power while in flight.
10	Breach in enclosed cabin risks sucking pilot or passengers out to a long fall.

Scarred Monoliths, page 142

Chapter 9: Travel-themed GM Intrusions, page 110

Nightswimmer   level 5 (15)   **Depletion:** 1 in 1d20 (check per month of use)

Large sweptback frame with enclosed cabin for the pilot and up to six additional passengers. In addition to being able to fly up to a long distance each round, or an average of 120 mph (190 km/h) during long-distance travel, a nightswimmer can change modes and rocket up into the void, becoming a craft capable of moving between the various children of the sun. A nightswimmer takes several weeks to several months to voyage between interplanetary locations that the pilot has specific knowledge of. Air is provided during this period, but no food or water, so additional resources should be brought aboard for such a trip.

> *Sometimes, several nightswimmers are found within the hold of a larger void-faring vehicle of the prior worlds.*

> *"Children of the sun" is a term sometimes used to refer to the various planets orbiting the sun.*

Ultraterrestrials living in New Yenth ride around on massive beetle-like mounts, fly to distant locations with dragonfly-like winged insects, and even move across vast bodies of water on the hard, carapaced backs of huge water bugs. Such mounts and similar transports would be useful in the Steadfast, but the portal connecting this parallel world with our own is too constrained to get most of these creatures through.

New Yenth, page 152

Void dreamer   level 10 (30)   **Depletion:** 1 in 1d100 (check per year of use)

This egg-shaped craft is about 500 feet (150 m) in diameter along its short axis and 700 feet (210 m) on its long axis. The exterior is matte white, featuring an assortment of crack-like lines wandering the surface. A single entrance provides access into what seems like a much smaller interior space with only a couple of chambers, including one for complex control mechanisms. The interior is large enough for up to 15 passengers. Any creature able to understand the controls can launch the void dreamer on interstellar trips that take only days to complete—even trips across the galaxy. However, many mechanisms aboard the craft are dangerous. In addition, the craft travels through an artificial sub-reality when moving, which has become corrupted with horrific predator entities over the eons since it was created.

Chapter 9: Travel-themed GM Intrusions, page 110

VOID VEHICLE GM INTRUSIONS

In addition to the general travel-themed GM intrusions provided in chapter 9, several GM intrusions specific to spacefaring vehicles are provided here. Choose which works best, or roll.

d10	Intrusion
01	Voidcraft struck by unknown material debris and begins to leak air.
02	Voidcraft power source unexpectedly stutters, runs out of fuel, or malfunctions in a way that could lead to detonation.
03	Voidcraft is holed by something large enough to risk a catastrophic blow-out.
04	Environmental controls malfunction; ship interior grows colder and colder (causing a buildup of frost and ice on interior surfaces), until the problem can be identified and repaired.
05	Drive system surges, causing the vehicle to move faster, farther, or to a different location than was intended.
06	Solar flare, gravitational gradient, or other unexpected phenomenon damages ship.
07	A malfunction, deliberate sabotage by a rival, or an automaton affects the environmental controls in a spacesuit or entire ship, turning good air bad. Affected characters, initially unaware of the problem, become more and more sleepy until they pass out.
08	Burst of light out in the void (a gamma-ray burst from "nearby" neutron star conjunction) threatens to fry ship and everyone on board.
09	External operations lead to a character being bucked off craft into empty space.
10	Environmental systems are compromised, requiring extensive overhaul to return to normal.

Modification, page 123

Builds Tomorrow, page 66

The Fourth Mark, page 146

Eldan Firth, page 166

Thaemor, page 148

Rhym Folona claims to have entered the synth hatch that lies at the top of the Fourth Mark, a feat no one else has ever managed. Inside, she found something she describes as a "phase tube" that promises fast travel straight through solid matter to distant locations. Whether or not Rhym Folona is telling the truth or lying for her own gain is anyone's guess. However, some note that she was in Eldan Firth one day, and then, just a couple of days later, she was sighted in Thaemor.

CUSTOMIZATION BY NUMENERA DEVICE

Vehicles (and sometimes mounts) can be—and often are—enhanced by one or more of the following customizations, which improve some facet of the vehicle or mount.

If one of the PCs is a Wright, or the characters know an NPC wright, customization by modification may be possible whether or not any of the following devices (which are essentially artifacts) are first found. Likewise, a character with the Builds Tomorrow focus might attempt to do the same.

But finding a customization and adding it to a vehicle or mount is also viable. Customization artifacts can be added to vehicles or mounts (or a mount's harness) with a successful understanding numenera or crafting numenera task equal to either the customization's level, or the vehicle or mount's level—whichever is higher.

WEAPON CUSTOMIZATIONS FOR VEHICLES AND MOUNTS

Most weapon customizations for vehicles and mounts are modified by Aeon Priests or Wrights from other devices of the numenera. Many weapons could also be mounted on a non-moving structure, at the point of maximum visibility, for defensive purposes. If a weapon is used against another vehicle, vehicular combat rules may come into play at the GM's option.

WEAPON CUSTOMIZATIONS

Choose an option from the weapon customizations table or roll randomly.

d10	Weapon Customization
01	Countermeasure module (clogger)
02	Countermeasure module (fogger)
03	Countermeasure module (slider)
04–06	Disruptor cannon
07–08	Drill ram
09	Force canon
10	Plasma lance

COUNTERMEASURE MODULE

Level: 1d6 + 3

Form: 6-foot (2 m) long canister affixed to hard point of vehicle's rear or to the underside of a mount on a harness; control box connected to the canister by a long umbilical

Effect: User can deploy a countermeasure against enemy vehicles that follow closely in pursuit. Most of these countermeasures are meant for use against overland pursuit, though some may prove effective during aerial or water pursuit. Any given countermeasure module customization contains only one type of countermeasure.

Clogger (gluey substance). If used against a pursuing mounted enemy or enemies within short range, a successful attack causes the enemy's mount (and possibly the enemy rider) to be coated in a quick-drying adhesive that holds them immobile for a few rounds, and potentially inflicts damage if breathed in (at the GM's option). If deployed during vehicular combat, treat the attack as a strike power or a core or vital spot targeting task eased by two steps. If successful, the gluey substance enters through an intake device and

renders the vehicle unusable for several hours (or longer) while the material is cleared out.

Fogger (dense orange haze). If used against a pursuing mounted enemy or enemies within short range, a successful attack causes the enemy's mount (and possibly the enemy rider) to be blinded for 1 minute. If deployed during vehicular combat, treat the attack as a disable defenses targeting task eased by two steps.

Slider (translucent oil): If used against a pursuing mounted enemy or enemies within short range, a successful attack causes a mounted enemy to slip and fall, causing them to lose their next turn (if not more, at the GM's option). If deployed during vehicular combat, treat the attack as a disable maneuverability targeting task eased by two steps.

Depletion: 1 in 1d6

DISRUPTOR CANNON

Level: 1d6 + 4

Form: Mountable device with a few simple controls

Effect: Emits a faint, long-range beam that affects only organic creatures and materials. PCs hit by the beam move one step down the damage track; NPCs hit by the beam lose one-third of their full health and are hindered.

This device is a rapid-fire weapon and thus can be used with the Spray or Arc Spray abilities that some characters have, but each "round of ammo" used or each additional target selected requires an additional depletion roll.

Depletion: 1–2 in 1d100

Aeon Priest, page 264

Vehicular Combat, page 405

Ishlav, page 160

Stirthal, page 151

Some among the latest generation born in Ishlav can see corridors in the air that no one else can. And, in a few cases, those able to see these corridors can enter them, only to suddenly find themselves transported many hundreds of miles across the land. Until recently, those witnessing youngsters beginning such a trip thought they were being disintegrated by a leftover effect of the ancient device that caused the destruction of the original city of Ishlav over twenty years ago.

Some cliff-dwellers in Stirthal sometimes use a living vine that can greatly extend or shorten its length to pull someone up from below or let them safely down. However, it's important to sing to the vine the entire time; otherwise, it might abruptly buck its passenger off. The secret of growing the vines is known only to a few.

DRILL RAM

Level: 1d6 + 4

Form: 3-foot (1 m) circular device that can be affixed on the front of a rigid vehicle (not customizable for most mounts)

Effect: When activated, the device fashions a drill-like ram from hard light, which persists for one minute. While the projection persists, the customized vehicle can be used as a weapon by the pilot who successfully rams a target. Against a creature, the drill ram inflicts damage equal to the artifact level (ignores Armor), or, if the creature is substantially smaller, inflicts double that and throws it a long distance. If driven into another vehicle (treat as a disable defenses targeting task, eased by two steps), a successful strike creates a breach in a vehicle whose level is less than the drill ram's level.

Depletion: 1 in 1d6

FORCE CANNON

Level: 1d6 + 4

Form: Mountable device forged of crystal

Effect: Radiates a force bolt at a target within long range. Successful attacks against a creature inflict damage equal to the force cannon's level. Attacks that succeed against a vehicle hinder all tasks related to operating that vehicle until repaired.

Depletion: 1 in 1d10

PLASMA LANCE

Level: 1d6 + 4

Form: Mountable device forged of synth and metal

Effect: Releases a blast of brilliant energy at a target within very long range. Attacks against a creature inflict damage equal to the plasma lance's level, and cause the target to burn for 4 points of damage on the following round. Attacks against a vehicle that succeed hinder by two steps all tasks related to operating that vehicle until repaired.

Depletion: 1 in 1d10

OTHER CUSTOMIZATIONS FOR VEHICLES AND MOUNTS

People adapt their vehicles and mounts with artifacts in lots of ways that have nothing to do with weaponry, including the following options.

OTHER CUSTOMIZATIONS

Choose an option from the other customizations table or roll randomly.

d20	Other Customization
01–02	Comfortable seat
03–04	Crash protector
05	Engine of light
06–07	Hover harness
08	Instant float
09–11	Language bridger
12–13	Pabulum dispenser
14	Portable garage
15	Shield module
16–17	Summoning module
18	Thief deterrent module
19–20	Vehicle grip

COMFORTABLE SEAT

Level: 1d6

Form: Device attached to saddle or seat

Effect: When a rider uses the saddle or seat for at least an hour while they have fewer than their maximum points in a Pool, the device injects a restorative substance into the rider's body. This restores 1d6 points to any stat Pool they wish (1d6 + 2 points if the artifact is level 5 or higher). Using this function does not require an action.

Depletion: 1 in 1d10 (for the healing ability; after depletion, it still functions as a seat or saddle)

CRASH PROTECTOR

Level: 1d6 + 3

Form: Mountable device with large glass dome

Effect: Once mounted, the crash protector remains inert unless the vehicle or mount would suffer a catastrophic crash or impact. Before the full effects of the event are felt, the crash protector siphons all inertia from the vehicle or mount (and any passengers) to prevent destruction or excessive damage. If the level of the vehicle or mount, or the level of the disaster that caused the crash, is greater than the crash protector's level, it is only partially effective. A partially effective crash protector instead provides Armor equal to the level of the crash protector against damage from the crash.

Depletion: Automatic

ENGINE OF LIGHT

Level: 1d6 + 2

Form: Large device securely mounted on vehicle (not customizable for most mounts)

Effect: When engaged, pushes a commonplace vehicle. Depending on the vehicle's normal capabilities, the engine can push it across the land, through the water, or through the air by expelling a jet of light for up to 10 hours per use (though the user can break this up into smaller units of time). This allows the vehicle to move a short distance each round or an average of 8 miles per hour (13 km/h) in good conditions. Artifacts of level 7 and higher can allow a vehicle to move a long distance each round or up to 50 mph (80 km/h) in good conditions.

Depletion: 1 in 1d100 (check each day item is used)

HOVER HARNESS

Level: 1d6 + 2

Form: Mountable device attached to wires that encircle vehicle or weave a harness around mount

Effect: Useful for a vehicle facing rough terrain or choppy water, allowing the vehicle to float up into the air or back down again an immediate distance per round, according to which direction the user adjusts the dial. The harness doesn't provide options for horizontal movement, but the user can push or pull the hovering object through some other means. The harness functions for ten minutes per use.

Depletion: 1 in 1d10

INSTANT FLOAT

Level: 1d6

Form: Mountable device attached to wires that encircle vehicle or weave a harness around mount

Effect: Once mounted, the instant float remains inert unless the vehicle or mount would be submerged in water. Before the full effects of the event are felt, the instant float deploys large, silvery bags filled with a buoyant gas that either prevents the vehicle or mount from sinking or rapidly lifts an already submerged one.

Depletion: Automatic

LANGUAGE BRIDGER

Level: 1d6

Form: Mountable device about 3 feet (1 m) on a side with several metallic antennas protruding at odd angles

Effect: For one hour per use, all creatures within short range of the vehicle or mount (or location) to which the device is attached can speak with each other if they have a language, whether or not any of the languages are the same.

Depletion: 1 in 1d100

PABULUM DISPENSER

Level: 1d6

Form: Mountable cabinet-like device (taking up the space of two human-sized passengers)

Effect: Slot on the front of the device extrudes chewy, nutritious, nearly tasteless white material. Each extrusion can satisfy the food requirements of one person for 28 hours.

Depletion: 1 in 1d20

PORTABLE GARAGE

Level: 1d6 + 3

Form: Mountable silvery box attached somewhere to vehicle or on mount's saddle

Effect: After delaying about a minute to allow riders to evacuate, the vehicle or mount is pulled into a limited artificial dimension (also called an otherspace). A small silvery fob is all that remains, which the user can carry with them. The vehicle or mount remains in storage and stasis until the residual fob is reactivated, producing the stored vehicle or mount in the nearest unoccupied space.

Depletion: 1 in 1d10

Living mounts subject to a rapid ascent from the watery depths may require treatment to avoid the effects of divers' disease (page 17).

*Vehicular Combat,
page 405*

SHIELD MODULE

Level: 1d6 + 2

Form: Mountable device attached to wires that encircle vehicle or weave a harness around mount

Effect: If a vehicle comes under attack while using the vehicular combat rules, a powerful energy field activates automatically and attempts to protect the vehicle. The same sort of field springs into being if the device is attached to a mount during regular combat. Any defense roll the user makes on behalf of their vehicle or mount is eased by one step. (A user riding a mount with this device attached also gains the benefit if attacked.) At artifact level 7 or higher, the shield eases defense rolls by two steps.

Depletion: 1 in 1d20

SUMMONING MODULE

Level: 1d6 + 2

Form: Mountable device attached to wires that encircle vehicle, plus a separate handheld device

Effect: If the handheld device associated with a mounted summoning module is activated, the vehicle activates and attempts to reach the user. Treat the vehicle as if piloted by a level 2 automaton that continually tries to reach the activated handheld device until it succeeds, either part is destroyed, or the handheld device is deactivated. If the summoning module is level 7 or higher, treat the vehicle as if piloted by a level 4 automaton.

Depletion: 1 in 1d20

THIEF DETERRENT MODULE

Level: 1d6 + 2

Form: 6-foot (3 m) long device affixed to hard point of vehicle or slung on the underside of mount via a harness

Effect: Once enabled (as an action), the device monitors a stationary vehicle's interior, exterior, and an area within immediate range of where it is parked, looking for unauthorized intruders. (If slung under a mount, the device monitors an area within immediate range of the hobbled mount.) Unauthorized access usually includes any person or creature that is not either the user or those the user specifically indicates

*Defensive automaton:
equal to the level of
the module; Armor 3*

*GM intrusion:
The thief deterrent
module accidentally
identifies a character
as an unauthorized
presence and activates.*

as authorized. If detected, a particular deterrent is activated. Any given thief deterrent module produces only one of the following options, though artifacts of level 6 and higher may have two options.

Warning: Blaring alarm sounds, easily loud enough to alert all creatures within long range.

Hiding: The vehicle or mount turns invisible for about a month or until a recognition phrase (which the user should have set while installing the customization) is audibly provided.

Lockout (vehicle only): A connection into the vehicle mechanism renders it unable to be operated until a recognition phrase is audibly provided.

Active denial (vehicle only, usually): For ten minutes, tiny, electrically charged automatons run through the vehicle, inflicting the module's level in points of damage each round to any creature in physical contact with the vehicle.

Recall (vehicle only): The vehicle attempts to return to some previously designated spot (a site the user should have designated while installing the customization) under its own power.

Defender: The device deploys a defensive automaton that actively stands off intruders for about a month or until a recognition phrase is audibly provided.

Depletion: 1 in 1d10

VEHICLE GRIP

Level: 1d6 + 2

Form: 3-foot (1 m) square device affixed to hard point of vehicle or slung on the underside of mount via a harness

Effect: Extends a metallic arm with manipulator for up to ten minutes per use. The user can verbally (or through internal control surfaces in an enclosed vehicle) command the vehicle grip to interact with the environment. This enables the vehicle or mount to anchor itself to something solid, grab a smaller creature or object, attempt fine manipulation of some external object, or even make a melee attack. The manipulator arm can extend up to about 30 feet (9 m) and remain effective.

Depletion: 1 in 1d20

TRAVEL DEVICES

The following artifacts are typically used directly by characters (as artifacts normally are) rather than being fitted to vehicles or mounts.

TRAVEL DEVICES

Choose a travel device from the travel devices table or roll randomly.

d20	Travel Device
01	Anywhere door
02–04	Companion light
05	Crashdown transporter
06	Endless coil
07	Flight armor
08–09	Glow skates
10	Instant vehicle
11–12	Jet gloves
13	Path lead
14	Personal canopy
15–16	Translation disc
17	Travel companion
18	Traveling shield
19	Void ring
20	Wayfinder

ANYWHERE DOOR

Level: 1d6 + 2

Form: A matched set of two 3-foot (1 m) long rolls of reflective gold foil, set with intricate metallic lines

Effect: If both sets of foil are unrolled and adhered by lightly pressing them to a fixed, generally flat surface, large enough to hold a rectangular shape 3 feet (1 m) wide by 6 feet (2 m) long, a creature or object can pass between the two anywhere doors as if a regular door, no matter how far apart the two doors are placed on the same world. Anywhere door sets of level 7 and higher can transmit between any two locations, regardless of whether they are in another galaxy or even dimension.

Depletion: 1 in 1d10 (check once each day used)

COMPANION LIGHT

Level: 1d6 + 1

Form: Crystal sphere about 1 foot (30 cm) in diameter, set in a collar-like device

Effect: For 10 hours (or until recalled), the companion light flies over the user's head at a height of up to 30 feet (9 m) where possible, all the while projecting a beam of light that brightly illuminates the area a short distance in radius around the user. Moves up to a long distance each round when deployed. Companion lights of level 6 and higher can brightly illuminate an area up to a long distance in radius around the user, should they desire.

Depletion: 1 in 1d20

CRASHDOWN TRANSPORTER

Level: 1d6 + 2

Form: Floating metallic device that hovers near user

Effect: Using the attached pointer, the user takes at least three rounds to draw a boundary on the ground, creating an area that can hold no more than ten standing people. While being drawn, the boundary also is visible as a faint, translucent line of light hanging in the air, though it can be passed through. When completed, the boundary line instantly transforms into a three-dimensional, many-sided shape that encloses any creatures standing inside. The geometric shape and its occupants teleport to a destination determined by the user. The destination must be somewhere in the solar system and be a place the user has seen before or knows for certain exists. When the polygon of light appears at the destination, it smashes down onto a solid surface from height, inflicting damage equal to the artifact's level to all creatures in an immediate area from its landing point who fail a Speed defense roll. However, all those within only feel a slight jarring right before the polygon of light evaporates.

Depletion: 1 in 1d10

ENDLESS COIL

Level: 1d6

Form: Pouch-like object

Effect: A coil of stranded synth can be pulled from the pouch (which contains an artificial extradimensional space) and used as a rope with a level equal to the artifact's level. The rope can be pulled out to any length, at a rate of up to a short distance each round. It can be cut or pulled back in; either way, the artifact can still produce more rope until depleted.

Depletion: 1 in 1d100 (check per 50 feet (16 m) of rope produced)

Users of an anywhere door usually unroll and adhere one end of a matched set at a safe location, then carry the other roll with them on their travels to be used at need.

FLIGHT ARMOR

Level: 1d6 + 4

Form: Full suit of synth and steel armor, covering the entirety of the wearer's body; features a bulky flight machine attached to the suit's back

Effect: For up to one hour, this armor allows the wearer to fly a long distance each round (by employing the jet-like machine) or an average of 120 mph (190 km/h) during long-distance travel.

In addition, the armor grants an additional +3 to Armor in addition to the 3 Armor that heavy armor usually offers. Further, it completely protects the wearer against poison gases and allows them to operate in an airless environment. The suit's Armor rating also applies to damage that often isn't reduced by typical armor, such as environmental damage (but not Intellect damage).

Flight armor is large and sturdy enough to support some weapon customizations, as determined by the GM, and could be found with a force cannon customization already installed if the artifact is level 9 or higher.

Depletion: 1 in 1d20 (Check each time flight is engaged. In addition, at any time, the GM can rule that the armor has sustained enough damage that the flight options cease, as do the atmosphere and environmental protections; the suit still functions as armor, however.)

Force cannon, page 34

Manipulating fine objects and similar tasks are hindered for someone wearing jet gloves.

GLOW SKATES

Level: 1d6 + 1

Form: Matched set of two bulky devices that can be strapped to user's feet like bulky boots

Effect: For up to one hour, projects a glowing hard-light extension from the bottom of each device, which the wearer can use to skate across any solid terrain, as well as up vertical walls. (Hard light created by the skates dissipates a round after the skates move past.) Over relatively flat terrain, a user can move up to a long distance each round or up to 50 mph (80 km/h); however, a user must make a difficulty 1 Speed roll each round to move so fast.

Depletion: 1 in 1d20

Slugspitter, page 301

Windslice blade, page 303

INSTANT VEHICLE

Level: 1d6 + 1

Form: Fob-like handheld device

Effect: Activation causes the fob to unfold into a simple two-wheeled vehicle (level 2) with an exposed seat for one rider for up to 28 hours. Ideal for wild terrain and off-road travel; moves a short distance each round in rough terrain or an average of 30 mph (48 km/h) during long-distance travel.

Choose or roll a d100 to determine if the vehicle has additional qualities. Add double the level of the artifact to the d100 roll if rolling randomly.

01–35	As indicated.
36–50	Vehicle speed is doubled.
51–65	Vehicle speed is tripled.
66–75	Vehicle can carry a passenger.
76–90	Vehicle can fly at indicated speed.
91–00+	Vehicle can fly at double indicated speed and carry a passenger.

Depletion: 1 in 1d20

JET GLOVES

Level: 1d6 + 1

Form: Bulky, gauntlet-like devices with a control surface on each

Effect: For up to one hour, the user can fly a long distance each round or an average of 50 mph (80 km/h) during long-distance travel, pulled through the air by the jet gloves. However, precise control of flight is tricky; anytime the user takes off, lands, or attempts some other flight maneuver that requires a degree of precision, the wearer must succeed on a Speed roll (minimum difficulty 1) for each round the situation persists.

Jet gloves of level 6 and higher typically have an additional ability such as invisibility, a built-in slugspitter, or a windslice blade; each activation lasts ten minutes but requires an additional depletion roll for the gloves.

Depletion: 1 in 1d20

Every traveler needs a vehicle or mount, reliable food and water for the trip, impeccable directions, and some method to speak to strangers who speak strange languages encountered along the way.

PATH LEAD

Level: 1d6 + 2

Form: Spherical handheld device

Effect: Animates to become a small flying automaton (level equal to artifact's level minus 2; navigation is equal to the artifact's level plus 2) for up to 28 hours per use. The automaton can lead the user through mazes, across difficult terrain, and through similarly confusing locations with many possible routes, moving up to a short distance each round. A path lead may also guide a lost user to the nearest exit of a contiguous ruin or to the nearest location otherwise specified by the user.

Depletion: 1 in 1d10

PERSONAL CANOPY

Level: 1d6

Form: Silvery pellet set in handheld device

Effect: Pellet expands to form a rigid, capsule-like protective barrier around the user, which lasts for up to 28 hours or until the user deflates it. The barrier is useful as a personal shelter in cold weather or storms, like an almost-form-fitting tent with hard sides. Half the barrier is transparent, allowing the user to see their surroundings. While deployed, this artifact does not impede the use of personal aerial travel devices such as a hover belt or various special abilities that grant the user flight.

Depletion: 1 in 1d20

TRANSLATION DISC

Level: 1d6

Form: Silvery disc that adheres to wearer's head

Effect: For ten minutes, the user can speak with any target creature within short range as if they shared a common language. If the user is within a couple of miles of an active language bridger, they can reproduce that effect instead for ten minutes, if desired.

Depletion: 1 in 1d20

TRAVEL COMPANION

Level: 1d6

Form: Doll-like figure of squeezable synth

Effect: For one hour, the travel companion animates, imitating a pet-like creature that can also speak simple sentences in dozens of different languages—many no longer spoken, but including the Truth (after a bit of training). The travel companion is helpful but limited in what it can accomplish, given its small size and limited active time. However, some find it a useful companion on long trips.

Depletion: 1 in 1d100

TRAVELING SHIELD

Level: 1d6 + 2

Form: Thick shield set with devices

Effect: Can be used as a regular shield in combat, providing an asset to Speed defense rolls. In addition, the user can command the shield to wrap themself, and all creatures within immediate range, in a protective envelope that becomes a flying vehicle under the user's control. The vehicle can fly a long distance each round or up to 50 mph (80 km/h) for up to one hour per use.

Depletion: 1 in 1d20 (check each flight)

VOID RING

Level: 1d6 + 3

Form: Ring set with a bulky device

Effect: For up to ten hours, wearer can fly a long distance each round or an average of 120 mph (190 km/h) during long-distance travel. During travel, the wearer is protected from buffeting by wind, cold, and heat (gaining 10 Armor against damage by any of those sources) by a thin envelope of force, visible as a faintly glowing translucent light.

Void rings of level 8 and higher also protect the wearer from poison gases and allow the wearer to operate in an airless environment while flight is engaged.

Depletion: 1 in 1d10

WAYFINDER

Level: 1d6 + 2

Form: Handheld device featuring a crystal sphere about 4 inches (10 cm) in diameter set in a metallic frame with controls

Effect: User can call up a map-like representation of the surrounding area within about a 50-mile (80 km) radius for up to one hour per use. The representation is holographically projected above the sphere. The user can set waypoints to known locations (or points selected on the representation), which ease navigation tasks by three steps. Wayfinders of level 6 and higher may have previously set waypoints leading to ancient ruins or other sites of interest to the prior worlds.

Depletion: 1 in 1d6

Characters may find some comfort in deploying a personal canopy while flying through a rainstorm or at high speeds.

Hover belt, page 297

Language bridger, page 35

Some travel companions recall ancient pieces of knowledge long forgotten by humans of the Ninth World.

COMPREHENSIVE TRAVEL OPTION LISTING

The Comprehensive Travel Option Listing includes all the new travel options introduced here in Break the Horizon, *as well as options from other books as noted.*

The Numenera game line includes two corebooks and dozens of sourcebooks and adventures. Scattered through those 1,000+ pages of prior-world wonders are all kinds of vehicles, portals to elsewhere, and other numenera related to roaming afar. The following listing is an index to the majority of those items. Because this is a "comprehensive" rather than "complete" travel option listing, some options were too minor, or judged too repetitive, to include.

Each entry indicates the name, the option's level (if applicable), a very brief description, and the book title and page number where you can find full details. The listing is broken down by type, including mounts, land vehicles, sea vehicles, and air and void vehicles. The land, sea, and air vehicles are further divided by whether they are commonplace or travel options of the prior worlds. Cyphers and artifacts, portals, and abilities that grant travel are also categories.

Level and Short Description: The level and a short description are provided with each travel option presented in the comprehensive list so that you can use any given option in a pinch, even if the book it appeared in isn't at hand.

For example, the comprehensive listing indicates that a portable steed is level 5 and describes it as a cypher that creates a mechanical steed for seven hours. That's enough information for you to use even if you don't have access to the *Technology Compendium*, which is where the portable steed is fully described.

Movement vs. Travel: For the purposes of this listing, options were selected that provide a user with the ability to travel to relatively distant locations. Options that provide a user with enhanced movement abilities that last less than an hour, or allow travel between points with a maximum range of less than a mile (1.6 km), do not appear here.

THE CODEX OF TRAVEL

An Aeon Priest called Markham has set themself a massive task: to create an impressively sized tome called *The Codex of Travel* that describes every method of travel—known or rumored—including mounts, vehicles, portals, devices, and more. It also includes Markham's best guess as to where an example of each option might be found. A character with this treatise eases tasks to find any given travel option by two steps. (The Aeon Priest's book contains many of the entries found in this chapter.)

If a travel option didn't note the level in the original source but should have, an estimated level is provided. If an option's level is normally presented as a range, as is often the case for artifacts, the average level for the option is presented as its level in this comprehensive listing.

SOURCES

The following books were used to compile the Comprehensive Travel Option Listing.

Numenera Discovery	*Into the Outside*	*Technology Compendium: Sir Arthour's*
Numenera Destiny	*Liminal Shore*	*Guide to the Numenera*
Beyond All Worlds	*Ninth World Bestiary 1*	*The Devil's Spine*
Break the Horizon	*Ninth World Bestiary 2*	*The Octopi of the Ninth World*
Building Tomorrow	*Ninth World Bestiary 3*	*The Thief, the Clave, and the*
Edge of the Sun	*Ninth World Guidebook*	*Ultimatum*
Into the Deep	*Priests of the Aeons*	*Vertices*
Into the Night	*Slaves of the Machine God*	*Voices of the Datasphere*

MOUNTS

Mounts appearing under this heading are generally living, or at least biomechanical.

Travel Option	Level	Short Description	Sourcebook
Aneen	Level 3	Pack animal and mount	*Numenera Discovery*, page 225
Apricari	Level 4	Land mount for octopi who wish to come ashore	*Ninth World Guidebook*, page 224
Brehm	Level 3	Reptilian courser, fast and lightweight	*Ninth World Bestiary 1*, page 13
Dissicaeli's mount	Level 8	Biomechanical carnivorous, mammal-like reptile	*Ninth World Bestiary 1*, page 146
Espron	Level 2	Large, antelope-like creature that leaves no trail	*Ninth World Bestiary 1*, page 13
Eurieg	Level 4	Ice-climbing lupine creature with spidery legs	*Ninth World Bestiary 3*, page 188
Ferno walker	Level 6	Six-limbed mammal with hands; can go for weeks without water	*Ninth World Bestiary 1*, page 13
Firestrider	Level 4	Swift mount for up to two riders; temperamental	*Break the Horizon*, page 21
Guin	Level 3	Bioenhanced, cybernetic mount that speaks using a combination of whistles and machine language; travels great distances at great speeds; carries one to three	*Ninth World Guidebook*, page 178
Hirroc	Level 3	Six-limbed lizard with white fur and red scales able to walk for days without rest and able to carry very large loads	*Ninth World Bestiary 3*, page 189
Hurra	Level 4	Massive creature with tree-trunk legs bearing multitiered howdahs	*Into the Night*, page 124
Karestrel	Level 4	Large seabird that a small person might use as a mount	*Ninth World Bestiary 2*, page 79
Lorub	Level 5	Large water-dwelling beasts used as water mounts along coasts	*Ninth World Bestiary 1*, page 77
Malork	Level 4	Winged mount used by inhabitants of the storm-swaddled planet of Urvanas	*Into the Night*, page 146
Morwen	Level 3	Howdah-bearing (holds up to ten passengers) massive slug	*Break the Horizon*, page 20
Nacious	Level 4	Spider-like mount that carries a rider on its abdomen; good for travel across cliff faces or across the ceilings of subterranean vaults	*Break the Horizon*, page 21
Ollivant	Level 3	Protoplasmic creature that carries rider within interior vesicle	*Break the Horizon*, page 20
Oxyuratl	Level 6	Flying biomechanical creature that can serve as a mount	*Ninth World Bestiary 2*, page 124
Quaaen	Level 5	Flying reptile, bred and biomodded to serve as a mount	*Ninth World Guidebook*, page 239

Travel Option	Level	Short Description	Sourcebook
Queb	Level 4	Furry serpentine creature; carries 20 people at a time	*Ninth World Bestiary 1*, page 13
Rambu	Level 2	Many-legged creature that can carry a howdah or several riders	*Break the Horizon*, page 20
Raster	Level 4	Flying biomechanical creature native to the land of Ancuan	*Numenera Discovery*, page 248
Razorcat	Level 5	Massive, tigerlike creature; typically ridden by Llhauric priests and their holy knights	*Ninth World Bestiary 1*, page 13
Revi	Level 4	Four-winged avian; able to carry two riders	*Ninth World Guidebook*, page 109
Rukomol	Level 3	Biomechanical desert-dwelling insect; carries two	*Ninth World Bestiary 3*, page 189
Saquin	Level 3	Spider-like mount that swings between attachment points; ideal for canyons, towering ruins of ancient cities, and similar terrain	*Break the Horizon*, page 21
Scuttling metheglin	Level 6	Beetle-like creature used as a mount	*Ninth World Bestiary 2*, page 141
Shantag	Level 4	Leather-skinned beast with apelike forelimbs; often walks on all fours; can be trained for combat	*Ninth World Guidebook*, page 240
Shiul	Level 3	Four-horned herd animals, sometimes used as mounts	*Ninth World Bestiary 3*, page 186
Snow loper	Level 3	Tall, thin-legged, multi-eyed creature with long hair suitable as a mount in steep, rocky places	*Numenera Discovery*, page 253
Tarrow mole	Level 5	Burrowing creature, able to penetrate ruins and rock with equal ease; will serve as a mount for single riders for limited periods	*Ninth World Bestiary 3*, page 148
Tharink	Level 4	Motile plant; quick and lively enough to serve as a regular mount	*Break the Horizon*, page 21
Thurden	Level 2	Reptilian camel-like creature common in Uxphon	*Ninth World Bestiary 3*, page 189
Urtilla	Level 4	Many-legged crustacean underwater mounts with bioluminescent nodules	*Into the Deep*, page 155
Verx	Level 3	Swimming mount that can sustain an airbreathing rider with air bubbles	*Break the Horizon*, page 21
Voranoch	Level 3	Reptile on Naharrai large enough to be ridden when domesticated	*Into the Night*, page 39
Xi-drake	Level 5	Flying reptile; may serve an Angulan Knight as a mount	*Numenera Discovery*, page 259
Zennit	Level 2	Giant humanoid creature that can carry one rider a long distance each round	*Break the Horizon*, page 20
Zephil	Level 3	Swift quadruped insect that pulls carts	*Into the Night*, page 124

Ancuan, page 160

Uxphon, page 171

Angulan Knights, page 217

COMMONPLACE VEHICLES

LAND VEHICLES, COMMONPLACE

Travel Option	Level	Short Description	Sourcebook
Cart, hand-pulled	level 2	Can carry cargo or one passenger	*Break the Horizon, page 23*
Chariot	level 2	Carries one or two passengers behind hitched mount	*Break the Horizon, page 23*
Coach	level 3	Carries up to six people inside and two on the driver's seat outside	*Break the Horizon, page 23*
Wagon	level 2	Larger, sturdier version of a mount-pulled cart	*Break the Horizon, page 23*

SEA VEHICLES, COMMONPLACE

Travel Option	Level	Short Description	Sourcebook
Canoe	level 2	Carries two on calm water	*Break the Horizon, page 23*
Caravel	level 5	Three-masted vessel with at least 30 crew and considerable cargo	*Break the Horizon, page 24*
Carrack	level 5	Three-masted vessel, larger and more advanced than a caravel	*Break the Horizon, page 24*
Coaster	level 3	Two-masted vessel, able to carry several dozen and cargo	*Break the Horizon, page 24*
Cog	level 4	Single-masted vessel, able to carry more cargo than a longship	*Break the Horizon, page 24*
Kayak	level 3	Carries one; better for rough water	*Break the Horizon, page 23*
Pushboat	level 3	Crank-turning keeps the boat moving in calm conditions; holds six	*The Devil's Spine, page 73*
Raft	level 1	Least safe version of water travel, prone to breaking	*Break the Horizon, page 23*
Rowboat	level 2	Carries up to six plus cargo; moves a long distance each round on water	*Break the Horizon, page 23*
Sailboat	level 3	Carries up to ten passengers and some cargo	*Break the Horizon, page 24*
Subsurfacer	level 4	One-person submersible craft	*Break the Horizon, page 23*

AIR VEHICLES, COMMONPLACE

Travel Option	Level	Short Description	Sourcebook
Balloon	level 3	Hot air lifts a basket; usually moves with the wind	*Break the Horizon, page 25*
Dirigible	level 4	Lighter-than-air gas fills a cigar-shaped balloon that lifts a gondola	*Break the Horizon, page 25*
Glider	level 2	Single-person air vehicle; also referred to as a glide wing	*Break the Horizon, page 25*

In the undercity of Mulen, rat-like creatures can be hitched to wheeled carts to quickly move passengers and cargo between distant locations. However, the hitched creatures can't stand even dim light, so such trips usually pass in cool darkness with only the sound of dozens of tiny feet to keep a traveler company.

Mulen, page 154

CYPHERS AND ARTIFACTS

The distinction between devices that provide a method of travel and vehicles of the prior worlds is not always easy to distinguish. In this case, devices that unfold or unlock another travel method are listed here under the Cyphers and Artifacts heading. Easily stored devices that enable travel for just their user are also described under this heading. Artifact-like devices that already have the conformation of a usable vehicle by more than just a single user are listed under Vehicles of the Prior Worlds.

CYPHERS BY LEVEL

Travel Option	Level	Short Description	Sourcebook
Airfins	level 3	Allows user to swim through air as if water	*Technology Compendium*, page 33
Instant wings	level 3	Allows user to glide for up to one hour	*Technology Compendium*, page 64
Trail blazer	level 3	Gives user a 28-hour window in which to teleport once between locations accessed since the cypher was activated	*Numenera Destiny*, page 185
Travel bubble	level 3	Creates flying force bubble that persists for 10 hours	*Numenera Destiny*, page 185
Light flyer	level 4	Creates a winged flyer, allowing a four-hour flight	*Technology Compendium*, page 67
Light steed	level 4	Creates physical mount lasting eight hours	*Technology Compendium*, page 67
Augmech handset	level 5	Allows user to control a distant artificial body	*Edge of the Sun*, page 73
Bridge builder	level 5	Creates permanent bridge up to a very long distance	*Building Tomorrow*, page 91
Bubble flyer	level 5	Creates temporary flying membrane for a few passengers	*Liminal Shore*, page 86
Cloudskimmer	level 5	Lifts up to four humans into the air for hours	*Technology Compendium*, page 40
Flying cap	level 5	Rotors extend from cap, allowing user to fly	*Technology Compendium*, page 55
Portable steed	level 5	Creates a mechanical steed for seven hours	*Technology Compendium*, page 80
Augmech crown	level 6	Mentally transfers user into a distant artificial body	*Edge of the Sun*, page 73
Road builder	level 7	Creates permanent road up to 10 miles (16 km) long	*Building Tomorrow*, page 98
Teleporter, mass	level 7	Teleports several creatures hundreds of miles	*Technology Compendium*, page 92
Teleporter, traveler	level 7	Teleports user hundreds of miles	*Numenera Discovery*, page 288
Time skipper	level 7	Pushes user ahead in time by minutes, hours, or days	*Priests of the Aeons*, page 46
Transdimensional gate	level 7	Creates portal to an alternate reality	*Technology Compendium*, page 93

PLANS AS BUILT DEVICES

Some subset of the vehicles, artifacts, portals, and other devices presented in the referenced sourcebooks in this comprehensive listing appear as *plans* for creating said vehicles and artifacts rather than as the thing itself. However, the players can find a completely functional vehicle or device instead of the plan whenever you wish. The stats for an already completed vehicle or other travel device are easily derived from its plan. The plan's Minimum Crafting level is the constructed vehicle or artifact's level, and the Specifications text describes it and/or its effect. And the depletion indicated is the depletion for the constructed vehicle.

ARTIFACTS BY LEVEL

Travel Option	Level	Short Description	Sourcebook
Powered boots	level 3	Grants quick movement on most physical surfaces	*Building Tomorrow*, page 87
Temporary wing	level 3	Allows user to fly	*Numenera Destiny*, page 192
Burrowing boots	level 4	Allows user to burrow down through the ground	*Priests of the Aeons*, page 49
Flight pack	level 4	Pack-like artifact; grants user flight for one hour	*Technology Compendium*, page 114
Instant vehicle	level 4	Unfolds from fob to become a two-wheeled vehicle for 28 hours	*Break the Horizon*, page 38
Pico wheel	level 4	Produces enclosed overland vehicle; holds one	*Building Tomorrow*, page 87
Traveling shield	level 5	Can be used as a shield in combat; becomes a flying vehicle for user and several passengers	*Break the Horizon*, page 39
Carapace component, wings	level 5	Biomechanical being; can be fitted to another creature as an artifact, which can be further customized with wing components	*Into the Night*, page 72
Flying harness	level 6	Grants wearer flight	*Ninth World Guidebook*, page 118
Foldable coach	level 6	Unfolds, becoming a self-powered coach	*Technology Compendium*, page 114
Node interface	level 6	Provides asset to understand and use a line node teleportation network	*Into the Night*, page 17
Augmech throne	level 7	Mentally transfers user into a distant artificial body	*Edge of the Sun*, page 78
Autarch actuator	level 7	Transcribes user into a distant artificial body	*Edge of the Sun*, page 78
Lacewing shirt	level 7	Unfolds lacy wings allowing user to fly	*Priests of the Aeons*, page 51
Liminal sail	level 7	Can be attached to a ship, allowing the ship to sail between the physical world and a simulated world contained in the datasphere	*Liminal Shore*, page 102
Photon transporter	level 7	Teleports users between two discs, regardless of the distance separating them	*Technology Compendium*, page 127
Xeobrencus stone	level 7	Transfers consciousness of user across the galaxy into the body of another creature living on a planet called Xeobrencus	*Into the Night*, page 90
Book of doors	level 8	Creates doorways into other dimensions	*Building Tomorrow*, page 70
Crossroads vestibule	level 9	Allows access to interdimensional hub	*Building Tomorrow*, page 71
Hover square	level 3	Hovering platform; moves a short distance each round	*Numenera Discovery*, page 297
Glow skates	level 4	Boots; allow wearer to skate across most terrains on hard light	*Break the Horizon*, page 38
Jet gloves	level 4	Bulky gauntlets; allow user clumsy flight	*Break the Horizon*, page 38
Wings of the Liminal Shore	level 4	User gains permanently grafted wings (which deplete after a week away from the Liminal Shore)	*Liminal Shore*, page 106
Anywhere door	level 5	Matched set of endpoints that become a door between any two points once both segments are installed	*Break the Horizon*, page 37
Crashdown transporter	level 5	With a few rounds of prep, teleports small group via a polygon of light that smashes into destination	*Break the Horizon*, page 37
Flux suit	level 5	Wearer can swim a long distance per round	*Into the Night*, page 91
Void ring	level 6	Ring; grants user flight and some degree of protection from environment	*Break the Horizon*, page 39
Flight armor	level 7	Battlesuit-like armor with flight capabilities	*Break the Horizon*, page 38

VEHICLES OF THE PRIOR WORLDS

LAND VEHICLES, NUMENERA (ALPHABETICALLY)

Travel Option	Level	Short Description	Sourcebook
Battle cart	level 7	Multi-wheeled enclosed vehicle with embedded weaponry	*Numenera Destiny*, page 170
Burrower	level 6	Enclosed burrowing vehicle; holds six	*Numenera Destiny*, page 171
Catena, hovertrain	level 7; estimated	Series of cars that magnetically levitate on a set track	*The Devil's Spine*, page 25
Chainpod	level 4	Single-person vehicle; resembles a large wheel	*Numenera Destiny*, page 171
Crawler tank	level 9	Enclosed, combat-capable tank; holds one	*Technology Compendium*, page 107
Cthonic bore	level 7	Enclosed vehicle; can travel on surface or burrow underground; holds five	*Technology Compendium*, page 108
Drit wheel	level 2	Two- or three-wheeled open-air vehicle; carries one	*Break the Horizon*, page 27
Domed wheeler	level 4	Enclosed cab; carries five safely, even in airless places	*Break the Horizon*, page 28
Dynamic roller	level 2	Wheeled frame with stabilizers that ease driving tasks for this overland vehicle	*Building Tomorrow*, page 83
Ectopic rover	level 6	Enclosed cab of this overland vehicle is actually a small artificial dimension that thoroughly protects driver and up to six passengers from external threats	*Building Tomorrow*, page 84
Flitting board	level 3	Hovering board holds one; traverses land or water	*Building Tomorrow*, page 85
Galloping gambado	level 6	Enclosed vehicle that runs and jumps; holds five	*Numenera Destiny*, page 174
Ghru articulated temple	level 7	Multi-chambered enclosed metallic vehicle	*Into the Night*, page 47
Glidon	level 3	Covered wagon built on a levitating platform	*Technology Compendium*, page 99
Homecoming vector	level 6	Overland vehicle with enclosed cab; can drive itself	*Building Tomorrow*, page 86
Jumper	level 4	Single-pilot vehicle that relies on jumping for locomotion	*Numenera Destiny*, page 175
Land wheeler	level 5	Enormous overland vehicle with four connected enclosed cabins	*Building Tomorrow*, page 86
Lava eel	level 6	Enclosed vehicle can traverse viscous liquids (such as lava); holds six	*Numenera Destiny*, page 176
Light wheel	level 6	Vehicle made of solidified light; carries one rider on exposed seat	*Break the Horizon*, page 28
Moving fortress	level 8	Massive tracks allow this moveable castle to traverse the landscape	*Building Tomorrow*, page 86
Mud roller	level 3	Simple open-air wheeled vehicle; holds four	*Numenera Destiny*, page 176
Omni wheel	level 3	Open-air vehicle with adaptable wheels capable of transforming to move across most terrain and even up near-vertical surfaces; carries up to two	*Break the Horizon*, page 27
Portwalker	level 3	Cab able to hold up to six supported by extendible legs perfect for wading through deep water	*Break the Horizon*, page 28
Roving abode	level 4	Wheeled vehicle with enclosed living accommodations	*Building Tomorrow*, page 88
Runner	level 2	Exposed cab on two biomechanical legs	*Break the Horizon*, page 27
Scream wheeler	level 2	Narrow exposed two-wheeled vehicle; single-pilot; loud	*Numenera Destiny*, page 177

Travel Option	Level	Short Description	Sourcebook
Skim flitter	level 3	Open-air vehicle able to traverse most physical surfaces	*Break the Horizon*, page 27
Snowskimmer	level 2	Exposed craft slides across snow and ice; single pilot	*Numenera Destiny*, page 177
Speedster	level 4	Open-air hover frame; carries two; moves especially fast	*Break the Horizon*, page 28
Speedster, battle	level 5	As speedster, plus offensive and defensive options	*Break the Horizon*, page 28
Strider	level 4	Enclosed cab with room for seven; usually has at least one weapon	*Break the Horizon*, page 28
Tendril crawler	level 5	Overland vehicle uses tendrils for movement; holds five	*Building Tomorrow*, page 88
Terapede	level 6	Exposed many-legged land craft; holds several passengers	*Numenera Destiny*, page 177
Transport cart	level 4	Enclosed multi-wheeled land vehicle, capable on both rough and smooth terrain; holds five	*Numenera Destiny*, page 178
Touring city	level 9	Vehicle on massive legs with accommodations for thousands	*Building Tomorrow*, page 89
Two-legged wayfarer	level 3	Enclosed cab with room for five supported by two articulated biomechanical legs	*Break the Horizon*, page 28
War chariot	level 8	Enclosed multi-wheeled land vehicle; holds nine, each of whom can use an integrated weapon system built into the vehicle	*Numenera Destiny*, page 179
Wheeled vehicle, moon	level 5	Enclosed lunar vehicle capable of traversing the moon's terrain; holds eight	*Into the Night*, page 33

SEA VEHICLES, NUMENERA (ALPHABETICALLY)

Travel Option	Level	Short Description	Sourcebook
Deep diver	level 3	Underwater descender; holds six	*Numenera Destiny*, page 172
Deep swimmer	level 6	Underwater vehicle; holds twelve plus cargo	*Numenera Destiny*, page 172
Lorrother	level 7	Massive vehicle shaped somewhat like a lobster nearly 300 feet (100 m) across; clambers around the ocean floor armed with torpedoes; crewed by over a dozen creatures	*Into the Deep*, page 103
Roarboat	level 2	Open-air watercraft; carries nine; loud	*Break the Horizon*, page 30
Sailing abode	level 4	Watercraft with enclosed living accommodations	*Building Tomorrow*, page 88
Sea voyager	level 4	Very large watercraft with both open-air and enclosed decks; ideal for habitation during long water trips	*Break the Horizon*, page 30
Skelirroth dredge	level 7, estimated	Supermassive undersea dredging vehicle; scrapes clean the bottom-dwelling creatures along the ocean floor, continuing a centuries-long, automated mission of resource extraction	*Into the Deep*, page 77
Skimmer	level 6	Mechanical craft skims just above the water; carries six	*The Devil's Spine*, page 73
Sliver	level 4	Exposed watercraft; single pilot	*Numenera Destiny*, page 177
Solo submersible	level 6	Travel underwater for up to one week; holds one	*Into the Deep*, page 10
Submarine	level 7	100-foot (30 m) long vehicle, requiring crew of at least ten; carries 40 or more	*Into the Deep*, page 11
Submergine	level 5	Clearsynth bioship; able to dive up to 5 miles (8 km) beneath the ocean's surface and stay there for up to six years	*Numenera Discovery* page 219; *Into the Deep*, page 11
Swimming mount	level 2	Exposed underwater craft for two riders	*Numenera Destiny*, page 177
Venter	level 5	Three-person underwater vehicle, two inside and one outside	*Into the Deep*, page 120
Waterskimmer	level 2	Exposed craft jets across water; single pilot	*Numenera Destiny*, page 179

Submergines had a big role in the novel Tomorrow's Bones *by Shanna Germain.*

AIR VEHICLES, NUMENERA (ALPHABETICALLY)

Travel Option	Level	Short Description	Sourcebook
Battle flyer	level 7	Flying enclosed vehicle with embedded weaponry	*Numenera Destiny*, page 170
Blast wing	level 4	Single-pilot open-air flying vehicle with attack and defense options	*Break the Horizon*, page 30
Blazing Pillar	level 7	Massive floating three-level flying machine; moves up to a long distance each round	*Slaves of the Machine God*, page 115
Dynamic frame	level 1	Simple two-wheeled vehicle with exposed seat for one rider	*Numenera Destiny*, page 173
Ectopic wing	level 7	Enclosed cab of this flying vehicle is a small artificial dimension that thoroughly protects driver and up to six passengers from external threats	*Building Tomorrow*, page 84
Flit disc	level 5	Open-air flying disc; room for dozens of people and cargo	*Break the Horizon*, page 31
Flyer	level 6	Flying vehicle; holds six	*Numenera Destiny*, page 174
Growling wing	level 3	Flying vehicle with steep learning curve; holds two	*Building Tomorrow*, page 85
Hover disc	level 2	Open-air flying disc for one driver	*Numenera Destiny*, page 174
Hover frame	level 2	Open-frame surface good for hauling cargo	*Numenera Destiny*, page 175
Jet frame	level 4	Open-frame surface with options for fast travel	*Numenera Destiny*, page 175
Junkwing	level 2	Fixed-wing simple flying vehicle	*Numenera Destiny*, page 176
Lance wing	level 5	Enclosed cabin carries up to two; can fly through air or transition to fly higher into the airless void for about a day; includes offense options	*Break the Horizon*, page 31
Lithe wing	level 3	Single-pilot open-air flying vehicle	*Break the Horizon*, page 30
Nightswimmer	level 5	Enclosed cabin carries up to seven; can fly through air or transition to fly into the airless void for extended interplanetary trips	*Break the Horizon*, page 31
Ossam's stage	level 5, estimated	Floating numenera platform; serves as transport for equipment and a hovering stage during performances	*Numenera Discovery*, page 159
Rachar observation platform	level 7	Floating structure of metal and synth hovers high above Rachar; could be used as a battle flyer by someone able to repair it	*Numenera Discovery*, page 155
Sky chariot	level 8	Flying vehicle shaped like a massive head; holds eight	*Technology Compendium*, page 131
Soarcraft	level 6, estimated	Biomechanical creatures; held aloft by massive lighter-than-air gases and propelled by numenera engines; can move 300 miles (483 km) per hour	*Ninth World Guidebook*, page 187
Surveyor	level 2	Very stable hovering disc; ideal for aerial observation but slow-moving	*Break the Horizon*, page 30
Thunder harness	level 2	Exposed single-pilot flying pack	*Numenera Destiny*, page 178
Void dreamer	level 10	Colossal egg-shaped craft with several interior spaces; can fly through the airless void for extended interplanetary and interstellar trips	*Break the Horizon*, page 32
Windrider	level 4	Metallic wing artifact just large enough for a single person to ride through the air on	*Numenera Discovery*, page 303
Windrider, Urvanas	level 4	Variable-length metallic wing artifact; suitable for flying above the storm-swaddled surface of the planet Urvanas	*Into the Night*, page 55

VOID, INTERDIMENSIONAL, AND TIME VEHICLES (ALPHABETICALLY)

Travel Option	Level	Short Description	Sourcebook
Blood Tracker	level 5	Pirate ship (a caravel); sails between the physical world and a simulated world contained in the datasphere	*Liminal Shore*, page 35
Blue Voyager	level 5	Small flying vehicle (room for one) that can also transfer across dimensions; usually found in the bay of a crystal ship (listed hereafter)	*Into the Outside*, page 13
Calram pod ship	level 4, estimated	Vehicles capable of traveling from Earth's surface to the moon or other orbiting habitat; hold a crew plus up to 10 human subjects	*Into the Night*, page 25
Chrono engine	level 8	Enclosed time-travel (backward only) vehicle; holds five	*Numenera Destiny*, page 172
Chronoboard	level 5	Flying board; holds one; allows pilot to see up to one hour into the past	*Building Tomorrow*, page 83
Chronolapse	level 7	Flying vehicle; holds one; can also travel one day backward in time	*Building Tomorrow*, page 83
Crystal Ship	level 6	Massive dimension-traveling craft with several interior chambers, including a control chamber, quarters, and a bay for a secondary exploratory vehicle (the previously listed Blue Voyager)	*Into the Outside*, page 12
Dimensional treader	level 7	Dimension-hopping vehicle; holds ten	*Numenera Destiny*, page 172
Dimensional wing	level 9	Flying vehicle with dimension-hopping capability	*Numenera Destiny*, page 173
Empyrean Coach	level 8	Transfers users to a structure in close orbit around the sun	*Edge of the Sun*, page 143
Fiery ascender	level 6	Tower-like frame that blasts up to six travelers into the void	*Numenera Destiny*, page 173
Fiery traverser	level 7	As fiery ascender, but with more capabilities once the void is reached	*Building Tomorrow*, page 84
Flit	level 5	Chair-like vehicle; suitable for low- and zero-gravity locations	*Edge of the Sun*, page 80
Harryd vessel	level 4	Enclosed interplanetary vessel for pirating; used by harryd	*Into the Night*, page 12
Loneshell	level 5, level 8 to break, cut, or penetrate	Interplanetary vessel; crafted from the biomechanical shell of void-adapted fauna	*Into the Night*, page 71
Nightcraft	level 6	A remnant interstellar spacecraft left behind from when Earth was the hub of an interstellar empire in one of the prior worlds	*Into the Night*, page 8

Caravel, page 24

The harryd are humanoid avian creatures that inhabit a structure deep in the void.

Travel Option	Level	Short Description	Sourcebook
Planetary escape pod	level 5	Single-person void-only traversal vehicle	*Numenera Destiny*, page 176
Raft, the	level 7	Teardrop-shaped silvery vehicle; suited to travel in water, air, space, or through alternate dimensions; when folded, appears as a pack-sized unit	*The Thief, the Clave, and the Ultimatum*, page 8
Rosenant	level 7, estimated	Interstellar vessel; piloted by a human not native to Earth	*Into the Night*, page 133
Silent Nyek	level 6	Dimension-traveling ship; sometimes takes on passengers	*Into the Outside*, page 55
Time machine	level 10	Massive arch; provides time travel into the future	*Technology Compendium*, page 138
Vindication	level 5	Trade ship (a carrack); sails between the waters off the western shore of the Steadfast and Anepus (a town on a simulated world contained in the datasphere)	*Liminal Shore*, page 34
Vlerryn	level 6, estimated	Wrecked prior-world interplanetary warcraft; orbits the sun	*Into the Night*, page 59
Voidglider	level 10	Enclosed interstellar ship capable of holding many passengers	*Numenera Destiny*, page 178
Voidstrider	level 5	Single-person suit-like vehicle with minimal movement capability; offers maximum passenger protection in extreme environments	*Numenera Destiny*, page 179

TELEPORTATION AND INTERDIMENSIONAL PORTALS (ALPHABETICALLY)

Most options presented in this category are at fixed locations.

Travel Option	Level	Short Description	Sourcebook
Cathedral of Lying Mirrors	level 5	Location that allows travelers to bodily transcribe into and/or out of the datasphere	*Voices of the Datasphere*, page 52
Celerillion Door	level 5, estimated	Direct "passage"; occasionally manifests as a door set high on a cliff face in the Black Riage mountain range; transfers those that enter to the bizarre dimension of Celerillion	*Into the Outside*, page 109
Celestial Beacon	level 7, estimated	Portal located at the center of a broken, floating ruin; connects to the Engine of the Gods, a structure in close orbit around the sun	*Edge of the Sun*, page 29
Cosmic slide	level 8, estimated	Transports users on round-trip journey; stops at several other points in the cosmos	*Into the Night*, page 80
Emperor of Green door to the University of Doors	level 6, estimated	One of several dimensional portal entrances, typically called diums, to the University of Doors	*Numenera Discovery*, page 137
Grinder of Infinities	level 7	Several cube-like devices, all manifestations of a single one; allow users who enter and successfully operate the complex device to travel to a selected alternate dimension	*Into the Outside*, page 11; *Break the Horizon*, page 130

Carrack, page 24

Long trips are improved in almost every way by the company of friends. Travel alone only if no other options are available.

University of Doors, page 209

Travel Option	Level	Short Description	Sourcebook
Lightning Crane	level 8	Location in the Clock of Kala that allows travelers to bodily transcribe into and/or out of the datasphere	*Voices of the Datasphere*, page 54
Line node	level 6	Teleportation device (once part of a larger network); teleports users to distant locations	*Into the Night*, page 16
Malgort	level 6	Organic structure; allows travelers to bodily transcribe into and/or out of the datasphere	*Voices of the Datasphere*, page 54
Mouth of Hell	level 6, estimated	Portal leading to a terrible extradimensional location	*Beyond All Worlds*, page 4
Naharrai tunnel	level 5, estimated	A direct "tunnel" connects the city of Lhauric on Earth and the city of Arthoyn on the dry planet of Naharrai	*Into the Night*, page 38
Niul transit system	level 4, estimated	Tiny creatures consume a traveler molecule by molecule, then reintegrate the person at another of their colonies in a distant location	*Into the Night*, page 124
Skybreaker vertice	level 5	Prior world ruin; contains a device allowing travelers to bodily transcribe into and/or out of the datasphere	*Voices of the Datasphere*, page 152
Snessic	level 5	Broken flying vehicle that still allows travelers to bodily transcribe into the datasphere	*Voices of the Datasphere*, page 54
Stellar door	level 8	Malfunctioning portal that—if repaired—provides transport to a predetermined location elsewhere in the universe	*Into the Night*, page 7
Transcendent cosmic door	level 10, estimated	Accessible via malfunctioning ancient spacecraft; offers amazing opportunities to travel to and from any other location in the dimension—to truly travel into the night and explore the cosmos	*Numenera Destiny*, page 402
Vendav Ring	level 10, estimated	Half-mile (1 km) wide circular hoop of yellow synth; sometimes transports those who enter it to an unknown location; occasionally "ghosts" of travelers show up later, flickering into and out of reality like two-dimensional projections	*Into the Night*, page 81
Violet Plateau vertice	level 5, estimated	Location in the Plains of Kataru allowing travelers to bodily transcribe into the datasphere	*Liminal Shore*, page 36
Winking Eye of God	level 5	Oval of flickering red energy transports those who pass through into a higher dimensional space known as the Trefoil	*Numenera Destiny*, page 375
World door	level 7	Creates a portal leading to two distant worlds (Perelande, another child of the sun; or the Gloaming, which lies in another part of the galaxy)	*Into the Night*, page 33
Yenth portal	level 6	Portal to a parallel universe full of weird landscapes and odd flora and fauna	*Numenera Discovery* page 152; *Into the Outside*, page 38

Clock of Kala, page 206

Lhauric, page 192

Plains of Kataru, page 179

Trefoil, page 375

OTHER

Travel options under this category are either identifying a class of travel-related locations or objects, or are areas, craft, or creatures so large (and/or weird) that they don't fit well in other categories. For this reason, the entries here are not provided with a fixed level.

Travel Option	Short Description	Sourcebook
Augmechs, various	A method of travel whereby a character "goes" to a location by inhabiting and animating a prosthetic body at the intended destination using special devices to make the connection	*Edge of the Sun*, page 89
Augmodrome	Location containing various "chairs" that allow a user to inhabit an artificial body (known as an augmech) as if it were their own body; located deep under the Earth's surface.	*Edge of the Sun*, page 28
Beanstalk	Base of a strand of material that reaches into the void; travel up the strand to a station situated at the edge of the void is possible using mechanisms associated with it	*Numenera Discovery* page 180; *Into the Night*, page 6
Cloud city	Thousands of cities float above the cloud-swaddled surface of Urvanas; many could be controlled like city-sized vehicles	*Into the Night*, page 51
Crowd City	City of fused, animated corpses; travels across the Cloudcrystal Skyfields	*Numenera Discovery*, page 169
Engine of the Gods	Vast structure in close orbit around the sun; has effectively made a vehicle of the entire solar system as it continually flees from an ancient threat	*Edge of the Sun*, page 8
Equation of summoning	Allows one who successfully assays this combination of numbers and strange symbols to call up a door to the Howling Pyramid, which lies in an alternate dimension where sound works differently	*Slaves of the Machine God*, page 73
Invisible corridors	Tunnels made of water threading through the oceans, stretching thousands of miles; inside, the water is breathable, water temperature and pressure are pleasant, and explorers from the surface can travel comfortably	*Into the Deep*, page 12
Lost Manufactory	Mobile creation-forge of the prior worlds; resembles a massive metallic insect standing 50 feet (15 m) high on machine legs; despite suffering serious degradation, the manufactory can still be piloted	*Slaves of the Machine God*, page 71
Nibovian lure	Any of an array of attractants designed for humans; those ensnared are ultimately transferred to the strange dimension of Reeval, home of Nibovian creators	*Into the Outside*, page 97
Nihliesh	Previously mobile vehicle-city on which a Ninth World city has since been constructed	*Numenera Discovery*, page 202
Quiet House	Physical structure opens onto a constantly expanding extradimensional manifold composed of myriad different types of rooms called the Endless Abode	*Into the Outside*, page 46
Rarrow rift	Connects the city of Rarrow with another location (or possibly far-future time) called Hidden Rarrow	*Numenera Discovery*, page 163
Rathatruum	Community built on the back of a multilegged automaton that patrols in a pattern, traveling many miles a year	*Numenera Destiny*, page 237
Sideslip Fields	Region allows explorers to walk into alternate realities (or get lost in them)	*Into the Outside*, page 10
Street behind the street	Limited dimension that echoes a single street running the length of Charmonde; entered by walking down any street in Charmonde with a specific key	*Numenera Discovery*, page 391

Swim portals	The perfected technology of instantaneous transportation allowing octopi to cross vast distances between hoop-like endpoints	*The Octopi of the Ninth World,* page 6
Sharp world portal	Transports the user—and up to five creatures they specify within immediate range—to a near-identical parallel dimension	*Vertices,* page 75
Taracal	Massive inhabited arcology that migrates across the Sea of Secrets	*Numenera Destiny,* page 217
Terminus	Ancient malfunctioning spacecraft 160 miles (260 km) long and 20 miles (32 km) wide	*Numenera Destiny,* page 396
Transport tube	Low-gravity maze of tubes whisks travelers to a distant location	*Technology Compendium,* page 8
Tumult tune	Symbols scribed on ceramic plates buried deep under the seas or scattered across the moon's dark side (or in other locations) can—if sung as a tune—transport the singer to a dimension of pure sound called the Tumult	*Into the Outside,* page 85
Umdera	Transportable town; periodically disassembled and hauled to be rebuilt in a new location	*Numenera Destiny,* page 196
Vertices, various	Various locations where physical creatures can be transcribed bodily into the datasphere and back out again	*Vertices*
Whaleboat	Creature as large as a city to which a great ship is affixed	*The Devil's Spine,* page 74

ABILITIES

Travel Option	Short Description	Sourcebook
Electrical Flight	Fly for ten minutes	*Numenera Discovery,* page 85
Dimensional Survey	Step into an alternate dimension for up to one hour	*Priests of the Aeons,* page 18
Flight	Fly for one hour	*Numenera Discovery,* page 65
Homeworld Bridge	Transmit yourself across the void to your homeworld and back	*Priests of the Aeons,* page 15
Into the Outside	Step into an alternate dimension without bouncing back	*Priests of the Aeons,* page 19
Mental Projection	Fashion yourself a psychic construct that can travel away from your body	*Numenera Destiny,* page 95
Return to the Obelisk	Teleport between any two crystals (including crystal obelisks) you are aware of, no matter how distant from each other	*Numenera Destiny,* page 77
Teleportation	Nano esotery; allows transport to any previously seen or visited location on Earth	*Numenera Discovery,* page 43
Time Travel	Travel to a point in time within ten years of the present	*Priests of the Aeons,* page 22
Traverse the Worlds	Nano esotery; allows transport to a previously seen or visited location on another planet or dimension	*Numenera Discovery,* page 43
Wind Chariot	Fly for up to ten hours	*Numenera Destiny,* page 102
Windwracked Traveler	Fly for an hour (or more with Effort)	*Numenera Destiny,* page 70

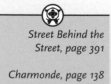

Street Behind the Street, page 391

Charmonde, page 138

Chapter 6: Creatures   56

Chapter 7: NPCs   72

CHAPTER 6

CREATURES

CREATURES BY LEVEL

Mind slime	2
Grindral	3
Howler	3
Road imposter	3
Seiskin	3
Dreamtooth	4
Gnath	5
Horticuller	5
Reality eater	5
Vestige	5
Datademon	6
Gray singer	6
Mazocacoth	6
Mirrored beast	6
Retenan	6

Encounters and Hazards Along the Way, page 78

Understanding the Listings, page 222

Reality eater, page 67

Dreamtooth, page 58

Road imposter, page 69

The creatures in this chapter are associated with travel. Of course, every creature described in previous Numenera corebooks, bestiaries, and sourcebooks is a potential candidate for characters to encounter while on a trip. The ones described here merely add to that list. In addition, most creatures described here are integrated into other sections of the book, including several in Encounters and Hazards Along the Way.

UNDERSTANDING THE LISTINGS

The most important element of each creature is its level, which also determines the target number a PC must reach to attack or defend against it. The target number is three times the opponent's level, and is listed in parentheses after its level in each entry.

A creature's target number is usually also its health, which is the amount of damage it can sustain before it is dead or incapacitated. For easy reference, the entries always list a creature's health, even when it's the normal amount for a creature of its level.

For more detailed information on level, health, combat, and other elements, see the Understanding the Listings section in *Numenera Discovery*.

THE SAFE WAYFARER TRAVEL GUIDE TO ENCOUNTERING CREATURES

One of the inevitable realities of traveling across the Steadfast and the Beyond, or even more distant locales, is that you'll encounter strange beings, dangerous entities, and hungry creatures. The first, best advice we can provide is to simply be prepared.

Preparation Is Never Wasted. The problem with preparing to explore ruins of the prior worlds is that almost by definition you don't know what kind of creatures you'll encounter inside. The best you can do is to have a hearty defense, a strong offense and, most importantly, some method of bridging communication gaps that would normally be insurmountable.

Not Every Creature Is a Foe. Sometimes the most horrific-seeming creatures can be negotiated with. It is always worth at least attempting to negotiate. Maybe you can defray a conflict that would otherwise happen, or maybe even gain an unlooked-for benefit. For instance, a successful negotiation with a reality eater could grant you passage to another dimension.

Humans or Something Else? Sometimes bandits pretend to be merchants or fellow travelers in order to spring an ambush. Other times, creatures pretend to be human for much the same purpose. If engaging strangers, be on the lookout for telltale signs of human mimicry instead of actual humanity. For instance, dreamtooths achieve their disguise through psychic manipulation, which can be detected by some Nanos. Road imposters are easier to detect, once you get close enough to see that their clothes are mismatched and not always worn properly.

DATADEMON 6 (18)

Like vestiges, datademons are born of vertices, which are locations that bodily transport characters into and out of the datasphere. However, unlike the ghostly phased vestiges, datademons are transcribed from the datasphere into physical bodies in the real world—bodies that are terrifying amalgams of flesh, synth, and twisted metal, a cause of constant pain for the creature. It is perhaps this agony that drives them to inflict such harm on any other creatures they meet, whether automaton, biomechanical, or fully living.

As a creature born of the datasphere, a datademon is able to physically tap into nearly every kind of automaton or machine it encounters, using the toothed umbilical that serves as its mouth. It also tries to do the same with purely living creatures, which usually ends poorly for the victim.

Motive: Violence

Environment: Almost anywhere, but especially near places where the datasphere can be accessed

Health: 22

Armor: 2

Damage Inflicted: 6 points

Movement: Short; very long when teleporting

Combat: A datademon can physically attack up to three creatures at once, inflicting 6 points of damage with each of two claw attacks and 6 points of damage with its toothed umbilical "mouth." However, a creature struck by the mouth faces additional troubles.

If the target hit by the toothed umbilical attack is an automaton or biomechanical, it must succeed on an Intellect defense roll or come under the datademon's direct control until the target escapes. The umbilical can stretch up to a short distance, during which time the controlled creature can continue to take actions mentally directed by the datademon, and the datademon can continue to make its two claw attacks against other targets.

If the target hit by the toothed umbilical attack is not mechanical or modified with machines, it must make a Might defense roll or the connection remains, automatically inflicting 6 points of damage each round until the target can escape.

Interaction: A datademon is a rage monster, though if PCs trap one, they might be able to communicate with it, and discover it is some distortion born out of the datasphere.

Use: The characters turn on an ancient machine. It spins up, begins to break, but manages to transcribe a datademon before failing.

Loot: A datademon's remains contain three or four cyphers.

Vestige, page 71

Vertices are locations that contain ancient machines able to transport characters into and out of the datasphere.

Datasphere, page 355

If characters attempt to sever the umbilical connection between the datademon and a victim by severing the umbilical or otherwise attacking it, treat the umbilical as a level 4 object.

Attacking Objects, page 116

GM intrusion: *The datademon grows a new toothed umbilical and attacks the character.*

DREAMTOOTH 4 (12)

Dreamtooths are somewhat-humanoid creatures able to telepathically disguise themselves to resemble other creatures they meet. (Any being with a mind, including biomechanicals and many automatons, are subject to the disguise, just like regular living creatures.) Dreamtooths adopt such disguises to pass unnoticed. Any given dreamtooth may act like a normal being of the kind it mimics, including being helpful to other creatures it encounters on the road. However, when night comes and sleep beckons, the dreamtooth feeds on the dreams of the nearest mind. When it does, the victim experiences unsettling nightmares, and upon waking is mentally drained, feeling even more tired than before they slept.

However, unless the dreamtooth finds itself physically threatened so that it must directly defend itself, that is likely the end of it. Dreamtooths yearn for diversity in their mental diet, and thus are constantly on the move, seeking out novel minds to mentally sample.

Motive: Devour the dreams of others

Environment: Almost anywhere, alone or in groups of three to ten

Health: 19

Damage Inflicted: 4 points

Movement: Short

Modifications: Disguise as level 7

Combat: Dreamtooths can use weapons, but their main defense against aggressors—and the manner they use to feed—is a short-range psychic attack against which a victim must make an Intellect defense roll. On a failure, the victim takes 4 points of Intellect damage (ignores Armor) and falls into a normal sleep. The dreamtooth can make this attack on a creature on the opposite side of a wall, but the attack is hindered.

If their disguise is ever pierced, a dreamtooth looks something like an animate, wrinkled prune that roughly conforms to a humanoid in shape.

Anytime the dreamtooth is damaged, startled, or the GM otherwise feels it is appropriate, a creature observing the dreamtooth can attempt a perception task to see past the dreamtooth's psychic disguise.

GM intrusion: *The character sees past the dreamtooth's psychic disguise, but the juxtaposition is so unsettling for the character that the dreamtooth can take a free turn to attack, run away, or do something else.*

Caravanserai, page 83

Most dreamtooths attack an already-sleeping target only once, and if successful are satisfied with their meal. However, if in an active altercation, a dreamtooth can continually attack each round. A target put to sleep by a dreamtooth attack can easily be roused with a loud noise or physical shaking, but this takes a round to accomplish, during which time the dreamtooth may attempt to escape around a corner, where it can take on a new psychic disguise to throw off pursuers. A victim that is affected by, but survives, a dreamtooth's psychic attack doesn't gain the healing benefit of their current (or next, if already used) ten hour recovery roll.

Interaction: Most dreamtooths seem like regular creatures of the kind they are disguised as. However, if their disguise is penetrated, they either flee or attempt to eliminate the one who has discovered their secret.

Use: A disguised dreamtooth family runs a caravanserai, feeding on travelers who stop by.

LADON

GNATH 5 (15)

Gnath are 12-foot (4 m) tall winged predators with enormous eyes that miss nothing. They spin up gooey, cocoon-like nests on ceilings and on the sides of tall structures or growths where they can watch their surroundings from a height. When a gnath discovers potential prey, it releases an enervating hunting howl, then wings down to snatch a victim affected by its screech, before finally returning to its nest where it can feast in peace. About an hour after completely consuming its prey, it vomits up a pellet of bones, clothing, and other items. Alternatively, instead of consuming paralyzed prey, it injects the eggs of its young in the unmoving, yet still-living target, then seals the victim into a sticky cocoon. When the eggs hatch, a warm and ready meal is waiting.

Gnath move from place to place, looking for remote locations where they can hunt for a time, before finally leaving a cocoon behind. There, the young will hatch, feeding on whatever morsel they emerge from.

Motive: Hungers for flesh; reproduction

Environment: Gnath hunt alone, but sometimes are found in pairs during mating periods.

Health: 24

Damage Inflicted: 6 points

Armor: 2

Movement: Short; flies a long distance each round

Modifications: Perception as level 8

Combat: A gnath can emit a piercing shriek that disables the motor functions of most living things (and in automatons that have any biomechanical parts), but only about once every minute. When it shrieks, all living creatures that can hear within short range must succeed on a Might defense roll or become unable to physically move. A victim so paralyzed can attempt to break free of the condition again about once each minute.

A gnath can carry a human-sized or smaller paralyzed creature back to its nest (which is usually not easily reached, except by other creatures that can fly). There it either begins to eat its victim, inflicting 6 points of damage each round, or it injects the prey with a fizzy bolus containing several pinhead-sized eggs, then seals the paralyzed target inside its cocoon. The eggs hatch about ten hours later, which is probably the end for a target who was unable to escape.

Use: Traveling PCs set camp in an area where a gnath hunts.

Loot: The pellets of digested prey (may contain equipment, shins, and items of the numenera that belonged to past victims).

GM intrusion: *The gnath coughs up a gelatinous sticky mess that sticks the character in place until they succeed on a Might-based task to break free.*

Cocoon: *level 3*

GRAY SINGER   6 (18)

One never knows where a gray singer will next appear. That question is put to rest when this red-eyed, equine-headed humanoid, shrouded in dappled gray wings folded like robes, appears in your camp—or, as sometimes happens, follows you back home after a long trip.

The gray singer begins any interaction with a song a couple of verses long. The song is often completely unfamiliar to those who hear it. However, every so often, the tune (and even the language) is familiar. Whether familiar or not, the gray singer finishes, then waits for a response. If you try to pick up the tune as best you can, you may gain the gray singer's favor.

A poor performance (which is usually one in which a character doesn't try at all), however, angers the gray singer. The bad luck that follows you afterward might be a sign of the gray singer's scorn.

Motive: Collect music

Environment: Almost anywhere

Health: 22

Damage Inflicted: 8 points

Armor: 1

Movement: Short; long when flying

Modifications: Music and performance as level 8

Combat: A gray singer usually only enters combat to defend itself, though it could attack someone that ignores its initial overture and refuses to reply musically in kind. If so, it can extend its wings and batter all creatures within immediate range for 8 points of damage.

If a character gains a gray singer's favor (as described under Interaction), the gray singer leaves behind a glowing, pearly gray feather suffused with transdimensional energy.

A character scorned by the gray singer may (or may not) later find a dead white feather among their possessions. Whether the feather is found or not, the next time the character attempts an important task (GM's discretion), it is hindered by three steps.

Interaction: A gray singer communicates only through music. It offers a random musical performance lasting a few rounds, then waits for some kind of reply. If a character attempts to reply in kind, in the same style, or otherwise attempts to follow the gray singer's initial musical foray, they must succeed on a difficulty 6 Intellect task to impress the creature. An impressed gray singer grants the character its favor. However, a character that doesn't try at all gains the creature's scorn.

Use: After the characters interact with a probability warping field or device, or after they pass into an alternate dimension, they notice an equine-headed creature following them.

Loot: The glowing feather signifying a gray singer's favor is a stim cypher.

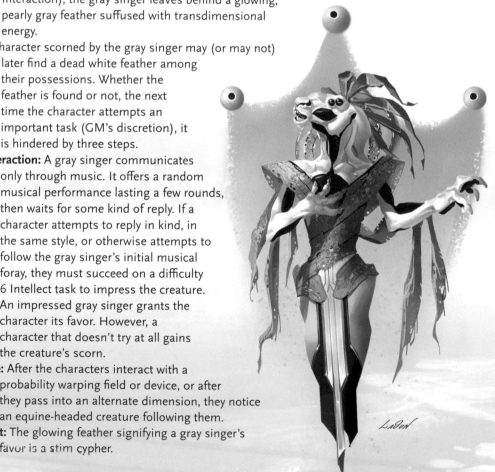

GM intrusion: *The character's attack on the gray singer is foiled because of an apparent unlucky coincidence: for example, the character slips, the character's weapon breaks, and so on.*

Stim, page 287

GRINDRAL 3 (9)

Many more fearsome abhumans exist in the Ninth World, but few are as roundly cursed out as grindrals. Existing purely on the efforts of other creatures, including other abhumans, grindrals steal to live. Because a stationary lair of thieving abhumans draws attention to itself, after which it is likely to be quickly located and burned out, grindral thief groups (usually consisting of a single extended family) mostly target travelers passing through an area rather than locals. In addition, they sometimes travel, themselves, rather than create a permanent lair.

Grindrals are slick-skinned creatures with five limbs (two legs and three differently sized arms) who have the ability to change their integument to take on the coloration and texture of their surroundings in moments. Adept at hiding, able to cling to almost any surface, and champion absconders if noticed, grindrals make perfect thieves.

Motive: Defense, stealing

Environment: Anywhere near roads or trails with at least some traffic, either alone or in groups of six to twelve

Health: 9

Damage Inflicted: 4 points

Movement: Short; short when climbing

Modifications: Lockpicking, perception, and stealth as level 6

Combat: Grindrals prefer to run from combat, but can bite foes if caught.

Their first line of defense is a psychic burst of confusion that affects all creatures within an immediate radius that fail an Intellect defense roll hindered by two steps. Affected targets lose their next turn (nor can they remember it). Grindrals can use this distraction to slip away, aided by their ability to blend into their surroundings. Even if a target isn't affected by a psychic burst, a grindral's camouflage ability may still allow it to safely sneak away with whatever it stole.

Interaction: Grindrals speak their own language. If communication is somehow managed, they are not interested in negotiating unless given no other choice.

Use: A group of travelers who were robbed during the night incorrectly blame the player characters for the deed.

Loot: Temporary grindral encampments (which look like several human-sized bird nests smashed together more than anything else) contain bits of stolen food, equipment, 20–30 shins, and possibly a few cyphers.

GM intrusion: *The character's attack doesn't actually hit the grindral; the creature was not exactly where it seemed to be.*

HORTICULLER   5 (15)

This 9-foot (3 m) tall metallic automaton is often encountered either tending to or planting trees, grass, and other plants. However, sometimes it is encountered clearing away flora of all kinds and feeding it into the angular funnel mounted on its arm. A mechanism within the arm quickly reduces the funneled material to mulch, which it then spreads as a bed for the seeds it presses into the earth with its other long, segmented arm.

GM intrusion:
The apparently calm horticuller suddenly attacks.

Horticullers are artificially intelligent machines that seem to have partially forgotten their purpose, though not utterly. Now they act erratically as they alternately plant or destroy vegetation. They either ignore or attack any creatures they come across, for reasons unexplained.

Motive: Unpredictable

Environment: Horticullers travel alone or in pairs and can be found anywhere flora grows (or used to grow).

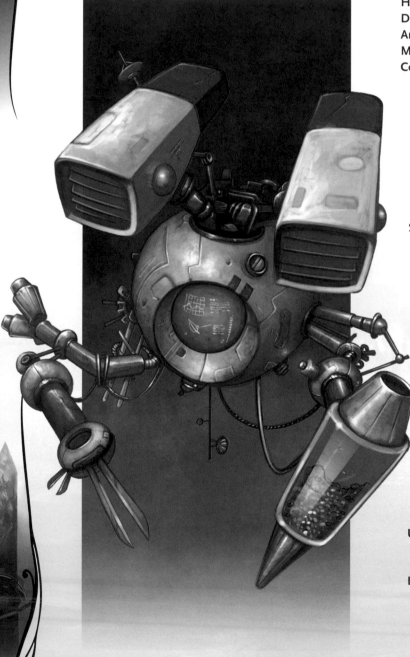

Health: 18

Damage Inflicted: 5 points

Armor: 3

Movement: Short (hovers)

Combat: A horticuller can attack twice on its turn; once with a shears-like implement on one of its arms and once with its segmented planting arm, using the spear-like seed ovipositor on the end. It inflicts 5 points of damage with each. If a creature is hit by either arm, it must succeed on a Might defense roll to avoid being dumped in the funnel leading to the mulcher (which inflicts 15 points of damage each round until a creature can pull its limb or itself free, or until it is dead and is mulched).

Sometimes, when a horticuller attacks a living creature with its seed ovipositor, it implants an especially exotic seed. This may have no effect on the creature. Then again, the target could end up sporting a strange growth from the wound within a few days, and/or go into anaphylactic shock (all tasks hindered by three steps until the growth—essentially a level 5 disease—is cured or recovered from).

Interaction: Horticullers are intelligent but unpredictable. They understand speech and, after listening to a language for a time, can often speak it in a very basic way. But a horticuller is just as likely to attack without provocation, perhaps even in the middle of a conversation. Still, a well-spoken, intelligent, and quick-witted character might be able to figure out what vegetation-related information the horticuller wants (at the moment).

Use: A horticuller attempts to cut down the tree being used in the PCs' camp (perhaps they've climbed into it or hung their hammocks from it).

Loot: The remains of a destroyed horticuller might hold 1d100 shins, 1d6 + 1 cyphers, an oddity, and perhaps a salvageable artifact. (Also, mulch.)

HOWLER 3 (9)

"Do you hear that? Out there in the night: something singing.
Many somethings, joining their voices in such a wonderful chorus . . .
Don't tell me to stay inside! Have you ever heard anything so beautiful?
It's like I'm dreaming while I'm awake. If you call it 'so much howling'
one more time, well, by Calaval's eyes, I swear you'll regret it!"

—*unfortunate last words of Kidrean Sasar,*
who fled her camp one night and was never seen again

Distant howls may be normal night beasts calling to each other. Or it could be a pack of howlers roaming nearby. The predators are always on the move, traversing lonely lands by night, and attempting to lure creatures who hear them into their presence, so they can feed without disturbance.

Motive: Hungers for flesh

Environment: Lonely locations, in packs of three to seven

Health: 17

Damage Inflicted: 4 points

Movement: Long; immediate when burrowing

Modifications: Stealth as level 4

Combat: Howlers bite and rend foes for 4 points of damage. A pack of three or more howlers can be treated as a single level 5 creature that makes two attacks for 5 points of damage each.

Howlers usually stay away from groups, preferring to draw one or two potential victims from a very long distance away by their song-like howls. A potential target may hear the far-off wail and think little of it; however, one in four people has a particular susceptibility to its draw. Within an hour or so of exposure, PCs selected by the GM must succeed on an Intellect defense roll hindered by two steps, or become so enamored of the sound that they try to slip away from whatever they're currently doing (which, given howlers only sing at night, is probably either sleeping or guarding camp) in order to find the source. This desire to get closer ends when the victim takes damage or the howling stops.

Interaction: Howlers are highly evolved predators, clever in how they trick or otherwise lure prey into an ambush.

Use: A nearby mazelike layout of weirdly regular canyons is known for the strange singing that sometimes echoes from its many entrances.

Howlers are usually encountered by those traveling through remote locations, away from communities and larger towns and cities.

GM intrusion: *A defeated howler utters a shattering death scream, which inflicts 3 points of ambient damage on all creatures within immediate range (except for other howlers or those with Armor versus sonic damage).*

MAZOCACOTH 6 (18)

Only a few mazocacoths walk the Ninth World. Each one has unique features, but all mazocacoths have two aspects, which vary by the sun's position. The aspect active at night is a massive phased entity towering at least 300 feet (90 m). It has many legs, like a spider, allowing it to move nimbly across mountain ridges and desert ravines alike. This "darkwalker" aspect is translucent and has the faintest of bluish glows, rendering it visible to some as it moves silently overhead like a scudding cloud.

The aspect that exists by day is the collapsed and solid version of the creature. This "sleeper" aspect is only 5 feet (1.5 m) in diameter, has only two legs and an almost-human face, and spends its time in a deep and almost-impossible-to-break sleep. Bright light intensifies this slumber.

Many who've seen a darkwalker get the sense that it's looking for something, though probably something that hasn't existed for aeons. Never succeeding doesn't keep mazocacoths from the search.

Motive: Searching for something lost

Environment: Anywhere

Health: 22

Damage Inflicted: 8 points

Armor: 2 (in sleeper aspect)

Movement: Very long in darkwalker aspect; short in sleeper aspect

Modifications: Perception as level 9

Combat: A mazocacoth has two forms.

Darkwalker: In its darkwalker aspect, the creature usually enters combat only if an attacker is able to affect its phased form, requiring a device designed to affect out-of-phase creatures or a weapon that relies on transdimensional energy. If threatened, a darkwalker can extend one of its many legs to stab a foe within 300 feet (90 m), inflicting 8 points of Intellect damage (ignores Armor). If the mazocacoth so chooses, all creatures within immediate range of the main target are attacked as well. Any who succeed on their Intellect defense roll still suffer 2 points of Intellect damage (ignores Armor).

Sleeper: A mazocacoth in its sleeper form is usually sleeping. If roused from slumber, the sleeper does not defend itself if attacked. It will move away at full speed if it can, and will transform to aid its escape if it is twilight or night. Bright light stuns them back into slumber if they are not already sleeping.

Either: If a mazocacoth is killed in either aspect, a psychic cry inflicts 8 points of Intellect damage (ignores Armor) on all creatures within about a mile (1.5 km) of the deed, unless potential targets are shielded by a structure or other intervening barrier. Even if shielded, potential targets are still stunned for a few rounds as they feel the mazocacoth's death. The body fades away over the course of a few rounds.

Interaction: A mazocacoth never speaks, but sometimes it grants boons to creatures that approach it respectfully—if they can get its attention. It may do the same to those who help a darkwalker in difficulty.

Use: The PCs hear of the "Nightwalker" that haunts a nearby mountain range. Locals in the area worship the nightly apparition as a god that, they say, keeps them safe from demons that would otherwise spill up out of the earth. See "The Roughest Day."

GM intrusion:
While the character uses a device in the proximity of the mazocacoth, it unexpectedly flashes with bright light, which stuns the mazocacoth or otherwise disturbs it greatly.

In its darkwalker form, the creature has access to a variety of additional abilities that include the power to heal creatures, teleport long distances, see several hours into the future, and probably more, as the GM determines.

"The Roughest Day,"
page 114

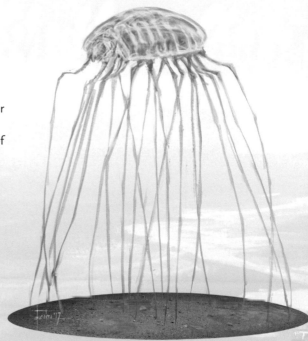

MIND SLIME   2 (6)

Vast networks of fungus-like life stretch underground for miles in some isolated regions. Evolved during, and probably touched by, the prior worlds, they pulse with psychic energy, passing information back and forth between nodes. Humans rarely ever discover their existence because they're mostly below ground, and tend to grow in places where the surface above is mostly empty of intelligent life, as if they are somehow sensitive to too much thinking.

The emergence of polyp-like translucent shapes that can grow to heights of 3 feet (1 m) is a clue that some might use to deduce the fungus-like network's existence. For most, however, the sudden appearance of "mind slimes" is just another danger of travel. They normally only appear in lonely areas, popping up out of the drit of one's camp in the middle of the night to make what seems like a predatory fungal attack.

Motive: Hungers for knowledge

Environment: Almost anywhere lonely, usually in clumps of six to ten

Health: 9

Damage Inflicted: 2 points

Movement: Immediate; immediate when burrowing

Combat: A mind slime can discharge a faintly blue-glowing, gooey substance at a target within short range. On a failed Speed defense roll, a target is partially covered in the substance, which hinders all physical tasks. The target can use their action to remove the material with a successful Might-based task. If a target's tasks are hindered by three steps because of an accumulation of gooey substance, the target becomes cocooned.

A cocooned foe is held immobile and can take only purely mental actions, or struggle to get free (a hindered, difficulty 4 Might-based task). Each round a victim remains cocooned, knowledge is siphoned from them and fed to the network below ground, inflicting 2 points of Intellect damage (ignores Armor) each round.

Interaction: Mind slimes are more like extensions of the networks that send them upward, and usually can't be negotiated with. However, a character with psychic abilities might be able to open communication through a mind slime to the alien network beneath.

Use: A single forager returns to the newly established outpost a few days after the group they were with left, with horrible stories about mind-eating mushrooms killing everyone.

GM intrusion: *The character that loses knowledge from a mind slime attack loses access to one of their abilities for several days or until they use a recovery roll expressly to regain the ability loss.*

MIRRORED BEAST   6 (18)

Named for the reflective nature of their skin, these many-legged, 12-foot (4 m) long automatons are acquisitive and territorial. They lurk in various ruins, draining energy from any still-active devices and machines they can find. They tend to remain at a location for only a few months or years before moving on and claiming a new location as their territory.

When a mirrored beast freezes in place, it can be very hard to distinguish from its surroundings, given its enhanced reflective surface. Unless a creature happens to catch its own reflection exactly head on, the beast may just reflect back more broken ruins to an oncoming viewer.

The mirrored beast's reflective defense, which disrupts other machines that might attack it, has the unintended consequence of mineralizing unlucky living creatures that trigger the defense. This means that mirrored beasts eventually accumulate a litter of "life-sized" crystal figures in their current territory.

Motive: Hungers for energy

Environment: Usually alone in ruins of the prior worlds

Health: 25

Damage Inflicted: 6 points

Armor: 1

Movement: Short; immediate when burrowing

Modifications: Speed defense as level 7 due to mirrored surface; stealth as level 8

Combat: The mirrored beast's two claw attacks inflict 6 points of damage each; however, the mirrored beast is first likely to use its ability to manipulate light in order to neutralize intruders.

The mirrored beast can use its action once each minute to adjust its reflective surface to bathe a target in short range with weird radiation. A machine or automaton of level 5 or lower becomes non-operational until repaired. Living creatures of level 5 and lower (and PCs who fail a Might defense roll) are mineralized, becoming solid crystal.

A crystallized target isn't dead. Someone who succeeds at an understanding numenera task while studying a mineralized victim realizes that placing the victim in a completely dark space for a few minutes should reverse the transformation. If the crystal isn't badly damaged, the target reverts to normal and is unharmed.

Interaction: Mirrored beasts communicate with other machines using invisible channels that most characters are completely oblivious to. However, a mirrored beast can sometimes attempt to trigger numenera carried by PCs to speak for it. When this happens, it's usually to deliver threats or demands for the characters to turn over their powered devices.

Use: Characters passing by an old ruin are noticed by a mirrored beast, which begins to stalk after them, drawn to their cyphers and other devices, as further explicated in What Follows.

GM intrusion: *The character that successfully strikes the mirrored beast must succeed on an Intellect defense roll, or discover they actually struck an illusion created by the beast's control over light.*

What Follows, page 109

REALITY EATER 5 (15)

Reality eaters are intelligent transdimensional gates. A 6-foot (2 m) diameter central blot of spherical darkness—the mouth—is surrounded by a halo of whirling metallic debris—the teeth. A mind exists as a telepathic overlay that survives on the outer "skin" of the mouth, visible as a purplish aura.

Even when it's not directly communicating, nearby creatures hear a muttering within short range. Reality eaters are thus sometimes referred to as muttering mouths, on account of the strange sounds they constantly produce. The sounds are likely distortions of sounds made in alternate connecting dimensions.

A reality eater can pull itself "inside out" to travel into any dimension it knows about, or into any adjacent dimension.

Motive: Knowledge, experience

Environment: Anywhere

Health: 26

Damage Inflicted: 5 points

Movement: Short while flying

Modifications: Transdimensional knowledge as level 7

Combat: A reality eater automatically attacks every creature within immediate range with its spinning "teeth" each round, inflicting 5 points of damage on targets who fail a Speed defense roll.

If a creature is killed while in immediate range of a reality eater, the victim is sucked through the gate at the creature's core (which sends the dead body to some other dimension).

If a reality eater is killed, the dimensional gate at the core loses cohesion. Two or three rounds later, it implodes. On a failed Might defense roll, all creatures within immediate range of the implosion suffer 5 points of transdimensional damage.

Interaction: A reality eater is not automatically hostile. But the mind impressed upon the gate is slightly aggressive and wild, and, despite being telepathic, the creature is easily confused and angered. However, it will negotiate, and may even offer to send PCs to another dimension, if PCs agree to be "eaten" by it.

Use: PCs stranded in another dimension use a device to summon a gate or portal, or seek the aid of a being who promises help. A reality eater appears.

Those who can get on the good side of a reality eater may be "consumed" as a method of interdimensional travel in a way that doesn't kill them.

GM Intrusion (Group): *Characters caught in a reality eater's death implosion must make a Speed defense roll or be sucked into an alternate dimension.*

RETENAN   6 (18)

What a character had for dinner yesterday is not considered a significant memory, unless that dinner included an important conversation or some other coincident event of significance.

GM intrusion:
The character who loses a memory (or who takes Intellect damage from an attack) is stunned until they succeed on an Intellect defense roll.

A toll "of your recollection" is required to pass upon a road, through a door, or across a region that a retenan has claimed as its territory. The nature of that memory can be nearly anything, from a creature's most cherished recollection to that one thing they did that they'd rather forget. The only requirement is that the memory have some significance. If asked what it does with the memories it exacts, the retenan indicates the experience will be "crystallized for later investigation."

A retenan is a biomechanical creature with several disparate head-like protuberances (none of them particularly humanoid), connected by metallic, flexible cables to a much thicker, serpentine metallic strand at least 15 feet (5 m) long. It can separate smaller strands from the larger ones to manipulate its surroundings.

Motive: Collects memories
Environment: Almost anywhere
Health: 20
Damage Inflicted: 6 points
Armor: 2 (4 against fire and electricity)
Movement: Short
Modifications: Most knowledge tasks as level 8

Combat: A retenan can use metallic tendrils to make two melee attacks that inflict 6 points of damage each round. As part of the same action, they can also make a short-range mental attack that inflicts 6 points of Intellect damage on a failed Intellect defense roll. When the retenan uses this latter ability on a willing creature, no damage is dealt; however, a previously-agreed-upon memory is extracted from that target.

Interaction: A retenan can speak almost any language, including machine languages, by using telepathy, sounds, light, or other methods of signal generation, as required. Most retenans begin any new interaction with an attempt at negotiation, asking for a toll from those attempting to pass through their claimed territory or passage. If a group isn't willing to offer up at least one memory, the retenan attacks.

Use: As the characters travel across a narrow pass or other restricted passage, a retenan appears to block the way.

Loot: The remains of a retenan can be salvaged for a couple of cyphers.

ROAD IMPOSTER   3 (9)

From a distance, these creatures resemble human travelers, going so far as to dress in clothing worn by their previous victims and equipping themselves in the same fashion. Up close, however, the eyeless nature of road imposters comes into focus. Eyeless on their faces, at least; their eyes grow on the palms of their hands. When attempting to go disguised, road imposters hide their eyeless faces by wearing masks or goggles.

Road imposters wander beyond the confines of communities and larger cities, preying on small groups of travelers so that news of their presence is prevented from being spread. Road imposters are motivated by a basic drive: to eat the flesh of humans, which they savor above all other things.

Motive: Hungers for flesh (especially human)

Environment: Road imposters travel in small groups of three to six, usually in regions where humans travel, rarely in the heart of a human community.

Health: 12

Damage Inflicted: 4 points

Movement: Long

Modifications: Deception and disguise tasks, and perception tasks that include smell, as level 6

Combat: Road imposters use the weapons and equipment taken from previous victims, so they may use swords or crossbows and even employ a cypher or two in their effort to bring down new prey. If possible, they attempt to begin combat against would-be prey with an ambush. However, a road imposter can also bare wicked teeth and bite a foe for 4 points of damage.

Interaction: Road imposters speak the Truth with a flat, affectless accent. If they don't begin an encounter with an ambush, they may interact with and appear to negotiate with newly met characters. It's all in aid of estimating whether the characters might make a good mark. If characters come across as too much for them, the road imposters make their excuses and go on their way (though they may still decide to double back and come after the characters when their guard is down).

Use: The PCs come across two groups of travelers on the road engaged in conflict. Both groups accuse the other of being "bandits" that first attacked the other.

Loot: A group of road imposters may carry two or three cyphers between them.

Road imposters may be abhumans. Then again, they may be extradimensional beings that have recently come here after eradicating the human population of the parallel plane they once called home.

GM intrusion: Unexpectedly, the road imposter bites the character.

SEISKIN   3 (9)

"Movement is prayer, travel is hymn, and arrival is preparation for the next pilgrimage."

—Seiskin saying

Seiskins trade to survive, though they may also act as couriers of messages or important objects between distant points.

These avian-like creatures sport colorful body feathers and bright clothes. They have human-like fingers and voices that can mimic human speech and birdsong with equal facility. They always travel together in groups, relying on several floatstone-enabled wagons (pulled by various beasts of burden).

Seiskins are usually on the move. They glorify the act of travel itself, believing that they are keeping alive the spirit of The One Who Walks for each span of distance they cross. Their rituals are designed with moving in mind, and include traveling chants, complicated skipping, and the marking of their passage through an area with specially constructed cairn-like structures.

Motive: Travel the world (as part of ritual worship)

Environment: Anywhere

Health: 9

Damage Inflicted: 4 points

Armor: 1

Movement: Short; flies an immediate distance each round for brief durations

Modifications: Tasks related to travel (especially related to repair of saddles and gear) and foraging for food as level 6

Combat: Seiskins rely on regular ranged and melee weapons (usually medium) in a fight. However, they usually travel with various beasts, which they can release in a pinch to defend them. Such beasts range from a pack of broken hounds to one or two ravage bears. (These creatures aren't pets, but when released from their cages, they usually preferentially attack creatures other than seiskins.)

In addition, about one in four seiskins has a cypher allowing them to create a level 6 effect, such as a ray emitter or detonation.

Interaction: Seiskins understand that to travel widely, they must facilitate communication with whoever—or whatever—they encounter. Thus, they speak many languages (including the Truth). Seiskins may allow a small group of characters to travel with them for a time, especially if those characters abide by the rituals of the trip.

Use: Characters pinned down by bandits or some other threat notice a caravan of wagons drawing near; the caravan is a *flarnanx* of seiskins.

Loot: One in four seiskins carries a cypher (usually level 6 in effect) and about 10 shins.

Broken hound, page 226

Ravage bear, page 249

GM intrusion: *Before the negotiation continues, the seiskin asks the character to join in on a traveling chant. How well the character does on this level 5 performance task eases or hinders the negotiation task.*

VESTIGE   5 (15)

Quasi-real copies of creatures known as vestiges are sometimes encountered along lonely trails and at the mouths of weird ruins. Vestiges are generated by mind-snaring machines of the prior worlds, including machines that transport characters into and out of the datasphere (and keep residual copies thereof).

No two vestiges appear exactly alike, or even exactly like the creature or character that served as the seed of their generation. They appear as corrupted, phased versions of their original, and possess a warped version of the memories and motivations of the original. This doesn't necessarily mean a vestige is diametrically opposed to what their original wished to achieve, but they often are.

Motive: Unpredictable (but often a warped version of the motives of the character that seeded it)

Environment: Lonely places

Health: 15

Damage Inflicted: 5 points

Movement: Short

Modifications: Stealth as level 7

Combat: As a phased being, a vestige is hard to harm; it takes full damage from mental attacks and half damage from energy attacks, and can be damaged by physical attacks only if the attack affects transdimensional or out-of-phase creatures. In addition, the vestige can become invisible as its action, and remain so indefinitely or until it makes an attack or takes damage.

A vestige's touch inflicts 5 points of Intellect damage (ignores Armor), and, on a failed Intellect defense roll, the target begins to shift out of phase with reality—but not smoothly; the phase change is a destructive process, and the target falls one step down the damage track. In each subsequent round, a phased victim can attempt an Intellect-based task to fully reintegrate themselves as their action. If successful, the target returns to normal and reverses all descended steps on the damage track caused by this effect. Otherwise, they fall another step. A target killed by this is torn apart into so many phased particles.

A vestige can move through solid objects of up to level 7 as part of their movement.

Interaction: Some vestiges are talkative, some don't know they're copies, some want help for a task they failed to accomplish before they became a copy, but many are so corrupted they only wish to destroy.

Use: Someone the PCs need to confer with is dead or missing. However, PCs learn of or know that a vestige of that individual exists.

GM intrusion: *The partly phased character discovers they cannot make physical attacks until they become unphased.*

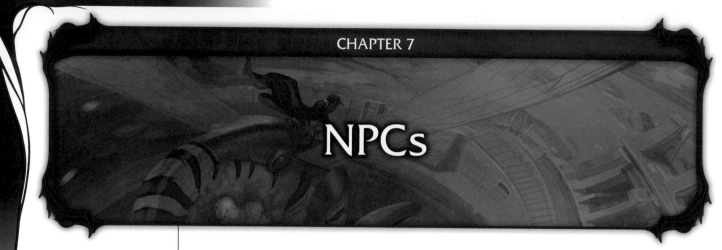

CHAPTER 7

NPCs

PCs encounter all kinds of NPCs while traveling, when visiting a strange new community, or even in the bowels of a ruin that both the PCs and other explorers happen to be investigating at the same time. Using the same format as the friends and foes presented in *Numenera Discovery*, the NPCs in this chapter can be found wherever the GM wants to use them. They work well for encounters on the road, in a town, or anywhere else. Choose an interesting NPC or roll for one randomly.

NPCs are assumed to be Ninth World humans, unless noted otherwise.

Friends and Foes, page 267

d10	NPC Met While Traveling
01	Croxton
02	Darli Kos
03	Divine Nex
04	Duchess Aranda
05	Jas the Eye Eater
06	Kresithan
07	Merthon
08	Sarrank
09	Storyteller
10	Zin the Wanderer

THE SAFE WAYFARER TRAVEL GUIDE TO MEETING STRANGERS

When you travel, it's certain you'll meet new people you've never interacted with before. How should you approach each new contact? Should you assume they're friendly and let your guard down? Or should you assume they're belligerent and show your strength to warn them off? The truth is that how you react initially will play a big part in how well or poorly the meeting ultimately goes.

Smile! When you meet humans for the first time, there's no better way to get off on the right foot than if you lower your own intimidation factor by smiling. Regardless of your actual intent, smiling at strangers puts them more at ease. Weirdly, smiling may also put *you* more at ease too.

Identify Likenesses. If you wish to interact with a stranger, begin with small talk. One of the best forays into small talk is to look for similarities between yourself and the stranger and just call attention to them. Believe it or not, this further helps both of you feel comfortable with the interaction.

Talk or Move On. It may be that you just want to avoid conflict with newly met strangers. Or, you may want to question them about the area or make a request. Either way, a great way to keep the conversation going for a bit is to simply follow any statements they make with a related question. Then, offer another statement or observation that applies to the situation and follow that with yet another question. And so on. Doing so engages the stranger and may actually accomplish the goal you're seeking in the first place, which could simply be to discover something new.

CROXTON

Appearance: Middle-aged man with grey dreadlocks woven with charm-like bits of numenera. Glowing eyeshades hide his eyes. The symbol for the Order of Truth is visible on a banner he sometimes unfurls when first seeing other travelers on the road.

About: Croxton publicly indicates that he is on a journey of discovery, moving from place to place across the Steadfast and the Beyond in order to update his *Almanac of the Ancients* (see below). He is quite proud of this slowly growing tome but also realizes it is quite valuable. To prevent others from trying to take it from him, he is usually happy to let well-mannered petitioners read from it for about an hour in return for a gift of food, spirits, or numenera.

The truth is that Croxton originally left his position in Qi ten years ago because a relationship with his lover ended badly. Hurt and humiliated, Croxton sought purpose externally. And, though that old pain still rears its head, it does so less and less these last few years.

Stats: level 5, Speed and Intellect defense as level 6; creates level 5 offensive, defensive, and utilitarian effects using various devices of the numenera secreted about his person

Almanac of the Ancients: After referencing this tome for at least one hour, one task related to the numenera is eased by two steps. Alternatively, a reader who succeeds on a difficulty 5 Intellect task after referencing this tome for at least two hours can predict the next occurrence of the iron wind within about 500 miles (800 km).

DARLI KOS

Appearance: Youthful but battle-hardened, Darli bears many scars and a set of impressive armor, pieced together from various other sets—some of which is obviously salvaged from the prior worlds. A broken hound follows Darli wherever she goes; she treats it like a pet and calls it "little guy."

About: Darli is happy to talk about battles she's fought in all across the Steadfast, which seems impressive at first. But the more she talks about the many wars in which she's participated, the more it seems like she is much too young to have had time to fight in so many different engagements. Whether she is preternaturally old in a young body or is masquerading as a veteran with war stories isn't immediately clear. If questioned or challenged on it, she just shrugs. Either way, her stories are entertaining enough to provide her free room and board most places, as well as leads for new mercenary contracts.

Stats: level 5, storytelling as level 7; health 22; Armor 3; two sword attacks inflict 5 points of damage each.

Broken hound, page 226

DIVINE NEX

Appearance: Slim, non-binary person of indeterminate age; usually wears a brilliant red and black cloak and one of several dozen masks. Some of the masks are beautiful, others are horrific, and many are sculpted to display a specific strong emotion like happiness, sadness, anger, or surprise.

About: Divine Nex makes a living moving from community to community, providing knowledge, entertainment, and news of distant locations. No one has ever seen Nex *not* in costume; when they are not singing, reciting sublime poetry, teaching ethics or some other kind of philosophy, dancing with amazing grace, or imbibing tea or wine while engaged in an extended conversation, Nex retires back to their Scarlet Tent.

Stats: level 4; entertainment (especially tumbling and acrobatics), healing, philosophy, disguise, woodworking, and persuasion as level 6

Scarlet Tent: level 6; has no exits or entrances, but Divine Nex knows the secret of entering and leaving at will

DUCHESS ARANDA

Tharink, page 21

Appearance: A white coach chased with glittering silver designs is pulled by a group of four tharinks. A young man named Delso (level 2) dressed in white livery drives the coach, and two soldiers (level 4; Armor 2) ride on the coach's back bumper.

Inside the coach is Duchess Aranda wearing a satin gown, black leather boots with high heels, and a bright red overcoat with matching gloves. One side of her face is hidden by what seems to be a mirrored mask. Both earrings are obviously some kind of mechanism—possibly a linked artifact.

About: As the wife of a powerful noble, the duchess enjoys many advantages—especially since the noble in question hasn't been seen in many years. When inquired about, she merely indicates that they are "on expedition" and will likely be back in just a few more years. In the meantime, the duchess continues to control the estate, which she does quite well.

From time to time, the duchess takes to the road (which she is partly responsible for keeping in good repair) so that she can visit a much larger community within a few days' travel, where theater performances are known to happen. Duchess Aranda never misses one. She is willing to forgive a lot in someone else who seems to have the same passion for theater as she does.

Stats: level 3, running an estate or similar larger household as level 6; Armor 5 (from earring artifact)

JAS THE EYE EATER

For more details about Jas the Eye Eater, see Ninth World Bestiary 3, *page 81.*

Appearance: Red-haired, she wears elaborate armor pieced together from numenera devices, and wields a great mechanical staff set with a metallic annulus that crackles with heat-sucking energy.

About: Jas moves from ruin to ruin out of a personal desire to explore and an even stronger urge to be alone. Gruff and untalkative at best, she physically lashes out at those who ignore her (sometimes unstated, but behaviorally obvious) warning to leave her alone.

Jas never shares the details of her childhood, even with the few people she counts as friends and contacts. She's sometimes encountered in various cities of the Steadfast selling rare iotum or other objects she's acquired during her constant explorations. One object she would never give up is an artifact she calls her "eye-eating loop," which is how she gained her appellation.

Stats: level 6, perceives and defends as level 7; health 24; Armor 2; two attacks inflict 6 points of damage each and, on a failed Might defense roll, targets take an additional 6 points of damage from cold and lose their next turn

KRESITHAN

Appearance: Bald, apparently in her late thirties, wearing road-stained clothing woven with gleaming wires and sparking devices. Her left eye is covered by a device with a red light that blinks erratically and is probably distracting to others. She usually carries two or three satchels bulging with broken devices.

About: On her best day, Kresithan can engage with others politely. However, if she is startled or otherwise put in a tight spot, she can come across as demanding, abrasive, and a bit entitled. As a nano, Kresithan has some mastery over the numenera—but never enough, in her opinion. She is always plotting to build more influence and power for herself, usually by finding something especially wondrous.

For Kresithan, power is not its own end. Instead, she hopes to find something worth enough to trade for the freedom of her brother, who is imprisoned in a nearby community. Or, failing that, something with enough power to break her brother free herself. So far, however, she still lacks what she needs.

Stats: level 3, resists mental effects as level 4; health 15; gain Armor 4 for ten minutes via a force field esotery; use force blasts, bursts of flame, bolts of electricity, and other esotery-derived attacks with long range that inflict 5 points of damage

MERTHON

Appearance: Man sporting a shock of black hair streaked with white and specks of varicolored paint. His clothing is similarly bespeckled. He usually has a paint brush, an easel, or some other artistic tool in hand. Thanks to a fortuitous encounter several years ago, Merthon is always accompanied by a handful of Oorgolian soldiers that guard him.

About: Merthon seeks to chronicle the Ninth World through artistic renderings, which he sometimes sells, sometimes produces on commission, and other times delivers to the Amber Gleaners. He has little fear of the weird mysteries that put so many other people off traveling, due entirely to his biomechanical bodyguards. Merthon is not entirely sure why they are devoted to his safety, but thinks it has something to do with how he lost his daughter in one of his first outings. The particulars of that incident are something Merthon prefers not to discuss.

Stats: level 3; painting, drawing, and similar artistic reproduction as level 7

Oorgolian soldiers, page 246

Amber Gleaners, page 245

SARRANK

Appearance: Sarrank is a middle-aged man with prematurely grey hair and a nervous, bustling energy. He wears a flowing purple coat into which a variety of intricate designs have been woven. The hem, however, has grown a bit ragged and travel-stained.

About: Sarrank is a diplomat from a nearby community on his way to a neighboring one (for the third time in the last few months). He is attempting to negotiate a trade deal involving the transfer of grains known as karsh rice, grown by farmers of the neighboring community, for fruit called papado, grown by Sarrank's community. He's not convinced that the karsh rice growers are negotiating in good faith. Each time it seems they are close to an agreement, they send him back to ask his own community for some new consideration.

Stats: level 4, diplomacy as level 6; Armor 2 (from worn robe, a numenera device)

It is better to travel in comfort than to arrive on time.

STORYTELLER

Appearance: Storyteller is an elderly man riding in a hovering chair. He wears a ragged cloak of exotic material that constantly changes hue and texture. Beneath that, his clothing is much more finely tailored but is obviously designed for travel. Golden cuff links flash on his sleeves, and his metallic belt glitters with various devices of the prior worlds.

Teller of Tales, page 104

About: Storyteller always portrays himself as assured and confident. For the most part, he is exactly that. He explains to those he meets that he is a collector of stories and offers to tell tales he has previously collected in return for the same. In truth, Storyteller collects stories because he's forgotten his own past. He hopes that one day he will come across a story enough like his own true past that it will rekindle memories of what he's lost. Or, failing that, that he can find a story of such power that he can claim it as his own.

Stats: level 6, Speed defense as level 7 due to cloak; animate cloak attacks a creature within immediate range, which inflicts 5 points of damage and, on a second failed Speed defense task, transfers the target to a small artificial extradimensional space until it can escape; hovering chair (level 6) can fly a long distance each round

ZIN THE WANDERER

Appearance: Appearing to be in her early twenties, her hair is shaved close to her scalp. Portions of her skin are as reflective as a mirror. Otherwise, she wears mostly red.

About: Zin is an explorer who was doused by a leak of weird material in a faraway ruin. The contact gave Zin her skin condition and also left her a bit confused.

She lost her team of fellow explorers and has been searching for them ever since. How long she has wandered is not something she recalls.

Stats: level 4; health 25 (regains 5 health per round from skin condition); Armor 5 (from skin condition)

PART 3:
WHERE THE SYNTH MEETS THE ROAD

Chapter 8: Encounters and Hazards Along the Way 78
Chapter 9: Travel-themed GM Intrusions 110

ENCOUNTERS AND HAZARDS ALONG THE WAY

When traveling to new locations, everything is—by definition— unexpected. In the Ninth World, the unexpected is also often weird.

This chapter provides you with single encounters and hazards to sprinkle into your campaign whenever the characters undertake a trip. As written, the encounters are one-off happenings that PCs experience along the way to someplace else. Of course, PCs may befriend an NPC, get a disease, make an enemy, or otherwise incur longer-term consequences in your game, depending on how they react to the situation you present.

Using This Section: Consider including at least one of these encounters or something you make up—even just seeing something weird—each time the PCs travel for more than a few days. The longer the PCs take to reach a destination, the more encounters they potentially have.

Next, choose when during the day the PCs will have an encounter. When traveling, the PCs are most likely to have unexpected encounters or find a hazard when they stop to rest. Often, they may see something unexpected not far off their route, leading to the encounter or hazard. Other times, a hazard or encounter may happen whether the PCs do anything to initiate it or not.

ENCOUNTERS AND HAZARDS

Roll randomly or choose an encounter from the following table.

d100	Encounter	d100	Encounter
01–02	Accident	51	Obelisks of Observation
3	Artificial Face	52	Orchard of the Ancients
4	A Sweet Interlude	53–54	Pavilion With No Doors
05–06	Attracted by Smell	55	Pit in the Plain
7	Bewebbed Flora	56	Poison Fields of Gold
8	Bonus Compartment	57–58	Pool of Judgment
09–10	Border Patrol	59	Portal Tumble
11	Canopy Ambush	60	Preservation Station
12	Caravanserai	61–62	Purple Skies in a Sphere
13–14	Cliffs of Carnage	63	Red Door
15	Color Leakage	64	Red Pillar
16	Company of the Azure Skull	65–66	Rot Vines
17–18	Crashed Craft	67	Ruin Outcropping: Floating Spheres
19	Crying Cave	68	Ruin Outcropping: Specimens
20	Curious Travelers	69–70	Seepage
21–22	Dead Courier	71	Sickness in the Land
23	Disembodied Heart	72	Sky Stain
24	Eight-Armed Statue	73	Sound of Deforestation
25–26	Disused Village	74–76	Starving Survivors
27	Following Moon	77	Steed Merchants Having a Sale
28	Gable Fruit Harrowers	78	Surprise Occupants
29–30	Glowing Mites	79–81	Teller of Tales
31	Glowing Mortification	82	That's No Hill
32	Graveyard	83	The Blazing Pillar
33–34	Helpful Flier	84–85	The Osserak
35	Home Under Siege	86	Thieves in the Night
36	Inquisition	87	Time Trap Obelisks
37–38	Iron Wind: Dusty Wind	88–89	Tornado!
39	Iron Wind: Golden Radiance	90	Unearthly Cold
40	Iron Wind: Green Mist	91–92	Vapor Feeders
41–42	Leaky Pipe	93–94	Vehicle Jacking
43	Lost Traveler	95	Violet Rain
44	Matterpool	96	Wall of Light
45–46	Message From the Past	97	Warm Arch
47	Metal Monolith Lure	98	Weird Formation
48	Metallic Pylons	99	What Follows
49–50	Murmuring Lake	00	Winged Swarm

Nacious, page 21

Cliffs of Carnage, page 84

Howler, page 63

OPTIONAL RULE: CONVEYANCE SUPREMACY

Normally, when an NPC interacts with another NPC or object, the GM compares the levels between the two to determine the outcome of any contest. For instance, if a level 3 creature tries to batter down a level 4 door, the creature fails. But if that same level 3 creature fights a level 2 creature, the level 3 creature should win, everything else being equal. (GMs use their discretion if both levels are equal.)

However, when PCs become involved, the characters roll versus a difficulty set by the level of the creature, object, or other challenge. That's just how the Cypher System works.

As an optional rule, characters can sometimes use the level of their vehicle or mount to overcome a travel-related hazard if the level of their vehicle or mount is higher than the hazard's level, as if the conveyance were an NPC. If you use this optional rule, make sure the PCs are at least aware of the situation. That way, either they can appreciate how the inherent strengths of their conveyance just saved them some hassle, or they can try to jump in and use their own skills to deal with the situation if it seems as though it isn't up to the task.

For instance, if the character is riding a nacious (a level 4 creature that can climb on walls and ceilings), and they come upon a hazard involving the Cliffs of Carnage (also a level 4 hazard), the nacious could just allow the character riding it to bypass the hazardous issue of climbing the cliffs entirely.

However, if some other factor disrupts the conveyance's ability to bypass the given hazard, then PCs may have to become directly involved, as usual. To continue the previous example, if the ascending nacious is attacked by a group of howlers waiting at the top of the Cliffs of Carnage, it might still fall unless the PC can get control of their suddenly panicked mount.

Explorer, page 265

Portwalker, page 28

Mask: level 8

ACCIDENT

A group of three to five explorers stole a vehicle that stands on long stilt-like legs, called a portwalker. They lit out for a ruin they recently heard about, confident their newly acquired vehicle would prove useful. At some point during the PCs' journey, the portwalker collides with the PCs' vehicle or mounts, or crashes into their camp. Introduce the accident as a GM intrusion.

If PCs are in a vehicle themselves during the collision, their vehicle is damaged and requires repair. If the PCs are mounted, one of their mounts is severely hurt and requires care. If the PCs were walking or encamped, three PCs traveling next to each other must each succeed on a difficulty 6 Speed defense roll or take 6 points of damage and be caught under the tumbled portwalker.

Immediately following the accident, the explorers spill out, a little bloodied but otherwise none the worse for wear. They are angry and upset that the PCs "caused their accident" (or so they claim, even if that's not true). The PCs could successfully talk the explorers down with a couple of successful persuasion checks, especially if they offer a gift of a cypher to go along with their apology. Alternatively, the PCs could offer to fix the damaged portwalker. Otherwise, the explorers may decide to attack the PCs while the characters are still reeling from the initial collision.

ARTIFICIAL FACE

Half buried in a stretch of desert sand is a massive artificial face over 100 feet (30 m) in diameter. If investigated, the face appears to be a mask-like device of ivory synth and milky crystal. One eye socket is empty, and sand spills through it. The other holds a massive red crystal that pulses ever so dimly. Touching it reveals a very slight vibration and warmth, but otherwise the face seems completely inert. Attempts to learn more are difficult given the face's level. But even a failed attempt to learn more suggests that the face is more than a simple mask. A success suggests it is the manifestation of a much more powerful entity, one that is hurt or perhaps damaged from long travel. The face is dangerous if roused (which probably only occurs if PCs attempt to destroy or fail to salvage it), becoming a raging being of crazed destruction as opposed to an inert object.

Attempts to salvage it might be enough to wake it on a bad roll (or as a GM intrusion that nearly—but not quite—wakes it), but those who press their luck successfully could gain some high-level rewards.

Salvaging, page 107

A SWEET INTERLUDE

A massive slug-like morwen carries a colorful coach-like compartment on its back (a howdah), set with many flags and streamers, and always accompanied by the delicious smells of baking. Four aged, white-haired human siblings—all with the surname Cottram— live and work in the coach, which serves not only as their home but as a kitchen and a place from which they trade their wares for needful things. The Cottrams are friendly and outgoing, having a seemingly outsized degree of faith in their ability to survive traveling the Steadfast and the Beyond. They give out free sample cookies to those they take a fancy to and sell large quantities of the same to those willing to trade.

The secret to the Cottrams' survival is that they have two "pet" balithaurs that follow them wherever they go. The balithaurs slink along in hiding, only emerging either at night to be fed, or to defend the Cottrams if the siblings or their morwen are threatened. Balithaurs are 30-foot (9 m) long creatures with many-clawed—and in some cases, mawed—limbs studded with piercing eyes. They have only a few joints, giving them a sort of "loose" look, but really that just means they can fold themselves into far-smaller spaces than their enormous bulk suggests.

ATTRACTED BY SMELL

A group of blood barms, broken hounds, or a couple of ravage bears finds the PCs' camp, likely attracted by the smell of their provisions (or some other element of their camp, like noise, visual displays, or even because they lingered too long in a place the creatures claim as their natural range). If the PCs previously indicated they took some palliative effort to prevent such an occurrence, whether by packing smart, reducing the camp's footprint, keeping quiet, or so on, the GM may simply decide the encounter doesn't happen. If so, the characters should still note the predators they avoided encountering in the distance, so they understand that their preparations had a positive impact on their journey.

Morwen, page 20

Cottram sibling: *level 3, baking sweets and trade as level 6*

Blood barm, page 226

Broken hound, page 226

Ravage bear, page 249

Packing Smart, page 12

Balithaur, page 255

Many-armed mechanism: *level 5*

Purple strands: *level 4*

Rejuvenator, page 286

Xi-drake, page 259

Angulan Knights, page 217

Angulan Knights, typical: *level 3; health 15; Armor 2; ranged and melee weapons inflict 5 points of damage*

Travel papers, page 15

Culova protector: *level 5, Speed defense as level 6, stealth and interaction tasks as level 7; health 25; Armor 2; moves a long distance each round (short when climbing); long-range crossbow attacks inflict 6 points of Speed damage from poison (ignores Armor) for two rounds on those who fail a Might defense task; for more details see* The Ninth World Bestiary 2, *page 38*

BEWEBBED FLORA

The path into the tree-like forest where the characters wish to travel (or near where they place their camp) is strung with sticky, gluey purple strands. The strands are not a cohesive wall, but they are significant enough that even PCs in an enclosed vehicle should be worried that pressing forward would risk getting stuck. These strands exist in a layer only about 18 feet (6 m) deep. Characters not in a vehicle who wish to press past them can attempt to do so individually by succeeding on a Might or Speed defense roll to maneuver through the webs. On a failure, the character becomes stuck, and all attempts to free themself are hindered by two steps. The driver of a vehicle can attempt the same, easing the task by two steps if the vehicle is higher level than the strands. The defense roll is hindered for characters attempting to ride a mount through.

Even on a success, the gluey substance clings to the character, vehicle, or mount and hinders all Speed, driving, or riding tasks until the substance is burned off or dissolved with alcohol.

The only question that remains: will whatever spun the strands in the first place be disturbed and investigate? If the GM decides so, then within a few rounds of the characters' initial contact with the strands, a couple of culova protectors arrive, angry at the intrusion.

BONUS COMPARTMENT

The PCs have a vehicle of the prior worlds! Every so often, it exhibits a strange behavior or ability. The latest is the appearance of a chamber that earlier exploration of the vehicle failed to reveal. This "bonus compartment" might be discovered weeks or months later due to damage done to the vehicle or a PC pilot failing a piloting task and hitting some previously unknown control.

The revealed compartment is tiny, just large enough to hold a small seat surrounded by the many-armed mechanism. Any character who sits in the chair activates the mechanism. One arm bends down to fit a film-like mask over the character's head and insert a thick needle into their neck, inflicting 1 point of damage and holding the character in place until they can escape. Though it may not be obvious, a character damaged by the device gains 5 Armor against damage from disease, poison, and radiation for 10 days. If the device is salvaged, characters gain 10 shins and a level 5 rejuvenator cypher.

BORDER PATROL

Several humans riding soaring xi-drakes approach. They fly a banner with the symbol of crossed swords on a field of green, red, and yellow. If the PCs do not recognize them, the lead rider announces loudly that the group represents an Angulan Knight patrol, and that the PCs should prepare themselves for some pressing questions.

It may be that the group of Angulan Knights has been hired by the kingdom or noble whose lands through which the PCs travel to question strangers, tax travelers, or find someone fleeing from an authority. Otherwise, the group is acting within its own charter: they are on the lookout for mutants, which they believe should be eradicated. PCs who cooperate—and aren't harboring a fugitive, a mutation, or something else the group is looking for—must succeed on a difficulty 3 persuasion task (or deception task, if attempting to hide something). The difficulty could go higher depending on the particular situation, such as if one PC is obviously a mutant. If PCs have travel papers, assuming nothing else goes wrong, they are automatically allowed to proceed after a bit of performative scrutiny.

CANOPY AMBUSH

A swarm of twelve insect-like chaliks lives in this forested area, feeding on other creatures that live nearby. They are drawn to bigger prey, such as PCs. The big insects scuttle up and down the trees with ease, leaving odd scorings in the smooth bark. PCs *might* notice these scorings when they travel through the area or set up camp nearby.

The chaliks prefer to attack an isolated PC (perhaps one standing guard or relieving themselves a little away from the camp) or make their move at an inopportune time for the group, such as while resting or sleeping. When the chaliks decide to attack, they prefer to drop down from branches overhead, if at all possible, which hinders perception tasks by PCs to notice their approach.

The chalik swarm continues to attack until it is reduced to three or fewer individuals, at which point the surviving creatures attempt to flee.

CARAVANSERAI

The PCs spy a caravanserai, also known as a roadhouse. The structure is a great enclosed square with faded, age-worn walls. Flickering lanterns are lit just after nightfall. Those who draw close hear snippets of exotic songs and smell a variety of enticing scents. An entrance in one wall large enough to drive a vehicle through leads into a wide, open-air courtyard with a central well. Besides the well, the courtyard holds several cart-drawn stalls that mainly sell travel supplies. The inner wall of the courtyard is riddled with doors to stables, rooms for sleeping, and other chambers suited to a roadside inn.

PCs discover they can lodge overnight for just a few shins, especially if they contribute something to the communal meal served once each day, prepared in one of the inner rooms.

The Tharmin family runs the place. The family numbers over a dozen, consisting of a handful of apparently human adults and several related children of all ages. The head of the Tharmin family is an elderly (but not frail) matriarch everyone calls Mata. She introduces herself at some point, asking if the characters' needs are being met.

The PCs' experience at the caravanserai may be entirely calm and restful.

Then again, one or more PCs may hear another group of travelers discussing a rumor of the roadhouse being haunted by dream-eating demons. If the PCs overhear such talk and decide to investigate for themselves,

it only takes them asking one member of the Tharmin family about the rumor for their restful stay to come to an end.

It just so happens that every member of the Tharmin family is actually a dreamtooth. Dreamtooths prey on travelers because they crave variety in their psychic diet, and the caravanserai offers them the perfect cover for such illicit mental feeding. A few travelers each morning wake up from horrendous nightmares and suffer from serious headaches, but are usually none the wiser or worse for wear when they continue on their journey.

If PCs inquire about the haunting rumor, they are assured by the Tharmins that the stories are just a bit of local color. If they do nothing else, they are allowed to leave the next day unharmed and unfed upon in the night. However, if the PCs actually mount any kind of active investigation, the entire family of dreamtooths comes after them. During their investigation, the characters may discover a series of secret tunnels that run beneath all the guest rooms. A dreamtooth situates itself directly beneath an occupied room and "sips" from the mind of the sleeping traveler above. However, a dreamtooth is a capable fighter outside of dreams, and if all of them come after the characters at once, the PCs face troubling odds. They might be forced to make a deal with Mata to survive. To do so, the PCs will have to convince Mata that they will leave and not raise the alarm to other travelers. A difficult task, but not impossible for especially convincing characters.

Chalik swarm: level 4; Armor 1; climbs a short distance each round; swarm bite attack inflicts 5 points of damage; a single chalik (level 2) can induce itself to burst, killing it but releasing a sticky residue that immobilizes one target who fails a Speed defense roll; for more details, see Ninth World Bestiary 2, page 33

Dreamtooth, page 58

CLIFFS OF CARNAGE

Cliff faces: level 4

Extremely rugged terrain—including a line of imposing cliff faces that rise like a wall a few hundred feet high—lies ahead along the PCs' route. To continue forward without losing lots of time trying to find an easier path around, the characters will have to either use some method to simply fly over or resort to climbing it. If the PCs have been relying on a vehicle or mount that is unable to climb, the characters may be forced to find a way around anyway.

However, a PC determined to find a way up with their non-climbing vehicle or mount can attempt to scout a path upward that their conveyance can take. Given that any PCs who look along the base of the cliffs discover a few shattered shells of synth and metal (vehicle chassis) and the bones of several aneen and other mounts, it's obvious that the path is still dangerous.

Scouting a route for a conveyance is an Intellect-based task hindered by two steps. On a success, the PC identifies a series of steep switchbacks up which they can attempt to bring their vehicle or mount. (On a failure, they fall while scouting the route, on a failed Speed defense roll.)

Carnivorous color: level 3, stealth tasks and mind-feeding attacks as level 5; health 12; flies an immediate distance each round; immediate-range mental attack inflicts 3 points of Intellect damage (ignores Armor); for more details, see Ninth World Bestiary 2, page 32

Chapter 11: Travelers Never Did Lie, page 132

Azure Skull of the Avatar, page 136

The series of switchbacks isn't really a true path, and portions of the cliff sometimes just break off and fall. To successfully make it to the top of the Cliffs of Carnage, each character leading or riding a mount, and each character piloting a ground vehicle, must succeed on two Speed-based tasks hindered by two steps.

COLOR LEAKAGE

The PCs travel through a region haunted by three creatures from a bizarre dimension that manifest as particularly vivid colors. If the characters are traveling in a vehicle, the carnivorous colors are first noticed on an interior surface of the vehicle. If the PCs are traveling in some other fashion, the colors manifest while the characters are resting. (If the PCs have managed to travel using some sort of instantaneous means, the colors might be able to interrupt them mid-trip and attack in a limited half-world of brilliant color.)

An attack by two or three carnivorous colors looks like a bright green light, a splash of brilliant scarlet on a wall, and/or a spontaneous change in hue from a neutral shade to sapphire blue on someone's clothing. The colors are beautiful—until they begin feeding on the minds of the nearest intelligent creatures! They don't speak a language the PCs can understand, even if psychic communication is attempted. But they're not mindless and can learn from experiences and solve problems.

COMPANY OF THE AZURE SKULL

The characters encounter a group of three travelers calling themselves the Company of the Azure Skull, as described (and pictured) in Chapter 11: Travelers Never Did Lie. However, if this is a randomly rolled encounter, the meeting between the PCs and the trio of Azure Skull mercenaries doesn't (necessarily) lead to the two groups traveling together. Instead, the mercenaries are surprised by the appearance of the characters. They immediately jump to the conclusion that the PCs are following them, having somehow discovered the Company is carrying the artifact known as the Azure Skull of the Avatar.

Presumably, that's *not* what the PCs are after, and if the characters can succeed on a couple of difficulty 5 persuasion tasks, they can talk the mercenaries down. If they do succeed and avoid a fight, the company of NPCs is conciliatory and goes so far as

to provide the PCs with several mushroom handpies baked by Sorino (which are fabulous). They also provide a couple of useful tips about the surrounding lands, if the PCs happen to be looking for something in the area. However, the mercenaries do not immediately reveal their own true purpose to chance-met strangers, except to say they like to stay on the road and see new sights.

CRASHED CRAFT

The PCs witness something come screaming in from the upper atmosphere, scratch a smokey track across the sky, then crash behind a distant rise. If the characters investigate, they find the wreckage of a great silvery vessel in a deep crater still red with heat. Once cooled, characters who break into the crashed craft discover one of the following interiors.

Dead Aliens. This interplanetary craft from elsewhere carried several aliens on a trip lasting several years. Unfortunately, it ended poorly, killing all those aboard. The only things left are the bodies of somewhat humanoid, blue-skinned people and an opportunity for some numenera salvage on the characters' parts, including 20 shins and a suspensor belt.

On the other hand, PCs with some talent might eventually get the craft itself functional again, at which point they could decide to use it as a nightswimmer with a depletion of 1 in 1d6.

Live Aliens. Whether or not they really count as aliens, several Oorgolian soldiers are aboard this crashed craft, and as PCs begin to investigate the crash, a few emerge and begin to set up a perimeter around the craft. They are unlikely to negotiate with characters and may even attack them, assuming that the characters had something to do with their crash.

Transdimensional Nexus. If PCs investigate, they find a chamber *much* bigger on the inside than the outside. The only solid flooring is a square about 50 feet (15 m) on a side floating in a haze of violet light. A control surface covered in dancing nanites sits at the center of the square. PCs who succeed on an understanding numenera task while using the control surface can open random portals in the haze to other dimensions.

Unfortunately, a human character simply doesn't have the brain functions to gain any better control than random openings to other places. Each new portal that opens is completely random, and any previously opened portal immediately closes. The worlds the PCs can randomly create a path into run

Sorino, page 136

Nightswimmer, page 31

Suspensor belt, page 302

Oorgolian soldier, page 246

Crashed craft: *level 7*

the gamut: they range from the eerily familiar to the downright strange, and everything in between. Some worlds are inhabited by life similar to that found in the Ninth World, while others are barren wastelands: drenched in radiation, choked by a poisonous atmosphere, or featuring temperatures that plunge far below freezing or soar past boiling. Unless characters want to get lost in another dimension, they should limit their experiments here.

CRYING CAVE

A faint sound like someone crying is detected. If characters investigate, they discover the noise emanating from a cave. The cave entrance is about 15 feet (5 m) in diameter. A strip of yellow synth lies loose on the floor, extending deeper into the cave until it disappears beyond sight.

One round after anything about the size of a human steps through the entrance, the synth strip begins to writhe. Anyone in any part of the cave must succeed on a Speed defense roll or become entangled. They remain stuck until they can escape, either by muscling free or destroying the strip of synth. If PCs attack the synth, its writhing grows violent, and in addition to entangling characters, it also inflicts 6 points of damage each round to each entangled target.

The crying noise is actually made by the strip of yellow synth, as its entire length vibrates almost like a vocal cord. A deeper exploration into the cave once the strip is dealt with reveals the cave is only about 40 feet (12 m) long, ending at a dilapidated mechanism from which the strip extrudes. It's impossible to say what the mechanism was once part of, but PCs could salvage it for 14 shins and a phase disruptor cypher.

CURIOUS TRAVELERS

Three humans approach the PCs, waving and smiling. The two women and one man wear wrappings of yellow and gold and bear an orange-colored tattoo of a triangle on their foreheads. Their wrappings are adorned with similar triangle-shaped beads, as well as tiny bones. If the PCs don't evade the three strangers, the leader introduces herself in the Truth as Jani, and her two friends as Meropi and Kando. In her strangely accented version of the Truth, she explains that they are pilgrims on the road to visit something called "the Osserak." (Whenever any of the travelers say the word "Osserak," they all bow and say "praise" quietly.)

If PCs ask about the Osserak, the pilgrims describe it as a pyramid-shaped structure about four weeks' travel from their small village. Each village member makes the pilgrimage every few years to gain the Osserak's blessing.

The pilgrims offer to share food with the PCs, but must soon be on their way. If the characters seem even a little interested, the pilgrims offer to show them to the holy site but warn that those who are not initiated into the way of the Osserak may become confused and forgetful, so characters should only come if they are willing to become initiated. Becoming initiated in the way of the Osserak is a long-term task requiring the PCs to spend one week studying with Jani, Meropi, and/or Kando (or another pilgrim). Those who undertake this task can properly approach the Osserak, performing the observances and prayers that prevent it from negatively affecting them.

DEAD COURIER

A body is found. The corpse was a human ravaged by some kind of predator's attack, which has left only about a third of the body behind. Characters who succeed on a difficulty 5 Intellect-based task believe the attack probably occurred no more than a couple of days ago.

If PCs check the courier's possessions, they discover a couple of cyphers (comprehension graft and gravity-nullifying spray), about 100 shins, and a document pouch sealed with red wax that bears an imprint of some kind of beetle with a human face. If investigated, the document pouch is found to contain a letter addressed to someone called Orannius, asking that they break off their storm chase as quickly as possible so they can return home and defend it from a "burrowing worm" awakened in the deep drit. The letter is signed Dalthius of Vebar but contains no additional directions or instructions. Obviously, the letter was never delivered.

The PCs can choose to ignore the document, attempt to find Orannius, or travel to Vebar themselves and attempt to solve the problem with the "burrowing worm" themselves. (The nature of the worm is left to the GM to determine, or it could be a cragworm with the ability to tunnel through solid rock.)

Long-Term Tasks, page 324

Strip of yellow synth: level 6

Attacking Objects, page 116

Phase disruptor, page 284

Comprehension graft, page 277

Gravity-nullifying spray, page 280

Orannius, page 267

Vebar, page 195

Cragworm, page 230

Jani, Meropi, and Kando: level 2, religion (the Osserak) as level 5

The Osserak, page 105

What you have to decide is how far you're willing to go away from the familiar and the known. Are you the kind of person who wants to see what's out there, or are you happy merely staying at home?

DISEMBODIED HEART

A mesa-like rock formation off in the distance supports a structure that looks remarkably like a disembodied human heart. And if one listens closely, an almost subsonic "thuuub . . . duuuub" can just be made out, repeating just once every round or two, vibrating through the ground.

If PCs investigate, they discover that the steeply rising escarpment is indeed topped by an approximately 140-foot (43 m) tall heart-shaped rock formation that looks even more like a heart up close, thanks to scarlet and yellow striations in the rock. The beating is also louder here and can even be felt through the air by anyone standing nearby.

If PCs look around toward the surrounding hills and valleys and succeed on a difficulty 3 perception task, they discern a negative shape all around them. It's as if they stand in a "valley" that could have been made by a vast humanoid shape that had fallen from a height and made an impression in the earth. If so, that entity is now long gone. However, the heart-shaped rock formation that remains does generally reside in the location where the entity's heart might have been.

If PCs don't have rock-penetrating abilities or devices, this is probably about as far as this encounter goes. However, if they do, and penetrate into the formation at least several feet, they find a biomechanical layer of substance within the stone responsible for the beating. No blood is being pumped, but an energy pulse does seep away into the ground. If PCs are reckless enough, they could destroy this relic of the prior worlds. However, if they are especially intellectual (and succeed on a difficulty 8 understanding numenera task), they could try to siphon off some of the energy from each beat. They could attempt to use this energy to repower depleted artifacts (such as a void ring) or for some other purpose later in their adventuring careers.

DISUSED VILLAGE

The PCs run across a village of about twenty homes, plus a few other buildings, surrounded by signs of cultivation and herding. If they look around, it soon becomes clear that no one is there, including animals. The place is obviously an abandoned human settlement: it's clear by the accumulation of drit and wind and water damage that no one has tended to the place for a year or more. That's the end of it if the characters remain for less than a single day or don't investigate further.

If the PCs investigate the abandoned village and succeed on a difficulty 3 perception task, they discover a metallic trapdoor in the ground near the village's center, obscured by drifting drit and other debris. A thick metal shard has been rammed through the mechanism, rendering it impossible for the door to be opened from below, although it's easy enough to open from above. If the PCs thoroughly investigate the village and succeed on a difficulty 8 perception task, they find the Cold Man, described hereafter, hiding below one of the empty houses—before he's ready to spring his trap.

If the PCs open the hatch and enter, they find a subterranean ruin that the villagers had apparently used as a sort of storm cellar. However, it seems that the approximately fifty people who took shelter here a few years ago perished in place, leaving remains of skeletal fragments in tattered clothing. Looking through their belongings, it could be speculated that the villagers rushed into this hiding place without time to bring much with them. However, someone has smeared a message on a prominent wall: "Beware the Cold Man."

Aside from minor items, PCs who search through the dead villagers' belongings discover a ray emitter (cell-disrupting radiation) and a motion sensor, as well as about 40 shins.

If all the PCs go down into the storm-shelter-ruin at once, the Cold Man (as named by the smeared message) makes his move. The Cold Man is a human who has a malfunctioning piece of numenera inset into

Heart-shaped rock formation: *level 8*

Void ring, page 39

Ray emitter, page 285

Motion sensor, page 283

Cold Man: *level 6; Armor 3 (immune to cold); two melee attacks inflict 6 points of damage each and, on failed Might defense roll, the target is chilled so thoroughly they are stunned, losing their next turn*

Flit disc, page 31

Iron hatch: *level 7*

Attacking Objects, page 116

Detonation, page 277

Detonation (flash), page 277

Eagleseye, page 279

Metallic statue: *level 5*

Conundary, page 257

Stilter: *level 4; moves a long distance each round; rearing attack inflicts 6 points of damage*

Harrower: *level 5 while high on gable fruit; level 2 normally*

his spine that affects his mind in unfortunate homicidal ways. When he sees his chance, he slides out of his smelly nest beneath one of the houses and attempts to lock the PCs into the subterranean ruin as he did with the original villagers a few years ago. If PCs become trapped, they'll have to bypass the iron hatch using an ability or device, or attack the hatch in an attempt to destroy it. If the PCs manage to break the hatch open, the Cold Man is waiting just outside and drops what is effectively a level 8 detonation (heat drain) cypher into the opening. The Cold Man is probably beyond help, his mind wrecked from the bad integration of a heat-draining device into his flesh. He fights like a rabid animal.

EIGHT-ARMED STATUE
Visible for some distance, this eight-armed metallic statue is only vaguely humanoid. It rises to a height of 60 feet (18 m) and seems to be caught in the act of exhorting the heavens above for an intercession. It doesn't have a recognizable face. Instead, runes run down its sides in slightly glowing red lines, constantly in motion. Characters who succeed on a difficulty 7 understanding numenera task can read the moving lines, which seem to name the statue as "Caller of Night." The remains of many past fires, as well as the bones of many kinds of creatures (including humans), lie half-buried around the statue.

A group of eye-warping conundary sometimes comes to the statue as a form of pilgrimage. They don't know what significance the statue may have once had. They just use it as a place for trapping confused prey from nearby abhuman tribes and, sometimes, human travelers caught up in the creatures' psychic illusions.

FOLLOWING MOON
The characters wake up, look up, or otherwise suddenly notice that at some point, they gained an aerial onlooker. A dull grey sphere hovers at some initially indeterminate height overhead, sort of resembling a moon. However, that's just an optical illusion. In fact, the dull grey sphere hovers not quite 200 feet (60 m) over the largest grouping of characters. If the characters are traveling, the sphere continues to follow them at that height for several days, until one day, it's just gone (it jets off into the night; an observing PC might see it flash away). That's the end of it, unless

the characters can devise some way to reach the observing sphere.

If so, they find it is a vehicle similar to a flit disc—except this one is about 30 feet (9 m) in diameter, and has an enclosed cabin large enough for several people. The long-dried and mummified corpse of a human Aeon Priest is strapped into a jury-rigged seat posted in front of a control surface. If PCs succeed on a difficulty 5 understanding numenera task, they discover the vehicle is operating on some sort of constrained series of instructions, possibly fed to it by the now long-dead Aeon Priest as a safety measure. Perhaps the vehicle is trying, in its limited way, to find help for its passenger? That help has come way too late, if so. If characters try to reprogram the vehicle, they must succeed on a difficulty 8 understanding numenera task to make it more amenable to their own desires. Even if they succeed, it's liable to return to its previous behavior in the future (present as a GM intrusion).

As to the nature of the mummified passenger, you could use this encounter as a hook to present your players with the map of some distant ruin, found on the Aeon Priest's body. Alternatively, it could just be a poor traveler who ran into a series of unfortunate events. In this case, searching his body yields a couple of cyphers, including a detonation (flash) and an eagleseye, and 35 shins.

GABLE FRUIT HARROWERS
A group of three humans riding stilters—red and white striped creatures with thin legs—confronts the PCs. They are dressed in ragged, pieced-together bits of road-stained clothing. The strangers call themselves harrowers and demand the characters offer them tribute. The PCs may notice that all of the harrowers have green stains about their mouths. If asked about it, they grin fiercely (revealing equally stained teeth) and say they are "fortified with gable fruit."

The harrowers are essentially brigands, but they've been driven into a strange frenzy due to the fruit they've been consuming. A lightly glowing green fungus infests their rations (and infects any new rations added), and they call the result gable fruit. When under the effect of the altered food, humans are stronger and faster, a lot more talkative, and driven toward violence. The harrowers who've accosted the PCs have been eating the infected food nonstop for several months. Dealing peacefully with the harrowers is difficult because even if the PCs offer tribute, the frenzied humans don't actually care. It's just a pretext for their eventual attack. (If a harrower could be non-violently neutralized, then prevented from eating any more gable fruit, they would revert to a much more peaceful state and wonder why they are so far from their stilter ranch.)

If the PCs defeat the harrowers and eat any food found in a harrower's bag, they risk becoming similarly affected by the gable fruit infection.

GLOWING MITES

Completely inert in the light, swarms of these biomechanical nanomites appear like so much dust, or sometimes as a thin residue of oil covering affected surfaces. Characters moving through or setting up their camp in an area afflicted with inert nanomites are unlikely to notice that anything is amiss by day. However, when it gets dark, the nanomites begin to swarm. They appear as a mist of tiny red dots filling an area at least a short distance across. Characters who are not completely enclosed or otherwise protected become infested.

An infestation can be treated by subjecting the character to bright light for at least three rounds or burning them off. Otherwise, the PC could be in serious trouble.

PCs who carefully explore around the area of their camp might gain a clue that something's not right; previous victims of the nanomites appear as vitrified, broken remains half-buried under the drit.

GLOWING MORTIFICATION

A storm thick with grit from a nearby desertified ruinscape blows in. Aloft on the winds are tiny flea-like metal bugs that are too small to see—at least at first. Everyone exposed to the storm must succeed on a Might defense roll. On a failure, they begin suffering from a disease known locally as glowing mortification.

At first, a sufferer is asymptomatic. However, after an hour, the character descends one step on the damage track, and one of their arms or legs—but only one—takes on a slight violet glow. A close inspection of the extremity shows tracks of very tiny glowing creatures beneath the victim's skin. These are nanobots, proliferating at an ever-increasing rate. Each hour after the first, the character must succeed on a Might defense roll or descend another step on the damage track. A success means the progression of the condition does not advance for that hour. Three successes indicate the character is cured. However, if the disease causes a character to descend a third step on the damage track, instead of dying, the character goes unconscious for 10 hours, during which time the affected limb drops off bloodlessly. Afterward, the character's maximum Might Pool is decreased by 2 points, and tasks that would involve the use of the missing limb are hindered, at least until a few months have passed. By that time, the character has adapted fully to using a different limb or otherwise accomplishing the task (at the GM's discretion).

If the PCs had forewarning of this particular threat, they might have secured preventative medicines. Alternatively, there might be someone nearby who can treat the disease before it runs its course—or even reattach a loose limb (which is perfectly preserved).

Glowing mortification, disease: *level 5*

Gable fruit infection: *level 4 disease; inflicts 4 points of Intellect damage each day a Might defense roll is failed. On a success, the disease ends. Until then, an infected PC chooses the most extroverted and aggressive option for any given situation.*

Nanomite swarm: *level 4; only active in darkness, otherwise appears as inert dust; only harmed by damage that inflicts damage in an area; all targets within immediate range must succeed on a Might defense roll each round or begin to vitrify (dropping one step on the damage track)*

Preventative Medicines, page 12

"We are harrowers! We ride where we wish, take tribute whenever we want, and put the fear of demons in whoever stands against us. Because our strength is equal to demons!"

—Typical greeting of a harrower

GRAVEYARD

Grave mound: *level 5*

A series of hive-like mounded structures visible nearby are arranged somewhat regularly in an otherwise barren location. Investigation reveals the mounds to be a variety of hardened mudstone. Symbols have been carved onto each grave mound. If it is a language, it is something other than the Truth, or any other language PCs are likely to know.

Raiders: *level 2; Armor 1; ranged attacks inflict 4 points of damage*

Kathos: *level 5; Armor 2; two ranged attacks inflict 5 points of damage each*

Speedster, page 28

More invasive investigation reveals that each grave mound holds the mummified remains of a humanoid creature, though ones with far-smaller heads and much more elongated bodies than humans of the Ninth World. No records of the creatures exist in the datasphere and, other than the nearby ruins of a community of similar construction, no other record remains of this small and now extinct people.

HELPFUL FLIER

Flit disc, page 31

Grek: *level 7*

Thief deterrent module, page 36

A flying craft flashes by overhead, then swings back around to get a closer look at the PCs on the ground below. The craft is a flit disc piloted by a young man with a silver mohawk named Grek. Assuming the PCs don't shoot at the vehicle or otherwise indicate their desire not to be bothered, Grek lands nearby. Then he steps off the disc and hails the characters with a big, friendly smile on his face. Grek, speaking the Truth, asks the characters if they need a ride or if he can offer some other kind of aid.

Convergence, page 216

Convergence magister/ magistrix: *level 5, resists mental effects as level 6; gain 4 Armor for ten minutes via esotery; long-range terrorizer attack inflicts 4 points of damage, and targets who fail additional Might defense roll lose their next turn*

Grek really is the friendly, outgoing person he comes across as. He travels simply to see new places and to meet new people. It's true he's had a few run-ins with ne'er-do-wells, including at least one group that accepted his offer of a ride then tried to steal his flit disc (an effort foiled by an installed thief deterrent module). However, that hasn't deterred him from continuing his friendly behavior. Just because he's nice doesn't mean he's foolish.

If PCs do take Grek up on an offer of aid, he'll provide parts, food, water, or a ride lasting up to a few days before indicating he needs to be moving on.

HOME UNDER SIEGE

Merian, Ghan, and sons: *level 2, farming and repair as level 5*

A family of frontier settlers has built a home and farm in an out-of-the-way place. The home is built from a cupola-like building (a prior-world structure) and is surrounded by an orchard of trees with elaborate purple blooms.

The family is composed of Merian, the sturdy and confident matriarch; her husband Ghan, who never speaks but has a ready smile

and helpful manner; and their three grown sons, all of whom defer to Merian. The farm has done well over the preceding four years, growing all their own food and making all their own equipment. The latter has been achieved thanks to an installation built by Ghan that is able to extrude various parts and materials that can then be assembled in his shop.

The home came under attack recently by a group of raiders riding speedsters led by an automaton named Kathos. Kathos wants the family's home (which it believes is an entrance to a much larger ruin) for itself. Those who follow it just want to loot the farm for food and goods.

PCs happen upon this home under siege during an interlude between attacks, possibly having enjoyed a bit of hospitality on Merian's and Ghan's parts, when the sound of speedsters is heard roaring in the distance.

INQUISITION

A group of humans, wearing robes and insignia marking them as members of the Order of Truth, are wandering this region with two purposes in mind: first, masquerading as Aeon Priests in order to blend in and gain the trust of both residents and travelers; second, to learn of any interesting happenings or locations that the Convergence can exploit. Rumors of a buried obelisk nearby (which the PCs may not yet be aware of) have drawn this group here. The humans are actually magisters and magistrixes of the Convergence, which seeks to grow its power.

IRON WIND

As horrible as extreme weather can be, the iron wind still takes center stage in the Ninth World. The iron wind is a little-understood phenomenon where wind moves with a mind of its own, tearing at flesh, objects, and structures and, often enough, altering them. Some places are more prone to iron wind activity than others. Unfortunately, with the residue of the prior worlds literally everywhere, the iron wind can also spring up almost anywhere if activated by an extreme weather event.

Each instance of iron wind can manifest differently from other episodes. That's just one reason it's so pernicious.

IRON WIND: DUSTY WIND

This instance of iron wind (level 4) appears as a particularly strong series of gusts that kick up what at first appears to be a lot of extra-dusty drit. However, closer examination reveals that it is uniformly fine and grey, more like ash than drit. Within a few hours, most humans who experienced the dust storm must succeed on an Intellect defense roll. On a failure, the targets become quarrelsome, sullen, and easily enraged. If around other humans, they turn their ire on each other. If alone, they turn that anger on themselves. Without intervention by someone able to detoxify their blood of the tiny nanites pumping out a cocktail of aggression, all those affected die by their own hand or at the hands of another victim within a few days.

IRON WIND: GOLDEN RADIANCE

This instance of iron wind (level 6) manifests at night as golden veins of light twinning across the ground in a gradual, traveling wave a very long distance across. It moves a long distance each round over the course of several hours before dying away. From a distance, the effect is enticing, even beautiful by human standards. However, a creature touched by the radiance must succeed on a Might defense roll or become infected with nanites that thread through their skin as they do the landscape. The radiance doesn't initially seem to have any effect other than giving affected individuals a sparkling, golden webwork across their skin. However, a couple of days later, affected creatures must make one additional Might defense roll. On a failure, their physical form collapses into so much dust all at once. The mind of a dusted creature may take up residence in a nearby machine, if one is available.

IRON WIND: GREEN MIST

This instance of iron wind (level 5) manifests as a miniature cloud of green mist a short distance across. A creature touched by the mist takes 4 points of Speed damage (ignores Armor) each round as its body begins to warp and alter in random ways. The effect ends when the creature successfully resists with a Might defense task; however, if the iron wind instance is still manifest, the creature could be subject to the damaging transformation once again.

LEAKY PIPE

A distant, shrill whistling sound is heard. If PCs follow up on it, the sound grows louder and louder until, after they've traveled a very long distance, they discover a metallic pipe about 6 feet (2 m) in diameter and 9 feet (3 m) long protruding from the bare ground. The pipe is capped, but a rent in the side is venting a white vapor and creating the whistle. In fact, the sound is so intense that characters must succeed on a difficulty 2 Might defense task for each minute they spend within immediate range of the venting pipe. On a failure, PCs are hindered on all perception tasks requiring hearing for at least an hour after they are no longer exposed to the noise.

One way to relieve the pressure is to remove the cap; PCs can do so by successfully attacking the object and causing it to fall one step on the object damage track. Other methods PCs think up and try may also get the job done. When the cap is removed, the venting gas is no longer forced through a tiny crack, and the whistling stops. In addition, a vertical tunnel is revealed (the pipe's interior) leading down into the darkness. A strong, warm, and highly humid flow of air continues to rush out of the tube, but not strongly enough to inhibit the fall of anything characters drop into the pipe (including themselves, should they wish to personally explore).

You have a few options if characters explore. One is to use this unexpected encounter as a character hook to some new adventure: maybe as an entrance to a larger area of your own creation, or as a way to begin a published adventure. Alternately, use the following:

The tube descends over a mile (2 km). However, even if a character should fall in without preparation, the strong upward flow of warm, humid air means that a character who plummets all the way to the bottom without successfully slowing their fall is not smashed, but instead takes 4 points of ambient damage. The chamber discovered is quite large and is dominated by a skyscraper-sized machine set in a pool of liquid, although only the top of the machine protrudes above water. Tiny orange glows glitter across the machine's surface, emerging from crevices and vents. The water surrounding the machine boils, but there is enough space around the pool to stand without coming to harm.

Pipe: *level 5*

Attacking objects, page 116

Machine: *level 7*

Options for iron wind (green mist) alterations can be found on the Harmful Mutations table (Numenera Discovery, page 398).

Don't wait; go now. Life is short and the world is big.

Salvaging Iotum, Parts, and Other Numenera, page 108

Ranked Disasters, page 309

Matterpool: *rank 4 natural disaster*

Fasia: *level 4, hunting as level 5*

Flit disc, page 31

Fountain of light: *level 6*

Unless the GM wishes to explicitly tie the image from the fountain to the Engine of the Gods (as described in Edge of the Sun, Message From the Past *is merely a weird encounter, though it could provide a couple of cyphers to PCs who attempt to salvage at the fountain's base.*

The purpose of the machine isn't apparent, though someone who succeeds on an understanding numenera task believes it is some kind of power node (for what, isn't obvious). If the PCs care to risk crossing the short distance of boiling water to the machine's face, they could attempt to salvage it for several hundred shins and other numenera.

LOST TRAVELER

A 30-foot (9 m) diameter, crystalline disc stands at an angle, partially embedded in the ground as if it fell from a great height. Here and there, wood, cloth, and metallic debris are scattered across the landscape. If PCs investigate the disc, Fasia pulls herself from under some nearby wreckage. She is hurt (with only 1 health) and unable to recognize the PCs as anything other than a potential threat given her fever—not that she can do anything about it.

If the PCs nurse Fasia back to health, she tells of how she is a hunter for her village called Meren's Lake (which the PCs have probably never heard of). One day, she found the edge of a crystal device. Uncovering it, she found a great disc (the very disc the PCs first spied). Fasia learned how to use the disc as a transport device capable of moving herself and her goods over great distances. However, one day she was attacked by a swarm of flying creatures, which damaged the disc. The disc took off at an incredible pace, and Fasia blacked out. When she came to, she found herself crashed here . . . wherever here is.

If PCs want to help Fasia further, they can invite her along so she doesn't perish of exposure out in the middle of nowhere. However, if they *really* want to provide aid, they can try to repair the broken disc (a flit disc) and also attempt to help her find her way back to Meren's Lake. (Where Meren's Lake is in relation to where the PCs find the lost traveler is up to you, but it is probably at least a couple of days' travel, if not *far* more.)

MATTERPOOL

A phenomenon known as a "matterpool" can spring up suddenly in wild regions of the Steadfast and the Beyond, threatening everything living or built on the surrounding landscape that can't fly. A matterpool swirls around and around, exactly like a whirlpool would do in a large body of water, somehow causing rock, soil, and other nonliving material to flow as if it were actually liquid. The active area of a matterpool is a long distance across, but terrain and landscape elements within a very long distance of it are somehow constantly drawn closer, over the course of several hours, until they too become snagged in the surrounding swirl and are quickly sucked under at the center. In fact, this may be how PCs end up encountering the pool, as their camp is slowly and nigh-imperceptibly "pulled" to the edge of the matterpool, at which point it begins to swirl around and around the hub.

Once a creature is caught within the swirling radius, the liquified matter acts like an adhesive. A character must succeed on a difficulty 4 Might defense roll each round to extricate themselves anew. If freed, a character can move normally on their turn across the face of the swirling matter, but the moment they take no movement on their turn, they become stuck again. Each round a character remains stuck within the swirl, they are carried inward an immediate or short distance. Any creature or object that begins their turn in the matterpool's center is gone (buried, sucked into another dimension, or teleported elsewhere; it's up to the GM).

Once a matterpool is active for about ten hours, it simply disappears, leaving the landscape scarred with a strange swirl of ridges.

MESSAGE FROM THE PAST

A rounded structure pokes out of the ruins with a regular, door-like opening on one side. Light sporadically flashes from it. If PCs investigate, they discover a chamber lit erratically by something like a fountain set near its center. Instead of water, a glowing blue substance sometimes surges out of the top. The lighted substance sprays up into the air then falls back into the surrounding basin, apparently evaporating as it does. To the touch (if PCs stick a hand or tool into the stream), the glowing substance seems to have no mass, as if it really is just some kind of slow light.

Should a character splash the fluid into their eyes or seek to consume it, that character unlocks an additional property of the fluid, which plays a visual message (at least that's what it feels like) to that character only.

The message begins with a burning sphere: a searing coal in the darkness. The bright sphere swells in size, becoming something large beyond comprehension, until the viewer sees a structure orbiting about the orb. The structure, in turn, swells in size, revealing it to be some kind of massive engine pointing directly at the burning sphere. The end closest to the burning orb emits a pale blue light, which seems to stabilize the structure above the ocean of fire covering the sphere. The engine's other end emits a flame thousands of miles long. It gives the impression that, despite how much larger the burning sphere is than the engine, the engine is actually pushing the sphere through the void.

The PCs can repeat this message as often as they want by splashing more fluid into their eyes (or consuming it). Some details change slightly each time it is played, but the overall sequence is basically the same.

METAL MONOLITH LURE

Something catches the light just so, reflecting sunlight or other illumination back into the PCs' eyes. Upon investigation, a 12-foot (4 m) tall, three-sided metallic monolith is discovered, mute and apparently inert, cut several feet into the ground.

The monolith is a lure: it was set to draw travelers from a nearby road or other place people sometimes pass, tempting them to travel a few miles out of their way to investigate.

Who set the lure? It could be a group of jiraskar-hunters who aren't interested in PCs who happen by. But the PCs may be in for a surprise when one or more jiraskar show up, too. If PCs drive off or kill the jiraskar, the hunters are cross with the characters.

Alternatively, entities specifically interested in collecting travelers for study might have set the lure, such as a group of tentacle-armed, numenera-savvy calramites that are curious about the pox of humans spreading across the Earth. If collected by calramites, PCs are taken to an off-world orbiting structure for a few days but are returned later, possibly with no memory of the experience.

METALLIC PYLONS

Several metallic pylons erupt from the ground here, each about 1 foot (30 cm) in diameter and over 50 feet (15 m) tall. Several are fallen, rusted, and probably salvaged, but a few are topped with shining pearls that constantly spit electricity. However, the pylons are safe to touch down near the base, though they are warm even at night. No obvious purpose for the pylons exists.

PCs can attempt to salvage the four working pylons for numenera. However, if they do so, an undetectable signal summons a human riding a nacious who appears within about

Nacious, page 21

Typical calramite:
level 4, all numenera tasks as level 8

Jiraskar, page 238

Wright, page 286

Megwill Cove, page 236

Titanothaur: level 10,
see The Ninth World
Bestiary, page 126

Obelisk: level 7

Synth cube: level 6

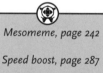

Mesomeme, page 242

Speed boost, page 287

Teleporter (bounder),
page 287

Visage changer,
page 288

Root structure: level 7

ten minutes. The human is Unacey, a Wright from the relatively nearby community of Megwill Cove. Unacey explains that the PCs must return what they have taken from the pylons to her, so she can repair them. She says the small village where she has set up shop depends on the active functioning of at least a few of the pylons to ward off the return of "the titanothaur." If asked to explain what a titanothaur is, she shrugs and simply says, "a creature vast and powerful beyond conception." Whether any of this is true or not, Unacey believes it—or at least she believes the villagers who have asked her to keep the pylons in functioning order.

If PCs comply, then all is fine. Unacey may even invite them back to the village for dinner—a ride of about ten minutes. If PCs resist, Unacey will have to decide whether she has the strength to insist (doubtful) or let the PCs make off with the salvage.

MURMURING LAKE

A reddish mist sometimes forms above this lake at night, then flows away a few hours after dawn. PCs who investigate this otherwise apparently natural body of water discover it is rich in aquatic life, including birds and insects, as well as edible fish. Relatively shallow, the lake's banks are thick with tall reeds and other plants.

Hiding amidst these reeds is a creature known as a mesomeme. PCs likely first become aware of it audibly: a strange choir of babble, including what sounds like human voices mixed in with animal croaks and other bestial calls. If the PCs enter among the reeds to investigate the sounds, they find a number of individual creatures—both people and animals—perhaps swimming or wading in the shallow water. Each person is speaking (nonsense phrases), and the animals are all making noises as well.

Of course, this tableau is actually the mesomeme's lure, and if the PCs see the heads, the mesomeme is almost certainly aware of the onlooking characters. It attempts to lure them as close as possible before revealing its true nature.

If the PCs manage to slay this dangerous beast and then search around the banks of the lake, they discover the camp of some previous explorers, including a few long-rotted bodies (missing their heads). Among several pieces of weathered standard equipment, the PCs also find several cyphers, including a speed boost, a teleporter (bounder), and a visage changer.

OBELISKS OF OBSERVATION

A series of gray, metallic obelisks stand in two long rows, forming an open-air "hallway" across the terrain about 30 feet (9 m) wide and 200 feet (60 m) long. The 30-foot (9 m) tall obelisks themselves are generally similar, each giving off a dim, bluish light from two eye-like slots set near their tops.

Should any creature enter the space between the obelisks, a floating synth cube about 9 feet (3 m) on a side appears at the farthest end of the "hallway" and moves towards the intruders, flying a short distance each round. As it approaches the characters, the cube side facing the characters displays events occurring within the "hallway" from the cube's point of view. The synth cube stops when it comes within an immediate distance of the closest PC. Staring at the stopped cube is akin to looking into a mirror.

If PCs succeed on an understanding numenera task on the synth cube, they discover the cube's edges are also a control surface. If fiddled with, they can change the scenes displayed on the floating cube's face. They learn they can manually change the display's point of view, at a rate of up to a very long distance per round. However, if they succeed on another understanding numenera task, they learn how to arbitrarily change the scene displayed to any location they have previously visited or know to exist.

If any violence is attempted against the synth cube or any of the obelisks, or if characters attempt to remove the synth cube from the hallway where it manifested, it phases to safety, becoming impossible to physically harm. On the following round, a couple of the obelisks animate as automatons (level 7) and seek to destroy the threat represented by the characters or other intruding creatures. More and more obelisks animate if necessary to contain the threat.

ORCHARD OF THE ANCIENTS

A series of approximately 40-foot (12 m) tall plants with ruby-colored fruits grow in fairly even rows covering an area a few miles across. The relative order the trees grow in may suggest to some that the trees have been planted purposefully. However, no humans or other creatures obviously live nearby. (All the trees making up the "orchard" are actually a single entity existing as a massive root structure beneath the ground, a remnant of a much larger system that existed in the area millions of years prior.)

If PCs investigate, they discover that the fruit of each tree is apparently edible, smelling tart. However, each bite delivers a random sensory effect (not necessarily one of taste). For instance, someone sampling the fruit might feel a sudden cold sensation, hear a strange animal roar, see unfamiliar glyphs flash before their eyes, or taste something horrible. Most sensations are completely safe, if novel.

It's possible that information could be gleaned by someone who meditates on a question before taking a bite of a piece of fruit and who succeeds on a level 7 Intellect-based task. However, bothering the root structure in this manner more than once or twice triggers a chance that an extremely painful or even potentially lethal sensation is induced by the next bite of fruit. Introduce the first dangerous sensation as a GM intrusion.

PAVILION WITH NO DOORS

The PCs spy a large scarlet tent that has no obvious exits or entrances. This tent belongs to Divine Nex, who PCs encounter after they spend a few rounds investigating the exterior of the strange pavilion.

Larger than life, Nex parades out of the tent as if on stage, projecting their voice loudly enough to reach the most distant seats in an outdoor theater as they introduce themself. They bring forth a basket of comestibles and a bottle of wine from a nearby community known for its spirits, and ask the PCs if they'd like a snack while they tell Nex all about their travels.

In turn, their host describes how they make a living moving from community to community, providing knowledge, entertainment, and news of distant locations. Nex indicates that if PCs are interested, they and Nex can travel together for a time. If PCs agree, the events described in the "Taker of Sorrow" adventure begin to unfold, though, of course, PCs may continue on their journey at any time without resolving the issues that come up.

PIT IN THE PLAIN

A square shaft, about 30 feet (9 m) to a side, punctures the terrain. It might not be obvious except from above, or if characters happen to run across the pit while exploring. Despite a small stream emptying into it and other signs of geologic erosion causing drit to fall into it, it is obviously very far from being filled up. The sides are metallic and bear a rough pattern of raised ridges that could be used to climb down to investigate.

If a character descends one way or another, the depth of the shaft is discovered to be about 200 feet (61 m). Around halfway down, characters may notice the increasing prevalence of a bluish tar-like substance smeared on the pit's walls and covering the bottom. Though it looks like some kind of stain or mold growth, the blue tar is, in fact, a creature—albeit one whose true physical form is far more complex in a dimension with more angles than this one. Still, it is dangerous to any physical material that it contacts, living or dead, whether solid, liquid, or gas. It incorporates whatever it breaks down into its form, which actually fills the shaft to a depth of over a thousand feet: over the aeons, it has increased its bulk enough to rise within just a few hundred feet of the surface.

POISON FIELDS OF GOLD

It smells strongly of flowers in this area, very pleasantly so. If characters investigate, they discover a field of bright yellow flowers whose petals are metallic. Despite their underlying rigidity, the metallic flowers grow like regular flora.

These steel blooms are more than a mere oddity, at least when they're growing in such a large quantity. If characters spend more than ten minutes within a short distance of any area where these flowers bloom, they must succeed on a Might defense roll or fall suddenly and deeply asleep due to the subtle poison interlaced with the fragrance. An affected character is allowed another Might defense roll every few hours, or each time they are forcefully prodded (or damaged).

Often, colonies of pincer ants keep cone-like colonies along the edges of steel bloom fields. Immune to the poison themselves, they move as a swarm to engulf sleeping prey, drag them to an edge, and build a new cone hive on the remains of their latest victim (whose entombed, sleeping body becomes another new pincer ant food source).

Tree: *level 3*

Pit: *level 7*

Blue tar: *level 7; health 50; two short-range pseudopod attacks inflict 8 points of damage each and, on a failed Might defense roll, target descends one step on the damage track*

Divine Nex, page 73

Scarlet Tent: *level 6; has no exits or entrances, but Divine Nex knows the secret of entering and leaving at will*

Steel bloom: *level 3*

"Taker of Sorrow," page 363

Pincer ant swarm: *level 3; immune to steel bloom fragrance poison*

Cone hive: *level 4*

POOL OF JUDGMENT

Ashy silt completely covers the way ahead, covering a region about 100 feet (30 m) in rough diameter. Ripples like those that might be seen on a pool's surface are frozen into the white substance.

Prodding the ashlike material with a pole or other long implement from outside has no effect other than smearing the ripple designs. Characters who succeed on a difficulty 5 perception task feel their skin tingle and notice their hair tends to stand on end when they are near the pool. If characters give the pool a wide berth, then that's probably that. (The white material is actually a mass of hibernating nanites.)

However, if characters continue to investigate by prodding or otherwise disturbing the pool, the entire volume of ash animates, rising up in a coiling white cloud. It solidifies as a massive, 100-foot (30 m) tall, statue-like slab with just a few design flourishes that make it vaguely resemble a standing humanoid. The entity formed is a telepathic mechanism calling itself a judge. It ignores the PCs if they do nothing else.

If the characters try to engage it, a completely alien consciousness responds telepathically, asking each to recount their crimes. Characters who refuse are subject to the judge's physical attack (just one, unless the PCs attack it back; then it's a combat).

Characters who comply (by admitting some experience that they feel even a little bit bad about how they handled) receive a telepathic balm, which essentially allows the character to put that event behind them. If this was something that was actually troubling the character, it no longer does.

A few hours later, the judge returns to its former state, assuming it is not further disturbed.

Marandor: level 7; Armor 3 (from suit); two long-range energy attacks (from suit) inflict 7 points of damage each

Hibernating nanites: level 3

Judge: level 8; Armor 5; two short-range melee attacks inflict 10 points of damage each

PORTAL TUMBLE

Weird atmospheric effects (lightning out of nowhere, strange colors in the sky, unexplained sounds) finally culminate in a fissure in reality through which an old man tumbles. If PCs saw the atmospheric effects and were drawn to investigate, they see the newcomer arrive.

The old man is Marandor. He wears a uniform-like leotard of golden fabric, though it is frayed and burnt. He arrives unconscious. A PC who tends to Marandor's injuries—a difficulty 3 healing task—rouses him. Otherwise, he wakes up a few hours later. Either way, the fissure in reality seals up behind Marandor after his arrival, and isn't immediately accessible again.

When Marandor recovers, he is confused. He apparently speaks a language other than the Truth, and not one currently spoken in the Ninth World. If the PCs manage to overcome the language barrier through an ability or device, Marandor explains that he was surveying something called the "Electron Reefs" in his vessel, which he refers to as a "quantum skiff." He was searching for signs of a breach by the lying and devious "Entropians." Some sort of malfunction on his vessel caused him to veer into an acausal storm that usually utterly destroys whatever falls into its grasp. He figured he was done for. Yet, here he is.

Whatever PCs make of him, Marandor essentially comes from a completely different reality and timeline than the Earth's Ninth World. At first, Marandor is eager to get back, but there doesn't seem to be any way for him to make that happen. In the meantime, he offers to accompany and help the characters on whatever task they might be about. He hopes that, in time, something of this new world he finds himself in will offer him an escape back to his own reality, where things between his own kind and the Entropians had reached a head.

"To move, to breathe, to fly, to float,
To gain all while you give,
To roam the roads of lands remote,
To travel is to live."

—*ancient prose from the prior worlds*

PRESERVATION STATION

Ranging out from a recently awakened ruin are unique automatons called preserverators. They initially appear as a mass of undifferentiated pinkish metal. However, each mass is composed of nanites able to take on the semblance of nearly any sapient creature they encounter. They take on such a façade in an effort to ease the qualms of strangers. The resemblance is purposefully rough: not enough for other creatures to actually believe they are being accosted by creatures of their own kind, at least not once an interaction begins.

Preserverators urge those they encounter to please accompany them to safety, drawing on a library of languages they've accumulated over deep time. The automatons won't explain the exact nature of the threat, but only tell those they accost that they will certainly die if the preserverators' offer of aid is not accepted. The preserverators' urging grows more strident, and if not eventually heeded, the automatons attempt to capture their targets and bodily drag them back to their "preservation station."

The preservation station is a multi-level buried ruin. The topmost level contains a cryogenic arch through which newcomers are directed by preserverators (or through which they might venture on their own). The arch is a mechanism that flash-freezes a target in perfect stasis, encapsulates them in a caul-like membrane, then hands them off to a nearby preserverator. The newly "saved" target is then stored in a vast chamber below, which is about half-filled with similarly frozen humans, familiar abhumans, and other contemporary sapient creatures (including some machine creatures) of the Ninth World. This space is just the highest chamber of several even-deeper chambers, each filled with preserved creatures of ever-earlier epochs.

All have been "saved" from dying through old age, misadventure, or death. However, attempts to resuscitate any but those stored within the last few months are only about 1% likely to be successful. Ninety-nine percent of the time, the re-warmed body is just a slush of exploded cells. And, of course, the preserverators take a dim view of any attempt to thaw already "saved" targets.

Preserverator: *level 5; short-range attack puts target into suggestible state for about an hour on a failed Intellect defense roll*

Cryogenic arch: *level 6*

Purple metallic sphere: *level 8*

Circular hatch: *level 5*

Datademon, page 57

Chirog, page 229

Titanothaur: *level 10*

PURPLE SKIES IN A SPHERE

A purple metallic sphere emerges dome-like from the ground. From a distance, it's easily mistaken for the exterior of an enclosed dome about 50 feet (15 m) in diameter. An investigation along the periphery of the "dome" reveals a sealed circular hatch about 6 feet (2 m) in diameter and warm to the touch (whereas the rest of the dome is cool).

A dangerous biomechanical menace, known as a datademon, watches the hatch from hiding a short distance away, behind a stand of short trees (easing its stealth task by two steps).

A successful understanding numenera task allows PCs to open the hatch, which produces a plume of warm steam that billows into the air. A glance inside reveals what seems to be a vast expanse of clouds, as if the PC were actually looking down at the sky from some vast height—if the sky were purple instead of blue. Among the clouds slowly tumble strange objects and ruin-like structures.

PCs can enter the sphere and explore (the weightless void has a breathable atmosphere), but before that, they must contend with the datademon's attack (possibly with surprise), launched as PCs gaze through the hatch.

PCs who discover the dome's interior (which seems to be either a pocket dimension or an entirely different dimension) may decide that they'd like to explore further. However, unless PCs make some sort of special effort to mark the entrance to the dimension, it's easy to lose track of it among the warm,

drifting clouds. Wandering around inside the sphere could generate many additional encounters, at your option. You can use the following table to help inspire them.

For each ten minutes that the PCs spend exploring, choose (or roll 1d6) to determine what they encounter.

1d6	Encounter
1	Two reality eaters are fighting each other. If PCs help one against the other and win, the victor may give PCs an option for returning to their home dimension.
2	Tower-like ruin with many smaller ruins and several options for salvaging the numenera
3	Colony of armor-plated chirogs eager to try new protein in human form.
4	Machine (level 4) 100 yards (91 m) across that is curious as a puppy, and about as bright.
5	Petrified corpse of a many-limbed, many-eyed titanothaur. Is it really dead, or just asleep?
6	Globule of smart water about 30 feet (9 m) in diameter (level 5) that initially just seems like a random floating volume of water, but if approached, actually attempts to suck in and drown creatures (but perhaps accidentally)

RED DOOR

Visible in the distance as a blood-red spot in an otherwise dreary landscape, this 20-foot (6 m) diameter circular red door set in the side of a rocky bluff has no apparent handle or control. If the door is destroyed or bypassed, the space beyond is the top of a well that descends about 80 feet (24 m), then opens into a 30-foot (9 m) diameter spherical chamber.

A writhing discontinuity hovers at the center of the great sphere. Completely black at the center, the discontinuity is limned with brilliant gold light. A ledge set in the chamber's side allows explorers to circle around the discontinuity, and along a single, aisle-like projection that reaches out from the ledge, even allowing them to approach within immediate range of the phenomenon. Those that do so feel as if something within the discontinuity is pulling them forward. Trying to touch (or dropping something onto) the discontinuity, however, is prevented by a protective temporal force field. If an object or character comes into contact with the force field, from the point of view of everyone else in the chamber, the creature or object becomes timestopped.

Returning a timestopped character to normal time requires someone to access one of several devices set into the wall along the ledge, and succeed on an understanding numenera task.

If PCs salvage the devices on the ledge, the discontinuity at the center of the chamber blinks out; however, anything timestopped remains in that condition until some other effect is able to release it back to the regular timestream. A successful salvage attempt yields about 30 shins, a reality spike, a phase disruptor, and a force screen projector.

TIMESTOPPED EFFECT

Time moves so slowly for a timestopped PC that, from the perspective of everyone else, they stand like a statue. From the PC's perspective, everything around them flits about with uncanny speed—so fast, in fact, that creatures might appear as stuttering blurs. Only fixed objects appear solid. The PC essentially takes no turns while in this state, at least relative to creatures not in the same state. Attacks against a timestopped creature are made as if they had Armor 10—timespace protects the deformation of flesh that most kinds of attacks deliver.

RED PILLAR

A great red pillar sprouts up from the earth, rising at least 500 feet (150 m) into the air and about 60 feet (18 m) in diameter. Projections that could be used as a sort of ladder-like stairs wind around it all the way to the top. Climbing is normally a difficulty 1 Might task, though a wind gust or other mishap could hinder the task along the way.

A flat surface on top of the pillar is marred by an off-center circular valve. The valve can be opened with a successful understanding numenera task. Inside is a great hollow filled with a matrix of metallic scaffolding. (The scaffolding could be used as a ladder-like aid in climbing about the interior the same way as the projections on the pillar's exterior.) The scaffolding holds hundreds of clear crystal spheres, like insects caught in a web. Every few minutes, one of the spheres flashes with light and an image. The image is utterly random, usually culled from the datasphere from some past epoch. However, a few are more recent.

Characters could attempt to salvage the location, or try to gain some greater understanding. If they attempt the latter and spend at least a few days crawling among the scaffolding, locating various control surfaces, and then succeed on an understanding numenera task, they can use the great device to query the datasphere about once a week, as if using a series of level 7 datasphere siphons.

However, the interior of the red pillar is guarded by a many-armed biomechanical protector who has one extendable mouth paired with each arm. If characters enter and do not leave within a day, it makes its quiet way up from the bottom of the hollow and begins to pick off characters one by one, usually by pushing them off the scaffolding to fall to their deaths at the bottom of the hollow, far below.

ROT VINES

A forest filled with tall trees stands in the travelers' path. Unless the characters can fly, or decide to find another way around (which presumably will add a day or more to the trip), the only way forward is through. The canopy above is dense and filters out most of the light, making things dim down below. Worse, the trees grow close together at times, which means those using vehicles or large mounts must wind around looking for a way through.

Red pillar: *level 7*

Red door: *level 5*

Force field: *level 8*

Salvaging Iotum, Parts, and Other Numenera, page 108

Devices on the Ledge: *level 6*

Protector: *level 4, stealth and dislodging attacks as level 6*

Reality spike, page 285

Phase disruptor, page 284

Force screen projector, page 279

Datasphere siphon, page 277

Mind slime, page 65

Rot vine: *level 4; pods burst in immediate radius and inflict 2 points of damage each round until target succeeds on a Might defense roll*

Circular door: *level 7*

Floating yellow sphere: *level 9*

Mechanism at the back of the room: *level 5*

Psychic communique, page 285

Several dangers lurk in the forest, including a group of mind slimes that may ambush those who camp beneath the boughs. However, even those who don't camp encounter rot vines. They grow both along the ground and in the branches, camouflaged by coloration and laden with pods filled with violet spores ready to burst and kill anyone who trips over, or becomes tangled in, a vine.

RUIN OUTCROPPING

Here and there, some ruins of the prior worlds persist as just a single chamber or two that were once probably part of a far-larger complex that has worn away. What remains is sometimes visible as a small structure jutting from a hillside or cliff face, with a door or other still-sealed accessway protecting (at least to some extent) what lies inside.

RUIN OUTCROPPING: FLOATING SPHERES

This ruin outcropping is visible as an artificially flat expanse along a cliff. It is perfectly smooth except for a circular door, which characters can open on a successful understanding numenera task.

Inside, PCs find a circular tunnel that quickly opens into a large room with a tangle of metallic tendrils that rise up from the floor to connect with several floating yellow spheres. These spheres glow slightly, and the characters can discern a faint smell of ozone. PCs who succeed on an understanding numenera task in regard to the spheres discern that they might be, or contain, individual intelligences that are either sleeping or communing.

One other obvious mechanism inhabits the room along the back wall; most of the metallic tendrils rising from the floor actually emerge from this device. If destroyed or salvaged (for about 12 shins and a couple of psychic communique cyphers), the yellow spheres rapidly blink in and out of existence for a few rounds, then blink out one last time, apparently gone for good.

RUIN OUTCROPPING: SPECIMENS

This ruin outcropping is visible as a purplish metallic cube, buried but for a single corner (which on the surface appears as a metallic pyramid protruding from the ground). Investigation reveals a sealed entranceway that characters can open if they succeed on an understanding numenera task.

Inside, explorers discover a purple chamber, though one whose floor slopes at a severe 45-degree angle. The large chamber extends a good way below the ground (a long distance per side). A strong chemical odor fills the air.

Nearly a dozen rows of transparent canisters fill the room, jutting from the angled floor. Each canister is about 12 feet (4 m) in diameter and stands 15 feet (5 m) tall, with a control surface circling it and wires connecting it under the floor. A reddish light emanates from a few of the transparent containers, though most are dark.

Once, each canister held a biological (or in some cases, biomechanical) creature preserved in a thick, clear gel. That preservation has failed in all of the dark canisters. Even so, the lit containers reveal multicolored worms, insects the size of humans, bird-like lizards, and several creatures that have no obvious analog. All of these are essentially dead, despite being preserved.

If PCs take a survey of all the canisters, they discover that a few are broken and their contents have spilled out (thus the chemical smell). PCs also discover three dead humans—apparently explorers who were investigating this chamber when something attacked them. Horrible, gaping wounds suggest something with many toothed mouths was responsible. But since the bodies have fallen to the lowest level where pooled preservative rests, they haven't really decayed much. Whatever killed the explorers is nowhere to be seen.

If the characters loot the bodies, they discover regular exploration equipment, as well as the following cyphers: a level 5 time dilation nodule (defensive), a level 3 warmth projector, a level 5 spatial warp, and a level 6 telepathy implant. One of the bodies also wears dimensional armor with a depletion of 1 in 1d6.

SEEPAGE

In the distance is a great crevice, and what appears to be red-hot, raw magma glimmers in its depths. The crevice is a long distance across and a very long distance wide. The molten rock itself is a long distance below the crevice's lip. PCs standing near the edge and looking over feel the heat, but aren't in immediate danger.

Scattered here and there around the edges of the crevice, like seashells along a beach, are blackened devices. Most are tiny, broken, or half-melted blobs, but a few are as large as houses. PCs who remain for an extended period discover the source as a geyser of molten rock spews unexpectedly from below, slopping over the edge of the crevice, then draining back into the depths. Sometimes, this leaves behind an object. PCs usually won't be close enough to a geyser to be in danger, unless you decide to introduce some risk as a GM intrusion.

Of more immediate concern than the geysers is a nearby colony of humanoid creatures with stone carapaces and red eyes (called anhedons) that periodically wander the edges of the crevice, looking for working devices among the mostly useless upwelling. The anhedons usually attempt to kill any creature they notice collecting items from the area. PCs who spend time combing the crevice's edge can collect one or two cyphers per hour, generally speaking.

Purplish metallic cube: *level 6*

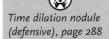

Anhedon, page 253

Time dilation nodule (defensive), page 288

Warmth projector, page 288

Spatial warp, page 287

Telepathy implant, page 287

Dimensional armor, page 294

Radiation: *level 3*

SICKNESS IN THE LAND

The area is saturated with invisible radiation from a buried ruin. The flora and fauna sparkle with an adaptive bluish glitter, but PCs without such protection are affected. Each hour a character spends in the area (either because they chose to rest or camp there, or because they are traveling through the area), they must make a Might defense roll. On a failure, a character suffers 6 points of ambient damage and takes a cumulative –1 penalty to recovery rolls. The penalty lessens by 1 for every 28 hours a character spends in an area not saturated by radiation.

SKY STAIN

Horticuller, page 62

One evening, the characters spy something new in the sky: a sort of faint stain, greenish and hazy like a nebula. Anyone with any knowledge of the stars understands that it's a new phenomenon. That may be as far as this encounter goes: something weird in the sky. However, if a PC has some means to reach further, either psychically or perhaps through a cypher-mediated channel to ask questions of the datasphere, they learn the image is "leakage" from an alternate, sentient dimension of hate. There is a chance that the "leakage" notices the PCs taking a direct interest in it. The character must succeed on a difficulty 5 Might task or gain a psychic disease known as green dream. The disease manifests as a sudden chill that passes, only becoming more serious after the PC goes to sleep.

Green Dream: People with this affliction (treat as a disease) begin to have the same dream: an iridescent emerald chamber filled with exquisite fractal growths constantly evolving and changing, creating a breathtaking vista that's hard to look away from. However, afflictions come after waking: fever, headaches, joint pains, confusion, and poor coordination. Those afflicted just want to go back to sleep, back to their wonderful "green dream." Unfortunately, many of those who experience the dream more than a few times never wake up again.

Green dream disease:
level 5; victim must make a Might defense roll each ten hours or all tasks are hindered one step (cumulative effect); three failed defense rolls before three successes drops victim into a sleep from which regular means cannot wake them (most waste away and die)

Explorer, page 265

SOUND OF DEFORESTATION

A strange, regular clanking noise becomes audible. It almost sounds like metal banging on metal in an even, unhurried rhythm that goes on for a few minutes, then stops. If the PCs are traveling, they may only hear the sound once or twice more, fainter each time,

before they move beyond the unidentified source. If the PCs are camping, it comes and goes, sometimes waking them up in the middle of the night.

Upon investigation, the PCs discover a 9-foot (3 m) tall automaton moving through an area thick with growth (trees or other tall flora). It seems intent on clearing the trees and/or other growth away by cutting it to the roots with one of its many implements, then feeding the material into an angular funnel on its upper surface. Some sort of process occurs within the body of the automaton, producing a clanking sound that is earsplitting in close proximity. Then, an orifice in the lower portion of the automaton spews out the plant material it fed into its funnel, looking essentially the same as when it went in. (The PCs have discovered a malfunctioning horticuller.)

If the PCs interfere, the horticuller is likely to attack. On the other hand, PCs who succeed on an understanding numenera task as they watch the automaton work realize that it must be malfunctioning. The material spewed out after the clanking process should be a fine mulch, useful for growing new plants. But something has gone wrong. It may be that the characters don't care, or that they'd prefer to simply overcome the automaton and salvage it. However, if they attempt to negotiate with the horticuller and succeed on a few persuasion tasks (assuming they can open up communication), the horticuller will submit to repair attempts. If the PCs succeed on that, the grateful machine reveals a cache of two or three cyphers it has collected during the course of its travels and drops them off to the PCs. (It might instead provide the PCs information about the area that they might not already know.)

STARVING SURVIVORS

The characters, traveling through a cold, hard-to-reach area, find three other explorers taking shelter in the shell of some structure previously built from prior-world ruins. The explorers were part of a larger group that found themselves accidentally teleported to this area some months ago. Their food rations gave out, and the three survivors only survived by resorting to eating those who perished before them. The bodies are stored in a snowbank (or some kind of numenera freezer-like compartment) behind the shelter, but only remnants remain. The three survivors are deeply affected by their horrible experiences and do not willingly tell characters what they've had to do in order to survive. However, they are very much in need of regular food and, more importantly, rescue. If PCs can't provide one of those things, the starving survivors begin to plot how to add the characters to their diet.

STEED MERCHANTS HAVING A SALE

The characters come across a caravan selling various mounts. The caravan is made up of several wagons that contain animal feed and water, saddles, and similar items that might be useful for those who wish to make a deal. The primary steed merchant is named Shorla, who, from a distance, might seem small and frail, but she has strange wires running through her skin that give her incredible strength and stamina. In addition to herself, about ten caravan workers make up the traveling band.

Shorla has several fine mounts available, but she is always looking to unload undersized or partly lame mounts to strangers first if she can get away with it—especially to buyers who don't take the time to size up the merchandise. If called on it, she pretends to be as surprised as the characters about the defect and offers them a "deal" if they'll take the mount off her hands.

SURPRISE OCCUPANTS

The characters' vehicle has a stowaway, which has been present (though undiscovered) since they first acquired it.

If the vehicle is only a single-person craft, the stowaway is, by necessity, small enough to fit into a storage compartment and go unnoticed for a time. A good option is a quiescent shinspinner that eventually wakes up and begins to secretly disassemble the vehicle.

A larger vehicle with room for many passengers could contain a small colony of shinspinners too. However, there's room for one or more larger creatures to be secretly stowing away. One possibility is that, after some period of travel in their vehicle, the characters discover a new compartment because of the sound of banging that occasionally emanates from a sealed opening. Upon breaking the seal, the characters discover a starving female nano called Kresithan there. She had put herself into stasis with a cypher, allowing her to survive for several years until the effect recently ended. Kresithan has her own agenda, as indicated in her NPC entry, and whether or not the PCs wish to indulge her determines how she reacts. Either way, at first, she is quite grateful for the rescue.

Shinspinner, page 276

Mounts, page 19

Shorla: *level 4, deception as level 6, physical tasks and defenses as level 7 due to implanted epidermal device*

Caravan worker, typical: *level 3*

Kresithan, page 75

TELLER OF TALES

A lone traveler—an elderly man wearing a ragged cloak of exotic material the PCs haven't previously encountered—accosts the characters during a rest. The man asks them to call him Storyteller. He explains that he collects amazing tales, and he asks the PCs for theirs. He offers his own in return, one for each story he is told. However, he warns the PCs that he will feed the teller to the "pet dimension" he keeps curled up in his cloak if he doesn't like their story.

The PCs can send the traveler on his way without consequence. Characters who wish can relate a story of their choosing and attempt a difficulty 4 persuasion task. On a success, Storyteller is delighted. He whispers a quick story to the PC whose story he liked. The story is so affecting that it acts like a level 5 cypher (if the PC hasn't reached their cypher limit), though it has no physical form. The PC can call on the power of the subtle cypher as if it were a normal cypher, despite it not being an object. Each PC can gain only one story (and associated subtle cypher) from Storyteller.

If Storyteller doesn't like the PC's story, he doesn't actually try to feed them to his pet dimension. He just frowns, then wonders if someone else has a story to tell. Of course, he defends himself if attacked.

Subtle cyphers from Storyteller have the following possible effects.

- Restores a number of points equal to the cypher's level to one of the user's Pools.
- Grants the ability to see in the dark for eight hours.
- For the next day, the user has an asset to Speed defense rolls.
- Grants the ability to see ten times as far as normal for one hour.
- Adds 1 to the user's Might, Speed, or Intellect Edge for one hour.

THAT'S NO HILL

An inviting-looking area, complete with a small pool and a nearby stream running through it, seems like the ideal place to rest (and recharge the energy reserves of a vehicle). The area features level ground, good sightlines, and a large outcropping of sky-blue rock the size of a large hill.

However, the outcrop of stone is actually a predator known as a choanid. If PCs camp near it or investigate it, it attacks. Even if the

PCs realize what the creature is before they draw near, it sees them and begins to track them to the best of its ability, and it may show up later when the PCs have mostly forgotten about it.

THE BLAZING PILLAR

The PCs spot something strange on the horizon, like a dark spot with a glow. It moves about as fast as a human can jog. As it gets closer, it's revealed to be a tilted, three-story building made of metal and synth, surrounded by pale yellow flames and emitting some kind of weird music. Various balconies and platforms have people on them who seem to be waving and pointing at the characters (unless the characters are hiding). One very prominent balcony has a person dressed in bright red clothing waving a long red and blue flag. None of the people appear to be hostile or carrying any weapons, and the vehicle continues to move vaguely in the direction of the PCs. When they get about a long distance away, the person with the flag calls out in a pleasant, high-pitched voice, "Hello, I am Sparadhi! Are you interested in trading with us? We have supplies and numenera, and we mean you no harm!" If invited closer, the flying building lands gently on the ground, at which point the yellow flames disappear, and the music stops.

Sparadhi is a traveling trader, using this strange vehicle called the Blazing Pillar to travel to various places and barter for goods. She is about thirty years old and wears fashionable and flamboyant clothing decorated with tiny numenera lights. Seen up close, there is an occasional septagonal pattern glowing under her skin (a subdermal artifact that gives her Armor). Her flag is just a long strip of cloth with alternating bands of blue and red, sort of like a wide scarf.

The Blazing Pillar floats about 10 feet (3 m) off the ground when it moves, and the flames are apparently a harmless energy discharge created by whatever engine the vehicle uses to move. Sparadhi inherited the machine from her mother and controls it by touching a metal orb on her balcony, but it doesn't seem to respond to anyone else trying to steer it (it might be attuned to her genes or to nanites in her brain).

Each of its three stories has two or three furnished rooms arranged around a central column, with a roof level surrounded by a

---

Storyteller, page 76

Sparadhi: *level 3; bargaining, partying, and positive social interaction as level 5; Armor 1 from an artifact*

The Blazing Pillar: *level 7 vehicle; floats up to a long distance each round for no more than ten hours out of twenty-eight; for more details, see* Slaves of the Machine God, *page 115*

Choanid, page 256

metal railing. Much of it seems like a very old machine, but there are many recent additions (such as the rails and furniture) that make it feel more like a home. The weird music seems to be a side effect of the engine or the flames, as it stops when the pillar lands and starts again when it flies.

If the PCs agree to trade, they are also invited to a party aboard the craft, which includes ten other guests who travel along with the Blazing Pillar as paying passengers. (PCs might be able to get a similar deal if they befriend Sparadhi.)

THE OSSERAK

Standing alone in the surrounding landscape is an ochre-colored, three-sided pyramid rising to a height of about 200 feet (60 m). This is the Osserak, resembling a much-eroded monument of especially hard stone. The ground around it is mostly flat and open, and shows signs of having hosted small encampments of humans in the past (mostly from castaway rags, broken tent pegs, the signs of a buried cooking fire, and so on).

PCs entering the clearing around the monument who have not learned how to "propitiate" the Osserak (see Curious Travelers) must succeed on an Intellect defense roll every few rounds to ward off a psychic emanation. Those who fail take 1 point of Intellect damage (ignores Armor) each time the effect is triggered.

Whether or not a character knows the observances and prayers to propitiate the Osserak, they can attempt to concentrate on the monument. This is an Intellect-based task that requires at least ten minutes of concentration. Those who are initiated ease the task by three steps. On a success, the character "gains the blessing of the Osserak." For the next ten days, they gain a sense of peace and balance, giving them 1 Armor against attacks that inflict mental damage.

THIEVES IN THE NIGHT

While encamped, the PCs are targeted by a group of grindrals. At first, this may seem like a one-off incident, but in fact, the initial foray that the PCs probably detect and stop is an intelligence-gathering probe launched by a magister named Harlod (who has Aeon Priest stats). Harlod has taken control of a colony of grindrals and uses them as his servitors and as a front. Harlod spies for the Angulan Knights, and is always on the lookout for traveling mutants he can capture and interrogate. However, most travelers that he finds are merely opportunities for him to enrich himself and the grindrals who serve him.

Harlod's lair is a cave mouth set in a cliff face near an occasionally traveled road. A cloaking device hides the cave mouth from casual scrutiny by causing the opening to appear as just more cliff face. Inside the lair is a central chamber used by the grindrals, a couple of side chambers where Harlod lives, plus one additional chamber where Harlod keeps his own vehicle, a strider.

TIME TRAP OBELISKS

On a nearby hillside float three black obelisks. Those who investigate discover they are floating about 18 feet (6 m) above the ground and at about the same distance each from the other. The obelisks are about 50 feet (15 m) tall, and are lightly inscribed with golden lines. The ground appears flattened beneath them. Searching among the weeds and shrubbery reveals the top of a cylinder-like machine forming a sort of platform where it emerges from the ground, though it is obviously degraded and even broken open in some places.

If someone steps onto the platform, the whole thing vibrates for a moment, then a control surface phases into existence at the platform's center. If a PC succeeds on an understanding numenera task while examining the control surface, they get the

Grindral, page 61

Aeon Priest, page 264

Angulan Knights, page 217

The Osserak: *level 8*

Cloaking device: *level 6*

Strider, page 28

Curious Travelers, page 86

Control surface: *level 5*

If one sees or experiences something new, that person is no longer the person they once were, but instead someone with a wider knowledge of themselves and of the world. Travelers understand this and constantly crave finding new places to visit for just this reason.

sense that the platform and obelisks can somehow alter time. The specifics are fuzzy at best, but the character believes (incorrectly) that they can target a creature or object they can see (or know to exist) and somehow displace it out of time. Other uses might also be possible, like seeing up to a year into the future. The user gets the sense they might be missing something, too, but can't determine exactly what.

Both uses require making an understanding numenera task on the control surface, hindered by three steps. Even if the task is successful, the most common outcome for anyone attempting to use the control surface is that the user (and anyone else on, or within immediate range of, the platform) is transferred into a bubble of space and time outside the normal time stream. Travelers don't initially notice a difference (though when they see a targeted creature disappear, they may incorrectly believe it was displaced, rather than themselves). In fact, the users are trapped in a time-space bubble and cannot leave the region—only a few miles in radius—until they successfully reverse the process.

If salvaged, the control surface yields around 20 shins, a controlled blinking nodule cypher, a couple of time dilation nodule cyphers (one offensive, the other defensive), and 1 unit of cosmic foam.

Controlled blinking module, page 277

Time dilation nodule, page 288

Cosmic foam, page 115

Unearthly cold: *level 6*

TORNADO!

The bruised sky spawns a storm of unusual ferocity, which in turn births a tornado! Typically a level 5–7 weather event, a tornado engulfs an area a long distance across each round, destroying every structure lower than its level and inflicting its level in ambient damage on everything else. A tornado typically takes about 1d6 + 2 rounds to pass any particular fixed point before moving on. PCs in a tornado without shelter (or whose shelter has just been ripped away) can attempt a Might defense roll each round, or take the indicated damage and be moved an immediate distance in a random direction. Even on a successful defense roll, the PC takes 2 points of damage from blowing debris. If PCs fail their Might defense roll twice in a row, they take additional damage equal to the tornado's level from piercing shrapnel and are stunned on their next turn.

UNEARTHLY COLD

Some element of the landscape—perhaps the corpse of a transdimensional being—is sucking heat from the nearby area for random periods of time. The unearthly cold inflicts 4 points of Speed damage per minute on a failed Might defense roll, or 2 points even on a successful roll (the unearthly cold ignores Armor).

VAPOR FEEDERS

This area near the route PCs are taking features several stalagmite-shaped clusters of rocky growth rising up from the ground to a height of about 3 feet (1 m). The mounds glow with a dull, brown-orange light that's difficult to notice during the day, but obvious at night. The mounds (vapor feeders) are essentially creatures, though each is composed of hardly animate drit and subsists on the air blowing across its surface. If left undisturbed, the mounds do not react to nearby creatures or PCs. However, those who investigate the mounds closely become targets of a stream of glowing, brown-orange, paralyzing acid expelled from the top of the mound. The outermost layers of flesh and other non-metallic substances touched by the liquid are changed from a solid to a gas, which is absorbed by the mound as particularly nutritious food.

Most mounds contain a few remnants of previous victims, though those are mostly animals and a few abhumans. However, a couple of mounds in the center of the cluster are bigger than the others and contain bone fragments, metallic bits of equipment, about 60 shins, and a comprehension graft cypher. But, of course, digging through them exposes searchers to the acidic attack.

VEHICLE JACKING

This event most likely unfolds in one of two ways.

One way this happens is if characters are staying at a location where they've left their vehicle (or mounts) unattended. Depending on the security the PCs left in place, either they return to find their vehicle missing, thanks to a group of four to seven vehicle jackers, or they find the jackers still in the process of trying to overcome the defenses or other security that protects the vehicle (or mounts).

The other way is that while traveling in their vehicle, they are flagged down by a group of four to seven "pilgrims" on a trip to Qi that seem to be in trouble. The pilgrims are actually vehicle jackers in disguise who spin a story about how their own amazing vehicle of the numenera broke down "just over that ridge," leaving them high and dry. If possible, the vehicle jackers attempt to put the PCs at ease in an attempt to separate the PCs from each other or from the vehicle, which means they're willing to play a long game to do so.

VIOLET RAIN

Due to an atmospheric anomaly, a purplish fluid drizzles down across the area. It's rainlike only in the sense that it's falling from the sky. Instead of liquid, the material falling in a violet rain event is composed of tiny, cube-shaped metallic "insects" that are violet in color. The tiny creatures swarm across whatever they touch, tearing it down to build up strange slabs about 9 feet (3 m) high and only a hand's breadth thick. The slabs are aligned so that one face looks exactly west.

Of more immediate concern to traveling PCs in the area where such a violet rain falls are the four or more violet rain cube swarms that come after them. These swarms attempt to tear the characters down to their constituent molecules so they can be rebuilt as more slabs.

WALL OF LIGHT

A shimmery wall made of nothing but air is faintly visible, rising from the ground into the sky. The wall discontinuity seems to extend for miles. It's possible to see the terrain through the discontinuity, though hazed with a multicolored residue like an oil slick.

A successful analysis of the wall by PCs with the means to do so reveals that it is akin to a minor fault in existence, similar to those visible in some exposed cliff faces.

A faint transdimensional energy is also associated with the wall. The PCs aren't sure if simply walking through the wall would be dangerous. Certainly, nearby wildlife seems to avoid doing so. Tossing stones or other objects through doesn't have a noticeable effect on the tossed items.

Going around the wall will add a few days to the characters' trip, but is possible.

If the PCs pass through the wall, select one character to make an Intellect defense roll (introduce as a GM intrusion). On a failed roll, the target disappears. Though it's not immediately clear what happened, the character is transdimensionally deflected into a parallel timeline. They reappear, as if they finishing walking through the wall, a full minute later, from the perspective of everyone who got through without incident. From the affected PC's perspective, they were passing through the wall one moment, and the next, they were encased (like an insect in amber) in red crystal that seemed to go on forever. They didn't need to breathe; they didn't feel warm

Red crystal (artifact)
Level: 2
Effect: adds 2 points to the wearer's Intellect Pool
Depletion: 1 in 1d6 (check whenever Intellect Pool is reduced to 0 points)

Abykos, page 224

Transdimensional ray projector, page 302

Doll: *level 1; hidden mechanism inside as level 4*

Mechanism: *level 5*

or cold; they just were. Time seemed to forget itself. Then, after an interminable period, the PC found themselves completing the transit, the memory of their time away already fading. The only souvenir of their unexpected trip is a red crystal embedded in their flesh, either in their forehead or in the palm of one hand. It turns out the red crystal is an artifact.

WARM ARCH

The thin span of a mighty arch is visible in the distance. Upon investigation, this roughly 700-foot (210 m) tall arch is discovered to stand above a series of broken prior-world ruins. The arch appears to be part of a larger structure that curves up out of the ground before plunging back. Various segments of silvery metal and crystalline blocks compose the structure. The material shudders ever so slightly if touched, and it seems as warm as human flesh.

At the base of the arch, a litter of four crude dolls lies: each is about half the size of a human. Made of stitched leather and fur, the dolls don't seem to depict humans, but possibly some sort of abhuman with no eyes but a rather large mouth and a long tongue. Though a bit weathered, the dolls have clearly only been here months at most. PCs who succeed on a difficulty 5 perception task find faint tracks that look almost like human feet, but with fewer toes and long, blade-like extensions in front. Weirdly, they seem to fade in and out in and around the arch.

Though not obvious, each doll also contains a mechanism in the stuffing. If a creature picks up the doll and walks "through" the arch, the mechanism acts like a key. The creature (and doll) are transported to an area far underneath the arch. A single doll will transport only a single character.

The chamber to which they are teleported is a wide, flat stone space, lit by a sourceless illumination and surrounded by darkness. Various mechanisms and devices are set into the stone, all dead and long-ago salvaged, except for one very large device set in the floor that buzzes and glows. Also, there are three ghostly humanoids—abykoses—standing about the chamber in what appears to be meditation, all facing the largest device. (Three additional dolls can also be found scattered about this main area.)

If PCs don't interfere or mess with the mechanisms here (or attack the abykoses), they can leave the area again simply by taking their dolls and inverting them 180 degrees from the position they were holding them when they entered. (This may take some experimentation.) If PCs attempt to salvage the main mechanism here (which resonates with transdimensional energy), the abykoses take issue with the intruders. If the characters persist and defeat the abykoses, a successful salvage attempt on the main mechanism yields about 30 shins and a transdimensional ray projector artifact. (However, this means PCs will have to find another way out of the underground location.)

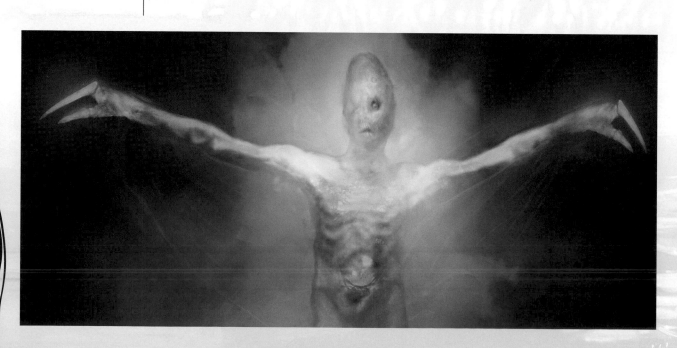

WEIRD FORMATION

Three reddish-orange glowing crystal columns protrude from the earth, each about 30 feet (9 m) high, arranged equidistantly around 20 feet (6 m) from each other. The triangular area within the columns is empty, though if anyone attempts to move into the area, they notice that the air feels somehow thicker.

The first creature to enter the area in any given week is phased into an alternate time state where they remain part of the normal time stream only every other round, though they may not initially realize it. From their point of view, creatures in their environment jerk suddenly ahead into new locations. From the perspective of creatures in the normal sequential time state, this character exists only every other round. Once it's clear what's going on, assign the affected player the responsibility of tracking which rounds their character exists and which rounds they do not. It's only important to track during combat, interaction, or anytime events play out round by round.

The unstable time-phasing effect gradually fades over the course of a week.

WHAT FOLLOWS

While the PCs investigate a ruin or other location where devices of the numenera can be found (as part of the main adventure or scenario that involves travel), they also discover a few broken crystal objects that almost resemble broken sculptures of vermin and, in one case, maybe an abhuman.

However, the damage is too extreme to make an exact identification. In what is presumably an unrelated incident, the PCs also discover that someone else has apparently salvaged a lot of the numenera at the location.

At some point, within a few days of the characters leaving the ruin and traveling somewhere else, they notice clues that something is following them. Initially, it manifests as a few incidents of visual distortion in a character's peripheral vision (the first of which you could introduce as a GM intrusion) that disappear when looked at head-on. What's actually happening is that a mirrored beast followed the PCs from their last stop and is sizing them up as potential targets rich in numenera it can confiscate.

What the PCs do next, their form of travel, and how long you want to stretch out this part of the encounter determine whether the mirrored beast attacks quickly, follows for a few more days, or gives up and moves off.

WINGED SWARM

Two to four swarms of winged creatures descend on traveling or camping characters. The creatures, called snipper moths, are individually 2-foot (60 cm) diameter, paper-thin discs of brown-black organic material that flutter through the air by folding their bodies rapidly as if they had wings. Scissor-like appendages are used to essentially attempt to snip sections of the characters' skin away and make off with the stolen integument for their own monstrous purposes.

Mirrored beast, page 66

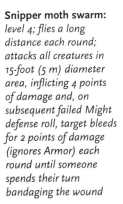

Snipper moth swarm: *level 4; flies a long distance each round; attacks all creatures in 15-foot (5 m) diameter area, inflicting 4 points of damage and, on subsequent failed Might defense roll, target bleeds for 2 points of damage (ignores Armor) each round until someone spends their turn bandaging the wound*

CHAPTER 9

TRAVEL-THEMED GM INTRUSIONS

*GM intrusions are designed to inject twists and challenges for players.
They are meant to be fun and interesting, not punitive.*

The material in this chapter can be used to generate creative—and unexpected—GM intrusions that can happen at any point while the PCs are traveling. Whether they are preparing for a journey, just leaving, on the road, camping rough, staying in a comfortable roadhouse, or just about to arrive at their destination, these intrusions can add a new wrinkle to the trip.

GM INTRUSIONS

Select a GM intrusion appropriate to the situation, roll a GM intrusion randomly, or use the list to inspire an intrusion of your own.

Many of the intrusions presented hereafter affect the group as a whole rather than just a single PC. These are tagged with (Group).

01–02 (Group): The landscape through which the PCs are traveling abruptly recomposes itself, folding up new surfaces and folding away old surfaces—thus revealing the area is artificial—with PCs potentially endangered in the process.

03–04 (Group): Iridescent sandstorm-like event lingers in the path where PCs intend to go; it isn't the iron wind, but it does consist of nanobots that tend to cling to and cover moving creatures and objects.

05–06 (Group): A wheel, leg, wing, or other mechanical failure means the PCs must take some time to repair their vehicle; alternatively, a mount becomes ill, injured, or exhausted, requiring it be healed or at least given a chance to rest up.

Grindral, page 61

07–08 (Group): Some unfortunate series of circumstances means the PCs have gotten themselves lost.

09–10: The character wakes after a ten hour rest to discover that the other characters have apparently left without them. In fact, the PC might have wandered off on their own because of some strange nearby influence. Or maybe the others really did leave the character behind because *they* were drawn off—in which case this is a group GM intrusion.

11–12 (Group): Some kind of massive flying craft of the prior worlds comes screaming out of the sky and impacts at a location somewhere within a few miles of the characters' route.

13–14 (Group): A mold, insect, or otherwise non-harmful nanite infestation renders the characters' food and/or water supply for the journey inedible and/or undrinkable.

15–16: The character trips or is thrown from their vehicle or mount by a jolt, startled mount, or similar accidental incident, risking a broken bone.

17–18 (Group): Weird music is emanating from nearby, though the musicians (if any) are not visible.

19–20: The character receives a message (telepathically, through a device they carry, or from a cypher used as a courier) from a friend or family member in a distant location—perhaps back where the character started their trip—indicating they require aid.

21–22 (Group): Thieving abhumans about the size of gophers called grindrals make off with camp gear and a few other needful things while PCs are distracted.

23–24 (Group): A mass of other travelers blocks up the route, causing delays and potentially leading to other issues related to irate travelers taking out their displeasure on others.

25–26: The character, new to their weird vehicle or the jouncing gait of their mount, becomes nauseated.

27–28: An NPC companion becomes irritated with the character for some reason (possibly not even for something that actually happened, but rather a miscommunication).

29–30 (Group): Ground fog is rolling in, except something is very strange about it; rain seems to be falling *up* into the sky from the low-level cloud bank.

31–32 (Group): Bandits lurk ahead; PCs may get a hint of them with a few rounds to prepare.

33–34: A personal nemesis of the character, who has been tracking them for some time, finally finds them during their trip.

35–36: Something about the new environment—maybe the dust, something the character ate, or a particular plant's pollen—causes a severe allergic reaction. The character must succeed on a Might defense roll or get a stinging rash across their skin that hinders physical tasks.

37–38: The character falls asleep while they should be navigating, piloting, or directing their mount.

39–40 (Group): The road ahead is washed out, covered in a landslide or cave-in, or otherwise inaccessible; the travelers will have to go around.

41–42: A nearby telepathic source has an adverse effect on the character, who must succeed on an Intellect defense roll or fall unconscious from the interference for about a minute.

43–44: On the road too long, the character must succeed on a Might defense roll or descend one step on the damage track from exhaustion.

45–46 (Group): A group of travelers who preceded the characters by days (or weeks or even years) is found dead along the way, all flash-mineralized by some not-immediately apparent source.

47–48 (Group): A three-sided, metallic monolith about 12 feet (4 m) tall stands in the middle of the road.

49–50 (Group): A small mercenary group, loud enough to disturb the characters' sleep, is encamped nearby.

51–52: A cypher used during the trip malfunctions, plunging the character into a subjective experience of time *years* long, but which doesn't have any external physical evidence to suggest anything is wrong. However, a round later (in external time), when the character's experience of time returns to normal, they must succeed on an Intellect defense roll or permanently lose 4 Intellect points. Even if they succeed, they take 4 points of Intellect damage (ignores Armor) from the grueling experience. On the other hand, the character learns something valuable during their mental sojourn.

53–54: In a roadhouse common room or another gathering of fellow travelers, the character is singled out by a rough-looking group of troublemakers looking for an easy mark.

55–56 (Group): A vertice in a nearby ruin activates and "prints" out a facsimile (level 4) of each character, but the copies are opposed to the goals the original characters share.

57–58: Some aspect of a nearby region or ruin is preventing the character's focus (or type) abilities from functioning, at least without great concentration.

59–60 (Group): Unexpected side trip! The road collapses, sending the characters into an underground region/ruin from which they need to escape. (Alternatively, their vehicle becomes disabled in an area that the travelers had assumed they'd simply speed through or fly over.)

61–62: Through misadventure, the character falls from the vehicle or mount, and no one else immediately notices.

63–64 (Group): A cypher meant to speed travel (or any cypher) malfunctions, sending PCs into a closed pocket universe that was set up as a trap in the region of normal space they were traveling through.

65–66: The character discovers that they've brought a stowaway along on their journey. The stowaway could be a complete innocent that somehow got "packed" away, a spy sent by an enemy, a fugitive, or someone the PCs have previously met in the campaign.

67–68: The character's accidental action (a loud sound, a flash of light, and so on) calls attention to the entire group's presence: on the road, at arrival, or during departure. This might not matter, but if the group was going for stealth, it likely matters a whole lot.

The subjective experience could simulate the character living the life of someone who lived long ago or in an alternate dimension, or perhaps exploring the memory of some strange alien creature.

Troublemaker, typical:
level 3, dirty tricks as level 4; Armor 1

Vertices are locations, installations, or devices with the ability to transcribe creatures and objects into, and out of, the datasphere.

111

Followers, page 17

Retenan, page 68

Broken hound, page 226

69–70 (Group): A toll is demanded. This might come from "official" sources, such as guards at a community gate, but it could just as easily come from a creature encountered on the road.

71–72 (Group): Somehow, the characters have arrived at their destination a month before they left.

73–74 (Group): Perhaps due to bad directions, the characters arrive at a location that's not the place they wished to travel to.

75–76: A piece of equipment dropped from the character, mount, or vehicle earlier, and the character who owns it only now realizes that it's missing, many hours of travel later.

77–78 (Group): A snowstorm sweeps across the region, forcing travelers to hole up for a time.

79–80: The character's mount dies (or the vehicle suffers a catastrophic failure). Some new form of transport must be acquired.

81–82: The character hears a desperate plea for aid from somewhere off the road they are traveling on.

83–84 (Group): A large pack of broken hounds attacks the travelers, from ambush if possible.

85–86: The character leaves camp to gather wood, wash up, or relieve themselves. Unfortunately, some landscape feature turns them around so they get lost and can't immediately find the camp again.

87–88: A companion, follower, or other NPC traveling with the character grows more and more irritable during the trip. The situation is everything they hate and, without some sort of serious intervention, the cordial relationship between the character and the NPC is finished.

89–90: An organization the character belongs to or a member of their family requests the character's immediate presence via a courier cypher (despite the fact the character is in the middle of a distant journey).

91–92: The character recovers a memory of something that happened earlier in the journey that no one else recalls (possibly an interaction with a memory-eating retenan).

93–94: The character develops a lump on their palm. Upon investigation (or if left undisturbed for a few days), the lump splits, revealing a mouth.

95–96: The character finds a strange device with several controls among their possessions. The character has no memory of having acquired it. The function of the device eludes immediate inquiry.

97–98: By pure coincidence (probably), the character recognizes a friend from long ago, who has also apparently traveled to the same location for their own reasons.

99–00 (Group): A friendly hunter offers to put the travelers up for the night in her family home. She offers them food, some hot spiced alcoholic drinks, and a warm place to sleep, and wants nothing in return.

PART 4:
ADVENTURE BECKONS

Chapter 10: The Roughest Day   114

Chapter 11: Travelers Never Did Lie   132

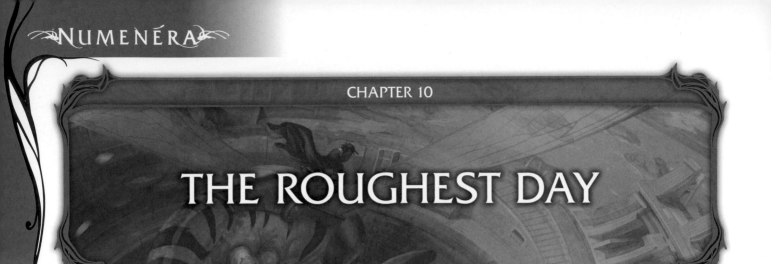

CHAPTER 10

THE ROUGHEST DAY

"The Roughest Day" is an adventure that can begin anywhere in the Ninth World. It's suitable for low- to middle-tier characters.

SYNOPSIS

The adventure has four sections, though the PCs may not get to all of them.

Trip Interrupted: Traveling PCs run across a community being attacked by dozens of abhumans. Against such a threat, characters might be tempted to just continue along their way. However, if they decide to lend their aid to the community, they could end up being drawn into the larger adventure.

God Is Gone: Characters learn the community worships a being called the Nightwalker. The Nightwalker kept the villagers safe from horrifying demons that would otherwise spill up out of the earth. Or it did until recently: after the Nightwalker failed to turn up for just a handful of days, the demons attacked. If something isn't done, the community's days are certainly numbered.

Blue Cloud, page 116

Into the Demon Caves: Characters who decide to help the community can easily find the caves that the "demons" inhabit. It's up to the PCs how they want to approach things. However they proceed, the characters don't find out what happened to the Nightwalker. However, they do find evidence that a mysterious someone from the village has been colluding with the abhumans.

Blinding Light of Betrayal: Several opportunities exist during the course of the adventure for the PCs to have slowly deduced that at least one NPC in the village probably knew more about the impending demon attack than anyone else, if you introduce any of the material under the "secondary plot thread" subheadings that follow. If you do and the PCs follow up on it and/or discover additional clues in the caves and wish to act upon them, they can probably piece together the evidence to learn the identity of the NPC responsible for causing the Nightwalker to disappear from the sky. (It's Ranger Kley!) Should they choose to engage in this lingering issue, the characters can find and release the Nightwalker, returning it to its nightly ramble across the sky.

TRIP INTERRUPTED

While the PCs are traveling, they pass through the village of Blue Cloud. Unfortunately for Blue Cloud, it is under attack by demons. Depending on your preferences, the PCs might reach the outskirts of town just as the sun goes down and the attack begins. Alternatively, the PCs could be lodging in the village overnight when the attack startles them from sleep. In the latter case, they have probably already met the important NPCs described hereafter under the main Blue Cloud entry.

When the PCs help a community deal with a vicious attack, they later discover that the attacks follow the loss of the community's protective totem. If PCs decide to offer additional aid, they find themselves exploring a margr lair, on the trail of an even deeper mystery.

For some reason, PCs need to find a dimensional doorway to accomplish their goals. This might be because of events that happened earlier in your campaign, or it could be a pretext if you are running this as a stand-alone adventure. In either case, PCs are following the tip from another explorer (or a datasphere glimmer) that such a door, known as the Grinder of Infinities, lies in the general area of Blue Cloud, within an ancient ruin. As PCs approach, they witness the demon attack on Blue Cloud.

If PCs help with the attack and ask about the door, none of the villagers know it by name. However, the NPC Ranger Diada indicates that the demons who attacked Blue Cloud live inside a ruin of the prior worlds. If there's an ancient transdimensional machine anywhere in the area, she supposes it's probably there.

DEMON ATTACK

About thirty demons come streaming down from a steep slope to the north of the village. Half the demons are mounted on lizard-like creatures that trail red-glowing tendrils behind them (aptly named firestriders). The demons themselves are humanoid creatures. No two look alike, but most have some aspect of a goat—a goat head, goat horns, goat legs, goat hooves, or some combination (or varying degrees thereof). They wear crude trophies on their belts and harnesses: severed heads on hooks, ears or fingers threaded on cords as necklaces, and so forth. PCs might (or might not) recognize these "demons" as margr: abhumans that live lives of terrible violence.

About half of the margr ride firestriders and half are on foot. Each attack made by a mounted margr is eased, thanks to coordination with the firestrider's action.

The margr intend to kill the villagers, loot their homes and fields, and burn the rest. They begin by attacking the villagers, regardless of age or infirmity. Some busy themselves setting fire to homes that contain cowering villagers. Most villagers know they're no match for the demons and try to run away rather than fight. However, a group of about fifteen villagers gather within the first few rounds of the attack and try to drive the margr off. The defense is led by three people wearing blue coats who the other villagers call rangers.

RESULT OF ATTACK WITHOUT CHARACTER ASSISTANCE

Without the PCs' aid, the villagers eventually manage to drive off the attackers, but at a terrible cost. The demons kill at least thirty villagers (out of about 230) and one ranger (Ranger Baraton) before the last few margr ride, or run, off.

RESULT OF ATTACK WITH CHARACTER ASSISTANCE

If the PCs jump into the fray, the margr that would otherwise have had free rein to sack Blue Cloud focus on the characters instead. Assuming characters fight on the villagers' side, the following challenges await them.

- **Fight the Margr:** If the PCs step in, the margr recognize them as a significant threat. The twelve firestrider-riding margr attack the PCs. Treat each group of three margr as a single level 4 mob, whose attacks are eased (by their firestriders), that inflict 5 points of damage. That means initially, PCs face four mobs of level 4 margr cavalry.

  Fighting the margr is the most important role PCs can take on. In fact, if the PCs can neutralize at least twelve margr (whether part of the attacking mobs or not), the villagers and rangers are up to the task of defeating and driving off the rest. In this scenario, apart from any losses the PCs themselves suffer, Blue Cloud suffers only three deaths. However, the town *also* still loses one of the three rangers (Ranger Baraton), leaving only the two rangers described hereafter.

- **Save Villagers From Fire:** Three villagers are trapped in a burning home. Extraction requires a difficulty 5 Might task to break down the door and a difficulty 4 Speed task to get each of the three villagers out.

- **Heal the Wounded:** Five villagers are severely wounded by the margr attack. Saving them requires a healing task or the use of a healing ability for each.

XP Award: The PCs each earn 1 XP if they tried to help defend against the attacking margr. In addition, they earn 1 XP if they saved at least one villager from the fire and another 1 XP if they healed at least two wounded villagers.

Ranger Diada, page 116

Firestrider, page 21

Ranger Baraton, page 117

Margr, page 240

Villager, typical: *level 2; tasks related to one aspect of village life as level 3*

Ranger: *level 4; navigation and perception tasks as level 6; Armor 1; ranged and melee attacks inflict 5 points of damage*

GOD IS GONE
Wherein PCs learn how the village of Blue Cloud was able to prosper for so long, and why its fortunes have changed recently.

The Nightwalker (also known as a mazocacoth), page 64

BLUE CLOUD   RANK 2 (6)

Blue Cloud is a village of about 230 people built in a valley pass in a mountainous area. The structures of the village—built of wood and picked stone—are backed up against the cliff-like face of one mountain. Cultivated areas, cleared by logging, fill most of the rest of the valley. The residents make their living by growing their own food, hunting, and fishing from a stream that runs through the area. A trade route runs through Blue Cloud, so the village sees outsiders pass through, once every few months or so, along what could only very generously be called a path.

For as long as the village has existed, residents have observed a nightly visitor of immense size picking its way across the mountaintops, passing like a faintly glowing blue cloud overhead before moving across the next ridge. In fact, the village was founded, and named for, the nightly visit. The entity itself was dubbed the Nightwalker. It came to be seen as a divine protector of Blue Cloud after it intervened over the course of years whenever raiders, demons, and other dangers threatened the community. Many villagers are in the habit of going outside at night to witness the path of the Nightwalker and give praise.

However, about a week ago, the faithful reported that the Nightwalker failed to appear. Moreover, the Nightwalker has failed to appear every night since. Unfortunately, this change is not merely cause for theological distress. The loss of Blue Cloud's guardian has most definitely been noted by the demons who live nearby. Every night, demons are sighted closer and closer to the edge of town.

Those sightings finally culminate in the attack described under Demon Attack.

KEY LOCATIONS IN BLUE CLOUD
Important structures in the village include the following.

Keeper Nalisor, page 117

Locked safe: level 6

Common House: The only two-story structure in Blue Cloud, containing a communal kitchen, dining area, and nine tiny rooms where single residents of the village stay until they can build or otherwise gain a house of their own. All those rooms—save one—are currently full, so there isn't room for all the PCs.

Baraton lived here (thus the now-empty room), and Diada currently does. Kley does not live here; he keeps a residence at the edge of town, though he often came to eat with the other rangers in the Common House when Baraton was still alive.

The house features a large room where food and spirits are served by Tyden, an elderly woman who lives in one of the small rooms.

Tyden: level 1; tasks related to running the Common House as level 4

Market: Various foods and basic needful things can be had from the gathering of carts and barrows that comes together every few days, out in front of the Common House.

Keeper's House: One of the largest homes in Blue Cloud, on account of it having an extra room for the current Keeper to use as they desire—Nalisor uses it for town business. The room also has a locked safe where he stores community treasures (such as a few cyphers and similar objects). He also has a weaver's loom where his husband turns out various articles of clothing, including the blue jackets used by the rangers. A couple of spare jackets are on hand already. (Though this fact probably doesn't come up right away, Kley recently lost his old coat and needed to requisition a new one.)

IMPORTANT NPCs IN BLUE CLOUD
The characters likely learn much of the context regarding the margr attack from Blue Cloud's residents.

Right after the demon attack, Ranger Diada approaches the PCs to question them on whether they had any part to play in inciting the demon attack.

Ranger Diada: Blue Cloud appoints three of its residents as "rangers" whose job it is to watch the approaches to the village, keep tabs on the demons that live in the caves to the north, and help defend the place should it come under attack. Ranger Diada is a proud, stubborn, in her mid-twenties with a prominent scar running down one side of her face and lots of tattoos. She wears the heavy blue leather coat of the rangers. To strangers, she is surly and suspicious.

If PCs talked to Diada before the attack (maybe she greeted them on the road), she directed them to Blue Cloud, assuming they seemed to be honest travelers rather than raiders in disguise.

If PCs talk to Diada after the attack (which she makes a point to do regardless of any prior meeting), she is suspicious of how their arrival coincided with the timing of the demon attack. If the PCs helped out, her initial instinct that the newcomers somehow caused the attack seems less tenable. But, because she's also stubborn, she'll bring it up in conversation more than once just to see how the characters react.

Secondary Plot Thread: If the characters mollify Diada and/or get on her good side, the ranger tells the PCs another of her suspicions: She thinks her fellow ranger, Baraton, knew something about the Nightwalker's disappearance. She remembers him saying over drinks in the Common House, "The sleeper has got to be connected with the missing Nightwalker. Perhaps I shouldn't have shared my discovery." This was after six nights without an appearance of the god and just one day before the demon attack.

When Diada pressed Baraton about what he was talking about, he waved her off, saying he would handle it. Now, of course, he is dead and beyond further questioning.

Keeper Nalisor: The currently acknowledged leader—called a "Keeper"—of Blue Cloud is a busy man in his late thirties who stands nearly 7 feet (2 m) tall. Nalisor and his husband Marl are well-liked by most of the villagers, especially since they give away any extra food they grow on their farm each year.

If the PCs talked to Nalisor before the attack, he was worried about the Nightwalker's absence but assumed it was just temporary. Either way, he believed the entity is just walking on a path longer than normal but will soon return to its old route. Such things have,

after all, happened before. Prior to the attack, he was more worried about the next harvest and had little time for other worries.

If PCs talk to Nalisor in the immediate aftermath of the attack, he thanks them for any aid they provided, then asks them to help out a bit further by putting out the last few fires, clearing out any remaining demons who might be nosing around the village, and otherwise cleaning up after the conflict. He also tells the PCs he wants to talk to them about something important the next day after everything settles down. If PCs agree, see Into the Demon Caves.

In the meantime, Nalisor makes arrangements for characters to stay at the house of a villager named Serri. The Keeper explains that Serri was the live-in caretaker for her ailing parents (both of whom recently died) and thus has a large house with extra rooms. If PCs demur, Nalisor isn't offended.

Ranger Baraton (Deceased): This slim man wore the heavy blue coat of the rangers. Before he died, he was a man of few words who lived in the Common House. He was killed while bravely defending Blue Cloud from the initial demon attack.

Secondary Plot Thread: If PCs become curious about Baraton, they may wish to investigate his room at the Common House. If they do check, they find it contains nothing out of the ordinary, other than a few extra weapons, old boots in need of repair, and a few small decorations. However (as Diada eventually volunteers), he didn't spend much time there. Until the demon attack, folks usually noticed him over at Serri's house, when he wasn't out on his rounds (as potentially volunteered by Tyden).

Serri. PCs are introduced to Serri if they accept the Keeper's offer of a place to stay. Alternately, the characters may find her while trying to piece together more information about Ranger Baraton.

Serri, happy to have guests, appears to be in her mid-twenties. She has large hands and a kind disposition. After the demon attack, worry haunts her eyes like everyone else's, plus a deeper sorrow. She and Baraton were courting, even before her parents died. He helped her run the small farm when he could, while she kept her parents comfortable.

Ranger Diada: *level 4; navigation and perception tasks as level 6; Armor 1; ranged and melee attacks inflict 5 points of damage*

Into the Demon Caves, page 119

Nalisor: *level 3; tasks related to leading a village as level 5*

Serri: *level 2; tasks related to running a small farm as level 4*

After Baraton's death, she keeps his blue jacket hung on a hook in the entry. She says it smells like him.

Secondary Plot Thread: If the PCs ask Serri if Baraton might have known something about the demon attack, about something called the "sleeper," or if he shared a discovery of some sort with her, she considers the question for a moment, then says that Baraton *did* mention finding something very odd up in the mountains about a month ago. When she asked him to explain, he only smiled and said he would, when the time was right.

If the characters ask Serri about the other rangers, she says that she dislikes Diada because Diada is always suspicious of everyone else. On the other hand, she likes Kley, who is always quick with a smile. (At least, for her.) In addition, she indicates that Baraton and Kley were friends, as they used to sometimes go on patrol together. Most everyone else in the village, she says, finds Kley's acerbic manner a little too harsh.

If the PCs think to check Baraton's jacket, they find a map in one pocket. The map is of the town and the nearby area, marking out a trail to something on the map called Grove of the Sleeper. Serri didn't know the map was there, but is happy to consign it to the PCs if they are interested in having it. A character who succeeds on a difficulty 2 navigation task while following the map's directions can find the grove after about a two-hour hike up into the mountains.

Ranger Kley: A tall man with grey in his hair and beard, Ranger Kley wears the blue coat of the rangers, one that looks brand new. (It is. He lost his old coat about a week ago.) Kley is quick with a smile and a compliment, at least when the characters are around. Unlike Diada, he is eager to get to know the PCs, whether he meets them before or after the initial attack. He attempts to insinuate himself into the characters' confidences by guiding them around the village, making introductions, and otherwise helping.

If PCs think back to the demon fight, they recall that he was part of the defense. He was lucky enough to have been on top of the Common House during the fight, allowing him to safely fire arrows from the rooftop without having to get into the thick of the fray as the other rangers and most of the other defending townsfolk did.

Ranger Kley has his own house at the edge of Blue Cloud. It's a small, two-room structure with a bedroom and a kitchen/general task room. The home also has a cellar and an unattached shed that contains a leather tarp, an empty wheelbarrow, and a variety of tools that are obviously old and in poor repair.

Secondary Plot Thread: PCs might notice that at least some of the other villagers seem surprised to see Kley being so helpful. If PCs ask Kley about it, he just laughs and says he's usually very grumpy, but the PCs' arrival has put him in a better mood. If PCs ask other villagers about Kley (except for Serri, who likes

Kley's Cellar, page 131

Grove of the Sleeper, page 119

Ranger Kley: *level 4; deception, navigation, and perception tasks as level 6; Armor 1; ranged and melee attacks inflict 5 points of damage; carries a ray emitter (paralysis) cypher*

Ray emitter (paralysis), page 285

him despite his ways), they are reluctant to say anything. However, if a character succeeds on a difficulty 4 persuasion task, Diada, Nalisor, or some other villager will shrug and say they don't know. It's just that Kley has always seemed bitter that Nalisor was elevated to the Keeper rather than himself. He's normally sarcastic and standoffish, but he's such a good ranger that the community remains grateful that Kley continues to wear the blue coat.

In truth, Ranger Kley has a secret. Several, actually.

The ranger always felt like an outsider in Blue Cloud, despite growing up in the village. He got all the hard breaks and none of the luck, he feels. Those feelings intensified as he grew older. The last straw was when Nalisor was chosen by acclamation to be Keeper, despite all Kley had done to advance the village. His feelings of ostracism metastasized into an angry grudge.

One day, about a month ago, Ranger Baraton showed Kley a discovery that he had made up in the mountains. Baraton called it the Grove of the Sleeper. Sure enough, by day, a strange creature only about 5 feet (1.5 m) in diameter with two insect-like legs and an almost-human face on its carapace was soundly sleeping in a cavity. Watching it as the day drew down into night, the entity went through a wondrous transformation, becoming the Nightwalker before their very eyes!

Baraton swore Kley to silence, but Kley couldn't stop thinking about it. He routinely made his way back to study the sleeper, wondering how to turn the discovery to his advantage. On one of those trips, a group of margr surprised and captured him. They took Kley down into their expansive lair, tortured him (in room 11), and prepared to kill him. Desperate to save himself, Kley promised the margr that if they let him go, he would see to it that the village of Blue Cloud would lose its protector. He wouldn't say how, but he promised that when it happened, the margr could raze the village to the ground, for all he cared. Somehow, he convinced them he was telling the truth, and that he would follow through on his promise.

Of course, Kley could have just run home, and that would have been the end of that. The thing was, he hated pretty much everyone in the village—including Baraton, who Kley despised for offering his friendship (which he thought was out of pity). So he was true to his

word to the margr: he procured a wheelbarrow from the market, went up to the Grove of the Sleeper, collected the unconscious being, and carted it down to his home on the edge of Blue Cloud without anyone the wiser. He installed it in his cellar, surrounded by three major glowglobes, whose constant light prevented it from becoming the Nightwalker again.

And so the situation remains—unless the PCs put together various clues scattered through the adventure and confront him; see the Blinding Light of Betrayal if so.

GROVE OF THE SLEEPER

The grove discovered by Baraton is about a two-hour hike for a typical human, in a generally northerly direction up into the mountains. The grove itself is a riot of color and pleasant odor, featuring all manner of flowers. An altar-like stone rise between two especially large and colorful trees is flat except for a 6-foot (2 m) diameter cavity worn into the surface, currently empty.

If PCs find the vacant grove and succeed on a difficulty 6 perception or reasoning task, they deduce that something *was* here for a very long time. Whatever it was occupied the stone rise for so long that a roughly human-sized concavity was eroded over hundreds (thousands?) of years. (As described earlier under Ranger Kley's description, it was the sleeper aspect of the Nightwalker, which Kley eventually stole.)

A successful difficulty 7 perception task reveals wheel tracks of the cart Kley used to haul away the sleeper and secretly hide it under his house. Unfortunately, the tracks peter out quickly. They could just as easily lead toward the margr caves or back toward the town, or even someplace else entirely.

GM Intrusion: A group of six margr ambush the PCs on their trip by starting a rockslide (level 5) to catch the PCs, then following it up with an attack. If PCs in the rockslide's path fail a Speed defense roll, they take 5 points of ambient damage and are pinned beneath boulders until they can escape.

INTO THE DEMON CAVES

If the PCs helped out with the margr attack, Keeper Nalisor invites them to a conference he holds in the Common House a few days after the conflict. In addition to the PCs and Nalisor, Ranger Diada and Ranger Kley are also present, assuming the PCs remain on good terms.

Blinding Light of Betrayal, page 130

The Nightwalker (also known as a mazocacoth), page 64

11. Scene of the Crime, page 126

Margr, page 240

Keeper Nalisor, page 117

Ranger Diada, page 116

Ranger Kley, page 118

Teleporter (bounder), page 287

Visage changer, page 288

Stunner, page 302

Nalisor lays out the situation: even though the demon attack was foiled, there are many, many more demons living in caves nearby. The only thing that kept them at bay was the Nightwalker's presence. As it seems more and more likely that the Nightwalker will never return, it is obvious that ignoring the demons will only lead to another attack.

In a nutshell, Nalisor asks if the PCs will help Blue Cloud once again. At the very least, he asks if they will scout out the demon caves and bring back a report on the true strength of the creatures that live there, and whether or not they are planning another attack.

Additionally, he floats the hypothesis that the demons may have actually had something to do with the disappearance of the Nightwalker. Their attack came suspiciously soon after the Nightwalker's final passage through the sky. Maybe the characters can find out if there's anything to that.

Finally, Nalisor argues, if the PCs put the demons into disarray, and eliminate a few in the bargain, perhaps it will keep them

occupied long enough for the Nightwalker to (hopefully) return on its own.

He offers the characters the small stockpile of salvage the village keeps for an emergency, stored in the locked safe in the Common House. It includes two cyphers—a teleporter (bounder) and a visage changer—and an artifact Nalisor calls a stunner.

If the PCs accept, Nalisor says that Ranger Diada will accompany them, both to help them achieve their aims and to guide them directly to the caves. Diada seems annoyed, but says she scouted a secret entrance to the place a few years ago, though she never previously had cause to use it. Ranger Kley, however, is ordered by the Keeper to remain in Blue Cloud and stay vigilant against any attack that slips through the PCs' advance.

PCs are asked to make any other arrangements they require quickly, as time is of the essence. If PCs do indeed delay for more than another three or four days, another margr attack similar in size to the initial attack materializes, everything else being equal.

DEMON CAVES

Scale: 50 Ft.

15 m

MARGR LAIR

The "demon caves" make up a large and rambling subterranean margr lair. Originally a structure of the prior worlds, most of the chambers inhabited by margr on a day-to-day basis have been covered in almost-sedimentary layers of filth and rotted carrion. A few pockets of weirdness still exist in the lair, which the margr have either adapted to their own needs or just learned to avoid.

Approximately 130 margr reside in this expansive lair, most with average margr stats, but a few with exceptional talents or who carry powerful devices of the prior worlds. If stirred up, they react as described under Lair Reaction to Intruders.

APPROACHING THE SECRET ENTRANCE

Diada indicates that to enter the caves secretly, the characters will have to do a bit of climbing. True to her promise, the ranger takes PCs on a roundabout path in a generally northerly direction that requires about three hours of hiking, rock scrambling, and one instance of actually ascending an 80-foot (24 m) sheer mountain face (a difficulty 4 climbing task) to succeed.

If successful, PCs come over a rise and see the following.

☞ READ ALOUD ☜

A colossal, beak-like metallic structure curves straight up out of the solid rock just past the last rise. Regular striations run across the structure's surface, glowing with a faint golden luster and forming strange designs. Near the base of the object, where it emerges from the stone, a narrow fissure opens into the interior.

Diada indicates that the fissure is the secret entrance. If PCs ask how she knows it opens onto the demon caves, she explains that she has observed the structure half a dozen times over the last several years, but never entered. On one occasion, she saw a demon emerge from it. (If PCs continue to quiz Diada on whether her observation is enough evidence to definitively say the fissure is a secret entrance, she angrily admits that it is not. *But*, she continues, they all had better hope it actually *is* a secret entrance, because trying to force their way in through the main entrance is probably suicide.)

If the PCs decide to try entering through the fissure, see 1. Secret Entrance hereafter.

APPROACHING THE MAIN ENTRANCE

If the characters fail to heed Diada's advice for whatever reason, or try the secret way and decide the challenges are too great, they can also enter the margr lair by way of the main entrance used by the margr themselves. Finding the main entrance is as simple as tracking the last set of attacking margr back the way they came (a routine task, thanks to the creatures not being concerned with stealth). This direct approach takes about an hour and a half's worth of hiking in a northerly direction from Blue Cloud into the mountains, until the main lair entrance comes into view.

☞ READ ALOUD ☜

A bonfire sends up a plume of oily smoke, most of which escapes into the sky. Some of the smoke, however, is caught by the overhanging lip of a massive cave mouth. Several demons mill about in a wide area just outside the cave mouth, apparently guarding the entrance when not squabbling among themselves. A huge, hornlike device is set just inside, probably to send a blast of noise into the cave if anyone sounds it.

If characters elect to approach this way, they'll have to escape the notice of the four margr watchers on duty, each of whom is armed with spears and bows. The watchers, despite their arguments, have one job: to alert the rest of the lair should any intruders approach. Their own lives are less important than that one task. Using the alarm horn is one way they alert the others of an attack; however, the sound of conflict is, in most cases, enough to alert the margr stationed across the bridge (in area 17 and beyond) that intruders are on the doorstep.

1. SECRET ENTRANCE

The fissure in the strange structure on the mountainside opens into a large space.

☞ READ ALOUD ☜

Drit and drifting snow have blown in through the fissure to partly cover this hollow, roughly cone-shaped chamber with a high, narrow ceiling. A slanted, bluish metal object emerges from the detritus, creating a sloping metallic surface of indeterminate size.

16. Main Entrance, page 127

Margr, page 240

Lair Reaction to Intruders, page 128

Margr watcher: *level 3, perception as level 5; Armor 1; ranged and melee attacks inflict 4 points of damage*

Alarm horn: *level 3*

Diada, page 116

Even cursory observation reveals that something disturbed the drifted snow and drit within the last few months along the base of the blue metallic structure, revealing a door-like hatch (currently closed) and a control surface. A successful difficulty 4 understanding numenera task allows the PCs to use the controls to cause the hatch to iris open. Revealed is a narrow metallic corridor contoured with regular striations, glowing with a faint golden luster, that form strange designs. The corridor corkscrews downward, leading to area 2.

2. SPRAY SEALANT

A narrow metallic corridor contoured with glowing striations connects area 1 to 2, corkscrewing downward to a depth of about 50 feet (15 m), and opening into a chamber.

⮞ READ ALOUD ⮜

This rectangular chamber, much longer than it is wide, is mostly clear of drifting drit. Glowing striations from the entrance corridor continue into the chamber, providing dim light. A machine hanging from the ceiling fills about a quarter of the available space, emitting an audible hum. A bulbous automaton lies inert on the floor almost directly beneath the mounted humming machine. An opening in the far side of the room provides a single obvious exit.

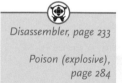

Disassembler, page 233

Poison (explosive), page 284

The inert automaton on the floor is a disassembler. PCs may notice the almost-transparent layer of synth-like substance that encases the disassembler from a distance, with a successful difficulty 3 perception task (or if they directly examine the automaton). Investigating PCs also find a concentrated mass of crushed bones, crude clothing, and a broken spear in a corner (see pellets, described hereafter).

Mounted Machine: If any character enters the chamber, the mounted machine deploys a spray arm, from which issues an immediate-range spray of nanoparticles that covers them in a transparent coating, on a failed Speed defense roll. Unless destroyed, the mounted machine sprays down anything moving within immediate range of it, but no more often than once every couple of minutes.

Coated PCs initially find that they can move and breathe normally and see without

Mounted machine: *level 5*

Large machine: *level 6*

Gnath, page 59

distortion through the selectively permeable substance. The coating grants +1 Armor. However, each minute thereafter, a coated character must succeed on a Might defense roll or suffer 5 points of ambient damage, as the material begins to have a deleterious, acidic effect on their skin. This continues until a PC can remove the coating, which requires that they succeed on a Might-based task to peel off the substance. A success on this task inflicts 5 points of ambient damage, as it takes some of the character's already bonded skin with it.

On a successful salvaging task, which also disables it, the PCs can recover a poison (explosive) cypher from the machine.

Coated Disassembler: If PCs peel the coating off the disassembler (which inflicts 5 points of damage to it), it whirrs back to "life." At first, it follows the PCs around in a somewhat friendly manner. That said, anytime PCs try to salvage the numenera going forward, the disassembler steps in and tries to eat whatever the characters find, be it cypher, artifact, or iotum. It remains friendly as long as the characters offer it at least one of whatever they find. Even so, over time, it begins to act more and more erratically. Eventually, the PCs need to figure out how to lose the automaton, or at some point, it attacks them for the numenera they're carrying.

3. SORTING APPARATUS

The exit in room 2 opens directly onto this chamber.

⮞ READ ALOUD ⮜

This large, square chamber, lit by dimly glowing wall striations, is crowded with a large metallic and crystalline machine. Each wall has a large, open exit, partly filled by pipe-like extensions reaching from the main machine. The sound of something rattling down one pipe then up another is audible every few seconds. Here and there, littered about the room like dropped toys, are concentrated bundles of cloth and bone. Goat-like skulls peer out of one of the bone masses.

The large machine filling most of the chamber is still somewhat active; however, before characters can interact with the machine, they must deal with the vagabond gnath that has temporarily claimed this chamber as its lair. PCs who succeed on a difficulty 5 perception task see it before it acts: a creature with huge eyes hangs in a sort of gooey half-cocoon on the ceiling, staring out at the chamber as if guarding it.

Large Machine: If the characters succeed on an understanding numenera task related to the large machine, they discover it is some type of sorting and treatment mechanism, apparently devoted to moving objects through the 2-foot (60 cm) diameter pipe bundles that extend into three satellite chambers (rooms 4, 5, and 6). For the brief period that the moving object resides within the bowels of the machine, it is treated with some kind of acidic wash, then sent along a pipe into one of the satellite chambers.

On a successful salvaging task, which also disables the machine, the PCs can recover an acidic resonator cypher from it. Doing this results in a potentially explosive buildup in chamber 5, as described there.

Pellets: If the PCs investigate any of the concentrated bundles of cloth, they discover they are apparently the remains of demons (margr) completely denuded of flesh; only bone, horn, hair, and clothing remain, concentrated down as if in some kind of organic compactor. (In fact, as regurgitated by the gnath.)

4. APT CLAY SATELLITE CHAMBER

A 12-foot (4 m) diameter circular corridor, half-filled with several 2-foot (60 cm) diameter pipes, extends about 20 feet before opening into this area.

⤜ READ ALOUD ⤛

This large, square chamber is lit by dimly glowing wall striations. The pipes extending from the machine in the previous chamber branch dozens of times before finally plugging into a grid-like shelving unit that completely fills the far wall. Each of the cubbies formed by the grid is sealed with transparent synth. Almost every one of these cubbies contains a few scraps of broken, degraded synth, but a few contain lumps of blue-grey material with a slight metallic luster.

About once each minute, the pipe bifurcation plugged into a particular shelving unit sucks the debris (or blue-grey lump) out

Acidic resonator, page 181

Apt clay, page 111

of one of the sealed (behind the transparent synth) shelving unit cubbies and transfers it to the machine in room 3, where it undergoes some kind of treatment. Then, a few rounds later, it is returned here. The debris gets slightly more degraded each time. The same thing occasionally happens to the lumps of blue-grey material—which PCs who succeed on a difficulty 3 understanding numenera task can identify as a useful crafting component called apt clay.

Characters who break into any particular cubby of the shelving unit can extract the scrap synth, or (in five individual cases), a unit of apt clay. However, when they break into a cubby, a repair automaton might spawn from the bottom of the overall shelving unit. The first thing it tries to do is eradicate the PCs, then repair the shelving unit.

5. QUANTUM SATELLITE CHAMBER

The corridor leading to this chamber is essentially a duplicate of the one between rooms 3 and 4. Likewise, the chamber beyond is nearly a duplicate, including most of the shelving cubbies containing debris and scrap. However, a total of three individual cubbies contain something different: an opaque synth box. PCs who break into one of the three cubbies and examine the synth box within discover that it contains glittering points of light. A successful difficulty 5 understanding

Shelving unit: *level 3*

Repair automaton: *level 4; Armor 3; immediate-range area electric attack inflicts 5 points of damage*

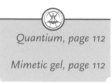

Quantium, page 112

Mimetic gel, page 112

Detonation, page 277

numenera task reveals the object to be 1 unit of quantium.

However, unlike regular quantium, the only thing keeping this material stable is the occasional treatment from the machine in room 3. If any unit of quantium from this room goes without treatment for a day, it essentially becomes a very unstable level 5 detonation, likely to explode at a mere jostle. A PC may realize this if, when they attempted their initial understanding numenera task to identify the material, they achieved a difficulty 7 result. Otherwise, it could come as a surprise. (The unstable quantium is not a cypher; thus, it doesn't count against the character's cypher limit.)

6. MIMETIC GEL SATELLITE CHAMBER

The corridor leading to this chamber is mostly a duplicate of the one between rooms 3 and 4. *Except* for one thing, which is probably only obvious to PCs once they enter: one more pipe traverses this corridor than in the other two satellite chamber corridors. This extra pipe is about 3 feet (1 m) in diameter.

Likewise, the chamber beyond is nearly a duplicate, including that most of the shelving cubbies contain debris and scrap. However, four of the cubbies contain something different: silvery canisters. PCs who break into a cubby with a canister and examine it discover that it contains a colorless, translucent goo. A successful difficulty 5 understanding numenera task reveals the object to be 1 unit of mimetic gel.

One additional feature stands out:

⟿ READ ALOUD ⟾

The largest pipe extending into this chamber doesn't join the others in branching to plug into the shelving unit cubbies. Instead, it curves down into the floor, apparently connected to something beneath. A wide split in the metallic surface leaves the pipe's hollow interior exposed and accessible.

Split Pipe: The fissure in the pipe is large enough to allow a human-sized creature access, though it's a bit of a squeeze. Examination shows fur caught along the edges of the fissure, where margr have probably crawled up and out, from a location some distance below.

PCs should be able to fit into the pipe if they wish to track back along the route taken by

the margr, though it's lightless and a bit tight. Luckily, it's not a sheer drop, but rather a slope that varies between 30 and 50 degrees. PCs who want to let gravity do its thing can treat the pipe as a slide that delivers them down about a 300-foot (90 m) chute that ultimately flings them into room 7. Those that do so, and succeed on a difficulty 3 Speed defense roll, can land without taking 3 points of damage from the velocity they built up.

PCs that enter the pipe who want to, instead, trace it back down the corridor into room 3 can do so; however, the pipe contains a filter-like obstruction that prevents them from continuing forward unless they clear it. If they do, they might get caught up in the treatment, which is a combination of radiation and acid washing (level 5) that triggers every few rounds while the machine remains active.

7. ENGINE OF THE ENTOMBER

A tube-like chute delivers explorers from room 6 down to this lower level. The only other exit is blocked by a sturdy wooden barrier.

⟿ READ ALOUD ⟾

Faintly glowing striations along the walls of this large, roughly hive-shaped hollow illuminate a central automaton-like figure standing well over twenty feet tall. The floor is covered in a rubble of metallic debris. Sculpture-like reliefs, resembling the demons that attacked Blue Cloud, are scattered here and there across the walls in random locations.

Entomber: What seems, at first glance, to be relief sculptures set randomly in the walls are actually margr who have been covered in a preservative metallic sheath and half-submerged into the wall by the central automaton-like figure—which the margr call the Entomber. In the normal course of things in the inhabited portions of the abhuman lair, margr who lose a fight to another of higher status are expelled into this chamber, where the Entomber "preserves" most of them. A few, however, survive long enough to climb up the chute (which the PCs may have just slid down; climbing back up is a difficulty 2 task) and access the ruin's higher level.

A couple of rounds after the Entomber detects movement in the chamber, it activates, attempting to catch and entomb intruders as it has done to so many margr.

Entomber: level 6, Speed defense as level 2 due to immobility; Armor 2; attack inflicts 6 points of damage and, on a subsequent failed Might defense roll, the target is coated in a hardening metallic substance that hinders all physical tasks until they use their turn to scrape it off; targets coated three times without removing the substance are entombed in what is essentially a level 6 airless casket

From Here On: The remaining numbered chambers in the complex are part of the same ruin described in entries 1–7. However, centuries of margr habitation have broken most of the remaining numenera, or hidden it beneath a layer of filth.

Sound of the Lair: At this juncture, characters can detect the noises of many bestial voices, some literally screaming in rage, others laughing or cruelly japing. The largest concentration of sounds comes from directly to the south (room 18).

Interacting With Margr Inside the Lair: If PCs go south and "poke the ravage bear," as it were, by revealing themselves as intruders, the Lair Reaction to Intruders likely kicks off against them, as if they had attacked from the main entrance. Of course, this time, the PCs are inside the lair.

On the other hand, margr don't expect other humanoids they meet *inside* their lair to be anything other than margr if an alarm hasn't sounded. If the PCs gather enough bones, skulls, and typical margr clothing, then hide their most-human features, any initial disguise and/or deception tasks the PCs attempt are eased by two steps.

9. FOOD PREP

⮞ READ ALOUD ⮜

The horrific stench emanating from this room is revealed to be the carcasses of all sorts of dead game. Some of the carcasses are hung from the ceiling and show signs of primitive butchering techniques; others are just lying on the floor. The corners of the room are thick with rotting skins and denuded bones.

Two margr share food preparation duties at a time. They could be sleeping between shifts, awake and arguing, shirking their duties, or—about 20% of the time—actually doing what they're supposed to be doing: rendering more meat for the other margr. They attack the PCs if they recognize they're humans, though that likely takes at least a few rounds. The sounds of a fight here don't necessarily alert the lair; margr are always fighting somewhere.

Lair Reaction to Intruders, page 128

Sturdy wooden barrier: level 4

Attacking Objects, page 116

GM intrusion: *A couple of margr appear unexpectedly with freshly killed game.*

Sturdy Wooden Barrier: A sturdy wooden barrier, crudely constructed but reinforced with synth scrap, closes off the only other exit from the chamber (a corridor that connects to room 8). If PCs resort to smashing the barrier by attacking it, any resulting sounds are mostly ignored by margr in the greater lair; they're used to prisoners who have been tossed in here frantically attempting to smash their way out.

8. CROSSROAD CORRIDOR

⮞ READ ALOUD ⮜

The corridor joins a four-way intersection. The sound of many creatures emanates from a couple of the corridors.

10. WATER WALL

☙ READ ALOUD ❧

The far wall of this chamber is apparently composed of a vertical wall of water. A 1-foot (30 cm) wide strip of metal frames the water wall. Devices set in the frame buzz and blink tiny white points of light.

This wall of standing water, created and maintained by the frame-like water forge, is one of the main sources of the lair's water. However, one margr champion likes spending several hours each day bathing in it, despite the fact it befouls the liquid for everyone else. If PCs arrive without alerting the lair, they probably find the champion here.

The water forge creates up to several hundred gallons of drinkable water each day, if necessary, and "stores" it as a cohesive wall, though it's easy enough to dip water from it—or jump right in and swim around. If PCs salvage the forge, it is destroyed. Water floods through this section of the lair, and the odds of being discovered dramatically rise as a few dozen margr arrive to investigate. However, a successful salvage task nets the characters 15 shins, a lightning wall projector cypher, and a living solvent cypher.

11. SCENE OF THE CRIME

An actual door (though crude) closes off this chamber. A bolt allows it to be secured from the outside, though it is currently open.

☙ READ ALOUD ❧

Barbed straps, iron rods and pincers, and a variety of cutting implements are scattered around an overturned stool covered in rawhide. Loose bindings lie on the floor near a cold firepit. A pile of discarded clothes lies in a corner.

When Ranger Kley was caught, this is where he was interrogated by the margr. This is where he ultimately promised the margr he would pave the way for their attack on Blue Cloud. And this is where they let Kley go. Mostly, they believed he was lying (after all, it's what they would do). Still, after listening to Kley's arguments long enough, they had decided the chance of being able to slaughter an entire village of humans was better than the certainty of slaughtering just one.

If PCs interrogate the margr in room 12, they may be able to learn most of this, other than the human's name (and his status as a ranger); to them, he was just a very annoying human who they still can't quite believe followed through on his promise.

Clothes in the Corner: If PCs investigate the chamber, among the discarded clothing obviously contributed by several different people is an intact blue coat. A blue coat, the characters notice, that looks remarkably like the ones the rangers in Blue Cloud wear.

12. TORTURERS' DEN

Four high-status margr champions live here in squalor. Usually, at least two are present, sleeping, eating, consorting, or fighting. Otherwise, the chamber is covered in filth, half-eaten meals, cast-off trash, and, if PCs have the time to search, about 40 loose shins.

Characters who successfully negotiate rather than fight the margr here may learn something of what happened with the human who wore a blue coat in room 11.

13. REMNANT DEVICE

☙ READ ALOUD ❧

A dark, metallic pedestal, festooned with ebony wires, is crowned by a faintly glowing greenish gem. An iridescent, translucent tendril of energy rises from the gem, slowly undulating in the air.

The margr avoid the still-functioning device—the phase changer—at the end of this hallway, believing its touch leads to a lethal outcome. If a creature approaches it, the tendril snakes out to touch them (Speed defense roll to avoid), although the device only functions once every few minutes. If successfully touched, the creature and its possessions go out of phase for a couple of minutes. (An out-of-phase creature can't interact physically with the environment, nor can any physical effect of the environment affect the creature.) If a salvaging task is attempted and failed, the device explodes like a detonation, but one PC goes out of phase for 28 hours if they fail a Speed defense roll. The explosion might still happen if the salvaging task succeeds, but before it does, the characters gain 6 shins and a phase changer cypher.

Water forge: *level 6*

Margr champion: *level 3; health 16; Armor 2; attacks inflict 5 points of damage; may carry a level 5 detonation or similar offensive cypher*

The blue coat in room 11 belonged to Ranger Kley. He had to acquire a new coat from the Keeper when he returned to town.

Lightning wall projector, page 282

Living solvent, page 282

Phase changer, page 284

Phase changer (device): *level 5*

Ranger Kley, page 118

GM intrusion: *On a failed difficulty 5 Intellect defense roll, the out-of-phase character begins to lose their grip on their phase state, potentially causing them to fall through solid material, inside of which the risk of becoming disoriented and lost is real.*

14. COURT OF THE DEMONS

Raucous laughter, mixed with yells, crude melodies, and the sound of fighting, echoes down the hallway leading to this chamber.

❧ READ ALOUD ❧

An unruly group of abhumans mill about this wide chamber, some ululating in what could perhaps be called singing, others clapping and laughing along, and a few wrestling. All the activity seems to be for the amusement of the especially large horned demon who sits at the far end of the hall on a throne-like heap of refuse and death.

The room contains four regular (level 2) margr, six margr champions, and, sitting in the "throne" at the far end of the chamber, the margr monarch (who calls itself Gorhash). Unless characters go out of their way to be noticed by the chamber's occupants, PCs can probably glance in, then retreat without having to engage.

Otherwise, if the PCs are revealed as humans, it's almost certainly a fight: the margr monarch must show strength in order to keep its place among its fellows. A fight also quickly alerts the rest of the lair that intruders are present, triggering the Lair Reaction to Intruders.

Especially ambitious characters might decide to kill the monarch and claim its perquisites. As noted in *Numenera Discovery*, killing their leader sends the margr into a frenzy of confusion and fear. In this situation, PCs could attempt to intimidate the remaining margr (difficulty 5) into doing as they command. A very powerful and forceful character could become the new leader, but such a position would be challenged so frequently that it would make the margr poor followers overall. However, in this role, characters could determine once and for all that the margr had nothing to do with the Nightwalker's disappearance; rather, some human did.

15. MONARCH'S RICHES

A crude barrier, which can be slid aside with a successful difficulty 4 Might-based roll, blocks access to this chamber.

❧ READ ALOUD ❧

Loose grain piled in untidy heaps, smoked meats hanging from the ceiling, spirits in casks and bottles, all manner of clothing scattered randomly about, and other valuables litter this room. A few metallic devices, obviously of the prior world, glint among the more commonplace riches.

If the characters have the time to loot this room, they could come away with lots of basic equipment and clothing stolen from humans over the decades, as well as food, water, and spirits (not all of which is stale, spoiled, or putrid).

In addition, characters can discover about 200 shins, several cyphers (sonic hole, shocker, and a remote viewer), and a cypher bag artifact.

16. MAIN ENTRANCE

This cavern-like space is found just past the area described under Approaching the Main Entrance.

❧ READ ALOUD ❧

The cave mouth opens into a massive, open hollow in the mountain's interior. The hollow's depths, lost in darkness hundreds of feet below, are difficult to gauge. A frayed-looking rope bridge spans the hollow, connected on this side by metallic spikes. Across the bridge, steady illumination, as if from a glowglobe, reveals another narrow ledge.

Normally, four margr watchers stand guard on the inner side of the bridge, looking toward the cave mouth. If PCs make it past the margr guard on the approach outside via combat, the guards here are probably aware of it. Or, if PCs slip by the watchers outside the main entrance, the margr inside may become aware of the intrusion when they see something causing the bridge to sway and kick in the characteristic way it does when someone is crossing it.

If so, one of the margr watchers runs back deeper into the lair to carry a warning.

Two of the three remaining margr shoot arrows from their shortbows at anyone attempting to cross the rope bridge. The final remaining margr has a level 8 ray emitter, which it uses when a PC gets within long range; in the meantime, it also fires arrows.

The roughly 100-foot (60 m) long bridge is treacherous, and PCs must succeed on a difficulty 4 Speed-based roll each round they move their full speed across it. The fastest PCs crossing the bridge can go without requiring a roll is about 25 feet (7.5 m) per round. This

Sonic hole, page 287

Shocker, page 286

Remote viewer, page 286

Cypher bag, page 294

Margr, page 240

Approaching the Main Entrance, page 121

Margr champion: *level 3; health 16; Armor 2; attacks inflict 5 points of damage; may carry a level 5 detonation or similar offensive cypher*

Margr monarch: *level 5; health 26; Armor 4 (from artifact); two attacks inflict 5 points of damage each; wears a level 5 artifact belt providing force Armor for 1 hour (Depletion: 1 in 1d6)*

Lair Reaction to Intruders, page 128

Margr watcher: *level 3, perception as level 5; Armor 1; attacks inflict 4 points of damage*

Rope bridge: *level 1*

GM Intrusion (Group): *One of the ropes on the bridge snaps. Everyone on it must succeed on a Speed defense roll or fall into the 230-foot (70 m) deep hollow.*

Ray emitter, page 285

means that, if moving at a safe speed, most PCs require about four rounds to cross, or, if going full speed, two rounds (assuming no misadventure).

If it seems like the PCs might successfully get across, one of the margr watchers uses its action to cut the bridge, attempting to send PCs swinging down into the 230-foot (70 m) abyss.

17. MAIN APPROACH

This wide corridor is covered in heads, mounted on either side wall on spikes, or hung from the ceiling. Most of the heads are too rotted to determine what they once were, but some are obviously human. Others are bestial, including a few that look demonic. A handful of automaton heads are also mounted here.

If not alerted, three groups of lazing margr (about twelve in total) stand idly around the main approach or recline on refuse heaps. They seem to be boasting about how cruelly each vanquished a particular human or other prey, thus securing it as a trophy on the wall (or on their person).

Automaton Heads: If PCs somehow have the opportunity to examine the automaton heads (six total) and succeed on a difficulty 5 salvage task, they can recover a field destabilizer from one particularly bulky head.

18. MARGR COMMON AREA

The bulk of the margr in the lair congregate here, assuming they are not roused.

Well over a hundred demons gather in this vast chamber. Some slumber and snore in unruly piles. Many tear into recently caught game or sip from crude cups of a faintly green-glowing thick fluid. Several cavort to the sound of atonal music around a towering machine at the center: the source of the emanation. Others on the edges wrestle each other, sometimes to the death. The smell of rot, filth, and unwashed bodies here is vicious, coating the tongue with its vile intensity.

Most of the over one hundred regular margr who live in this lair spend a lot of time here, unless they are out foraging, either through the main entrance or the chancy "hunting grounds" that can be reached through the strange device in room 20.

About a dozen margr watchers and four margr champions are also present.

Blend In or Combat? Assuming an alarm has not already gone out, if PCs take a modicum of preparation to disguise themselves, they might be able to blend in. Of course, even if PCs succeed in blending in, that doesn't mean they won't be handed a mug of the green drink (highly alcoholic; see area 19) and expected to down it, be grabbed and expected to dance around the "music machine" with a gyrating margr partner, or just randomly assaulted

Margr, page 240

Margr watcher:
level 3, perception as level 5; Armor 1; attacks inflict 4 points of damage

Margr champion:
level 3; health 16; Armor 2; attacks inflict 5 points of damage; may carry a level 5 detonation or similar offensive cypher

Field destabilizer, page 189

LAIR REACTION TO INTRUDERS

The margr aren't big planners, but emergent reactions to an intrusion detected at the main entrance go something like the following. (Generally speaking, as time goes on, more and more margr show up to aid in the lair's defense until the threat is chased off or neutralized, or the margr population is almost entirely expended.)

- **Round 1:** The margr watchers in room 16 become aware of intruders; one runs back into the deeper lair to carry a warning, while the other three hold off the intruders attempting to cross the bridge.
- **Every two to three rounds thereafter:** a group of four to eight regular (level 2) margr arrive from deeper within the lair to aid in its defense.
- **Every four rounds after the initial reaction:** Interspersed with the arrival of regular margr, a margr champion arrives to join in the defense.
- This process of more and more margr coming to help fight off the invasion continues until the intruders are vanquished or frightened away, or until almost all of the 130 margr living in the lair are accounted for. A handful attempt to flee or hide if the intruders prove to be so powerful they accomplish the latter.

for a wrestling match. Treat any of these occurrences as GM intrusions that could trip up the characters' disguised passage through the area, unless they play along.

Music Machine: Mostly defunct, this towering music machine can now only blink and produce atonal sounds, which the margr seem to like. If salvaged, all nearby margr attack the perpetrator because this disables the machine's sound-making capability. However, if successful, characters gain 30 shins, a couple of cyphers (an object replicator and a farspeaker), and 2 units of thaum dust.

19. GREEN DRINK

⮞ READ ALOUD ⮜

Amid the wreckage of degraded machines, a single panel on the far wall remains lit up. The panel features a control surface and what looks like a broken pipe. Dozens of crude containers crowd the floor of this chamber, each containing a smelly green sludge.

Unless the lair is alerted, there is usually a handful of margr about, filling emptied containers with green sludge from the cleaning fluid drain, transporting full containers toward room 18, or bringing empty ones back to be refilled. The green sludge is essentially hard alcohol, though mixed with disgusting contaminants likely to bring gastrointestinal distress to any PC brave enough to sample the margr "liquor."

Characters can try to salvage the lighted panel for numenera, but it's dangerous. On a failed attempt, they break the valve, and green sludge begins to flood the area. (On the other hand, maybe that's fine; PCs might decide to try to flood the margr out.) On a successful salvage attempt, the PCs liberate 5 shins and a poison (mind disrupting) cypher.

Cleaning fluid drain panel: *level 4*

Music machine: *level 4*

Object replicator, page 184

Farspeaker, page 182

Thaum dust, page 112

Poison (mind disrupting), page 285

B.D.

shifts between dimensions, constant hunting is possible without depleting the wildlife population. (Not that the margr care; that's just how it worked out.)

Entering the cube without knowing exactly how to do so safely causes the components within to spin up to lethal velocity. The intruder must succeed on a difficulty 4 Speed defense roll or suffer 5 points of damage. They continue spinning until someone succeeds on a difficulty 4 understanding numenera task to take temporary control of the device and cause it to stop. Once "safe," PCs skilled in the numenera can discover its full capabilities. They also learn that the Grinder is a shifting portal, leading to an infinity of alternate dimensions. (This understanding typically takes days of studying and experimenting, then finally succeeding on a difficulty 7 understanding numenera task to activate the portal.) If the attempt to understand it fails, the device loses its "safe" status, spinning up to lethal velocity once more.

If the PCs succeed, those within the cube see each interior surface shimmer, revealing strange scenes (all except the side through which PCs entered, which remains unchanged). The scenes can show nearly anything: incredible cities, floating mountains, never-before-seen creatures, empty pink space, volcanoes erupting with sound, tornadoes, peaceful forests of strange trees, red waves crashing on a beach of purple sand, and so on. Moving through any of these faces transports the character to a different dimension: the same as the scene shown. The GM determines the potential destinations.

A knowledgeable PC who succeeds on a difficulty 7 Intellect task with the device can select a destination, but only if they have specific knowledge of the dimension they wish to reach.

XP Award: The PCs each earn 1 XP if they scouted at least a few rooms of the margr lair. In addition, they earn 1 XP if they disrupted the margr in some fashion, and another 1 XP if they found the blue coat.

BLINDING LIGHT OF BETRAYAL

If the PCs return after having been away for a few days (possibly because they were scouting the margr lair), they find the village of Blue Cloud conducting a funeral.

If you used the alternate adventure hook (page 115), the Grinder of Infinities might be what the characters are looking for.

20. HUNTING PORTAL

Illumination, flickering like daylight through curtains, is visible from this room, even down the approaching corridor.

> **READ ALOUD**
>
> A cube twice as large as a human floats unmoored above the floor at the center of this chamber. Each of the cube's six sides opens into a space that isn't shared with any of the other sides—it's as if each side opens into a completely different location. Struts, components, and other devices of the ancients fill the cube's center. Several fresh carcasses of strange, furred animals lie along the edges of the room.

Margr cubekeeper: level 3, tasks related to the Grinder of Infinities as level 7

Usually, a single margr cubekeeper is found here. They are responsible for operating the cube in a way that doesn't kill every margr hunting party that ventures through it, or strand them in some distant dimension. The cubekeeper could ease the characters' attempts to understand the cube (or simply operate it for them) if they provide sufficient incentive—and if they can bring themselves to trust a margr.

Grinder of Infinities: level 7

Grinder of Infinites: The 9-foot (3 m) cube floating 3 feet (1 m) above the floor (also known as the Grinder of Infinities in some texts) provides, through hunting, most of the food (and much of the water) needed to keep the colony fed. Because the cube is an interdimensional door that constantly

GM intrusion: A hunting party of twelve margr led by one margr champion returns through the cube.

BARATON'S FUNERAL

A procession winds its way between buildings as the remains of Ranger Baraton are shepherded through town on a litter, over which his blue coat (donated by Serri) is hung. (If the PCs haven't yet put any clues together, maybe one character notices the map to the Grove of the Sleeper fall out, which could kick things off.)

Baraton is interred at the edge of the village, near several other markers made of artistically carved synth. Several people say a few words over his grave: about his bravery, his sacrifice, how he will be missed, and so on. Diada and Kley are both on hand to say a few words, too. Afterwards, Kley approaches the PCs, appearing happy to see them. If PCs voice no suspicions to him, he suggests they all go to the Common House and have a drink in Baraton's name.

CONFRONTING KLEY

PCs who put various clues (discovered during previous portions of this adventure) together—the most glaringly obvious of which was finding the old blue coat in the margr lair and learning of Kley's brand-new coat requisitioned a week ago—may come to suspect Ranger Kley of wrongdoing. If they confront him, he lies through his teeth about having anything to hide, first laughing it off, then feigning anger.

Of course, he knows that the jig is probably up, but outwardly continues to claim he is being unfairly disparaged. He wants to know just *what exactly* the characters think he could have done to bring the demons down on Blue Cloud. If the characters suggest he had something to do with the Nightwalker's disappearance, he just laughs. What could he, asks Kley, a simple man, do against a god?

If the characters ask to search his house, he agrees. If they just go to his house and search it without his permission, he acts outraged, going so far as to call others to his aid. However, he is really just trying to work out how to flee Blue Cloud unnoticed. He'll attempt to slip away and steal a mount or vehicle (if PCs brought one with them) if at all possible. Kley doesn't fight the PCs unless they attack him, and even so, he attempts to use his ray emitter (paralysis) cypher to delay them so he can escape. He doesn't want to face the consequences of his actions.

Kley's Cellar: A big, shed-like, slanted door on the side of Kley's house is locked (Kley has the key on his person). PCs standing right next to it might notice light coming through the cracks. If characters get past the door, they find steep stairs leading down into the dank cellar. Lots of drying vegetables are down there, as well as an old wheelbarrow. Around a half-wall, a bright light shines.

Moving around the corner, they find a strange creature, about the size of a human, with two insect-like legs, no arms, and an almost human-like face protruding from its carapace. It is curled up, as if sleeping, in the bright light shed by no fewer than three major glowglobes equidistantly spaced around it, so no part of its body is in shadow.

The slumbering entity is the sleeping aspect of a mazocacoth (known by Blue Cloud residents as the Nightwalker). If PCs remove or cover the bright lights, they will witness an amazing transformation (or, at least, they will when night falls, if it's not already dark). The sleeper expands as it rises up into the air, transforming into the gigantic form of the Nightwalker—destroying Kley's house in the process if it was not already outside.

CONCLUDING THE ADVENTURE

If PCs were merely passing through, they could continue on their way at any time. However, the town would be in their debt if they helped out.

If the PCs helped out with the attack and agreed to scout the margr lair, possibly disrupting it somewhat in the process, Blue Cloud still benefits, and PCs can feel happy to have helped.

However, if they figured out Kley was actually to blame for the problem and release the Nightwalker, the mere sight of its transformation is a heart-gladdening experience, one shared with every resident of Blue Cloud (except one). Indeed, even the Nightwalker itself seems to bow its strange, cloud-sized body in recognition of the PCs' actions before it passes over the nearest mountain peak, free.

XP Award: The PCs each earn 1 XP if they reveal Kley as the perpetrator, and another 2 XP if they release the sleeper back to its nightly travels.

Locked cellar
door: *level 4*

Serri, page 117

Mazocacoth, page 64

Ranger Kley, page 118

CHAPTER 11

TRAVELERS NEVER DID LIE

Geofra's Attack, page 141

"Travelers Never Did Lie" is an adventure that can begin anywhere in the Ninth World. It's suitable for mid-tier characters. It can be adjusted for low-tier characters by decreasing the specific numbers of creatures that appear by one, or in the case of the final encounter (Geofra's Attack), by two or three. The adventure can be adjusted for high-tier characters by ramping up the number of enemy creatures that appear during combat encounters by two or three. (The difficulties for social tasks do not need to be adjusted.)

Ideally, this adventure is one you layer into another adventure (or larger campaign) that requires the PCs to travel for at least several days between locations of interest.

SYNOPSIS

The adventure is time- and event-based, rather than location-based, suitable for taking place while characters are traveling in the company of other NPCs. Some events happen whether or not the PCs engage with the NPCs, though if the characters are involved, they'll have a greater insight on things, and have the chance to steer the adventure's final outcome.

Meet Your Traveling Companions: If this is a stand-alone adventure, characters begin already traveling in the company of a small mercenary group who call themselves the Company of the Azure Skull, having concluded that traveling together is safer than traveling alone. (Otherwise, you can use one or more of the adventure hooks described hereafter. The alternate adventure hooks provide the PCs and mercenaries with an opportunity to travel together.) This section describes the NPCs, then suggests a few initial encounters during the ongoing trip designed to further acquaint the PCs with the mercenaries.

Tested in Crisis: An attack by dangerous creatures allows the PCs and the mercenaries to work together (or not), granting the opportunity to potentially bond with one or more of the NPCs composing the Company of the Azure Skull. During this combat, PCs probably become aware that the mercenaries carry a literal object from which they take their name (the Azure Skull of the Avatar), which is a powerful artifact.

Troubled Relations: Relationships among the NPCs are strained for a couple of reasons. The PCs see, and possibly interact during, a few situations that boil over. PCs may choose to intercede as peacemakers, or just watch. The encounters in this section can occur at a rate determined by the GM, though guidance is provided, and the PCs' actions could alter that timeline.

Treachery or Redemption: A magistrix named Geofra, who has been tracking the company, finally launches her ambush. Part of her plan includes gaining the cooperation of one of the company members (Sorino), who she hopes to turn against the others. How the PCs previously interacted with Sorino and the rest of the company determines how the conflict plays out—and ultimately affects whether or not the PCs protect the company from its enemies.

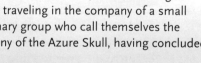

PCs have the opportunity to greatly affect the final demeanor of their NPC companions if they can muster a little compassion during the course of the adventure.

ALTERNATE ADVENTURE HOOKS

There are several possible ways that PCs could find themselves traveling with the mercenaries, including the following options.

Accidental Road Companions: By pure coincidence, the PCs and the mercenaries are traveling in the same direction, though probably for completely different reasons. So the first few interactions that happen prior to those noted under Meet Your Traveling Companions are random meetings on the road. After the second coincidental meeting, one of the NPCs (or perhaps even one of the PCs) suggests that the two groups travel together for as long as they share the same route.

Asked to Help: The characters are required by their patron—or asked by a friend, relative, or ally—to accompany a group of mercenaries across the Steadfast. The mercenaries say they are traveling to witness the scarred monoliths that float high above the gallen herds of Ghan: massive humanoid statues that drift slowly across the sky. According to the mercenaries' leader Qoreen, one of the statues may soon animate and fly off into the heavens, and she wants to be nearby to witness this event. (She won't explain how she has this foreknowledge, at least not initially, other than to say, "It is given to me to know such things.")

However, whether the scarred monolith animates and flies into the heavens (or does something more dangerous to nearby communities) doesn't play directly into this adventure. Instead, it serves as an excuse for the PCs to join the mercenaries for a time. This means that if you have a pretext for PCs joining the mercenaries more appropriate to your campaign, you should use that.

Glimmer: A character receives a hard-to-interpret message from the datasphere. The message is essentially the image of a translucent blue crystal skull and a feeling of imminent disaster. Luckily, the glimmer came with some directions attached saying where to start looking. If the PCs follow up, they find a company calling itself the Company of the Azure Skull.

LOWERING TENSION IN THE CAMP

During the course of this adventure, PCs will have the opportunity to interact with a group of NPCs—the Company of the Azure Skull—who are having a rough patch in their interpersonal relations. At certain points, PCs can choose to interact with an NPC. If PCs do so in a compassionate and convincing way, they have a chance to lower tension in the camp. Each time they do so, this lowered tension has knock-on effects among the Company of the Azure Skull's personnel so that instead of pushing each other further away, they begin to knit themselves back together.

Keep track of the number of times the PCs lower camp tension. The number becomes important in the last scene of the adventure, Treachery or Redemption.

However, don't tell the PCs that this is something you're tracking. Just let the PCs interact with the NPCs as they normally would, which could also be to do nothing. Of course, a few PCs could involve themselves in a way that actually raises tension in the camp. Count those occurrences too.

MEET YOUR TRAVELING COMPANIONS

The three principals of the Company of the Azure Skull are Eaylish the Shimmer, Qoreen the Crasher, and Sorino.

The mercenaries often take on small or short-term commissions brought to them by locals in the areas through which they travel. Qoreen has contacts in most major cities and in all of the nine kingdoms of the Steadfast. However, the company never stays in one location long. They seem driven to move about the world by some deeper, secret source. When they arrive at a new location, more often than not, they are just in time to witness a strange occurrence, find a completely new ruin, or sometimes even show up just in time to help those in desperate need. (The truth is that their impetus derives from an artifact carried by Qoreen the Crasher called the Azure Skull of the Avatar, described hereafter.)

What Blue Skull Are You Named After? If PCs ask about the company's name, everyone looks to Qoreen to answer. Early on in the characters' association, she says only that she sometimes has a feeling about future events, and that feeling is associated with a translucent blue crystal skull. Later, PCs probably learn the full truth, which is that she literally carries an azure skull, usually hidden away among her other equipment.

Scarred monoliths, page 142

Azure Skull of the Avatar, page 136

EAYLISH THE SHIMMER

Appearance: Goggled human female wearing elaborate leather armor. Phantoms of blue light play about her, seeming to obey her mood as well as her explicit instructions.

About: Eaylish comes across as mannered and privileged, friendly to other people she believes to be of equal (or higher) status, and a bit cold to those she thinks are of lower status.

She grew up as the eldest daughter of wealthy nobles. With no responsibilities, she was bored and spoiled. She enjoyed stealing things and causing trouble, knowing that her parents would fix it. One life-changing theft from an Aeon Priest was of a glass jar of sparkling blue motes, which she accidentally broke. The motes sank into her skin and somehow gave her the ability to manipulate light in the form of complex illusions and painful, searing blasts of radiant energy. These abilities allowed her to commit more interesting crimes and, because she always wore an illusory mask of someone else's face (often a rival noble scion who annoyed or offended her), these actions never came back to harm her.

Eaylish isn't a bad person—she's never killed anyone (in cold blood), she hasn't stolen anything that the victim couldn't afford to lose, and she doesn't go out of her way to mistreat people of lesser status than herself. Thanks to her privilege and power, she's never had to deal with the negative consequences of her actions, so she continues to escalate her "hobby," taking greater risks and stealing more valuable things just for the excitement of it—which is why she joined the Company of the Azure Skull. She saw it as an opportunity to expand her activities into distant locations, and she wasn't disappointed. At least, not on that front.

Personal Conflict: What she didn't expect was that she would develop feelings for Sorino, a fellow mercenary. Feelings that developed despite knowing Sorino is of lower status than herself. In order to try to deny those feelings, she is argumentative and cross with him, to the point of being rude. If her contrariness keeps up, it threatens to break the mercenaries apart.

Stats: level 5; disguise (due to illusion), Speed defense, and stealth as level 7; health 22; Armor 2; long-range light blasts inflict 6 points of damage; create a terrifying illusion that affects up to three people in long range who must make an Intellect defense roll or flee for one minute; create one or two human-sized illusions within short range and make them follow a specific series of actions (lasting up to a minute, then ending or repeating)

QOREEN THE CRASHER

Appearance: Human female who wears white and gold clothing and wields a weapon of the prior worlds in each hand. Her eyes seem to be missing pupils, her lower legs are at least partly prosthetic, and a golden circlet is melded to her head.

About: Qoreen is very matter-of-fact and not immediately given to small talk. That's because, for many years, she was unable to control her own location and never knew when she'd be snatched away to some other place beyond her control. That no-nonsense manner actually hides loneliness built up over several years.

Her previous random "deployments" were not by her choice but rather determined by a powerful and once-mysterious intellect that would teleport her where it wanted her to go, with no explanation or warning.

She gained some control over her own destiny when she discovered the source of her jumping about the world was an artifact she calls the Azure Skull of the Avatar (see description hereafter). She captured the skull when it finally materialized one day a few years ago after she spent several days in meditation, attempting to psychically contact it. This was a big turning point for Qoreen. She now keeps the artifact on her person, wrapped in gauze and leather so it isn't obvious. Though she has yet to fully crack the skull's origin or purpose, she now has some control over her life—but not as much as she had, at first, hoped.

Personal Conflict: Qoreen is constantly urged by the skull to investigate new locations and new situations. However, she maintains control over it, preventing it from bodily transporting her without permission by promising to investigate in due time and with a group to help her (namely, the Company of the Azure Skull, who she recruited both to help and to assuage her loneliness).

But now, conflicts in the group she put together are beginning to show. She thought that Eaylish and Sorino were perfectly suited to the company at first, but now it seems the two hate each other, which colors every interaction they have. Qoreen values them both, but their bickering is beginning to disrupt the group. Despite not having any evidence one way or the other, she's pretty sure Sorino is to blame.

Above and beyond that, the conflict reminded Qoreen that she is *tired*. Before she captured the skull, she traveled about for years without any ability to refuse. Things are better now, but she is still subject to the skull's psychic pressure to travel. She is beginning to wonder if she can pass the skull to someone else.

Stats: level 5; acrobatics (from prosthetics), initiative, ranged attacks, Speed defense, and Intellect defense as level 6; health 23; Armor 1; two long-range slugspitter (level 5) attacks inflict 5 points of damage each; carries the Azure Skull of the Avatar

Slugspitter (but with the form shown in Qoreen's illustration), page 301

Qoreen has a habit of turning up unexpectedly, sometimes in the middle of a lost ruin or right before some unexpected event occurs. One of the PCs may have even heard her name and of her reputation for "showing up where needed."

AZURE SKULL OF THE AVATAR

Level: 10

Form: Translucent blue crystal object: skull-like, with an elongated forehead

Motivation: The physical skull is the focus of a transdimensional entity's attention here. The skull's true motivations are probably unknowable, but manifest as a desire to observe various locations and events. Most of those are related to ancient ruins or momentous events somehow related to the prior worlds. Other times, what the skull wants to see seems inconsequential to its bearer. In either case, the skull is somehow able to anticipate situations that involve humans interacting with a long-inactive device of the numenera, or when humans are caught up in a dangerous phenomenon of the same.

Effect: A first-time bearer of the skull must succeed on a difficulty 6 Intellect defense roll, or the skull phases, becoming invisible but still associated with the bearer. In this situation, the bearer is sometimes randomly teleported to other locations in accordance with the skull's motivations. However, if a bearer succeeds on their defense roll (or later comes up with a method to successfully renegotiate the relationship), the skull is retained as a physical object.

The bearer of the physical skull is randomly subject to psychic pressure to visit various places around the Steadfast and the Beyond. The user isn't given the name of the location they are being pushed to investigate, but gains very specific directions via the psychic connection, as well as an offer to simply be teleported there (sans any companions). At first, the psychic pressure is fleeting, but if ignored, it grows to be something that the bearer must concentrate on if they wish to ignore it over the next few weeks. The pressure eases if the bearer accedes and begins a journey to the new location, or allows themself to be teleported.

A bearer of the Azure Skull (whether it is physical or phased) can also call on a couple of additional psychic abilities as an action; however, doing so causes crippling psychic pain for the bearer, which lasts for about a minute and prevents them from taking any turns during this period. The abilities that can be called upon include: a long-range psychic blast that inflicts 17 points of damage to a target; the ability to teleport (bearer or one unwilling target within short range) to a previously visited location (or one that the skull knows about); and the ability to command a target to take a specific course of action, though commanding the target to do direct harm to themself grants the target an additional Intellect defense roll eased by two steps.

Depletion: 1 in 1d6 (Upon depletion, the skull is powerless. It grows as black as pitch and, for the following three nights, the user has nightmares of falling into the heart of that darkness. On the fourth night, the nightmares are gone, the skull is back to normal, and no longer depleted.)

Creatures with sensitivity to transdimensional energy are drawn to the skull, so anyone bearing it faces threats from entities from alternate and/or bizarre dimensions from time to time.

SORINO

Appearance: Human male, late twenties, with a shaved head. Sorino's most distinguishing feature is a second mouth on his right palm with textured, green-black lips and a long tongue composed of blue energy. He sometimes wears a glove on his right hand when he doesn't want to draw attention to the oddity.

About: Once colorful and bold, Sorino used to have a joke or wry comment to make about any given situation. However, that light-hearted spirit has lately taken a beating, given the troubles between him and Eaylish, which have created troubles between him and Qoreen, too. So, by the time the characters first meet him, he can come across as brooding and a bit short-tempered.

Sorino is a master cook and baker, and still fulfills that role in the Company of the Azure Skull. (However, his once-elaborate meals have become fairly utilitarian of late, though he still enjoys making mushroom handpies.) While he was exploring a strange prior-world citadel in Navarene, west of the confluence of the Tithe and Jerribost rivers, he interacted with a machine that imparted his ancillary mouth. Delighted rather than horrified, he spent the next few years learning how to use it. About a year ago, he was recruited by Qoreen to join her company. Given his desire to explore, it seemed like a perfect opportunity, so he accepted.

Personal Conflict: Sorino actually thought he and Eaylish had become friends, despite her strange notions of class and station. Possibly a friendship that could become even more. But something changed, and he's started to resent the mere sight of her.

To make matters worse, Sorino feels that Qoreen blames *him* for the spat. She even went so far as to insinuate that he, Sorino, apologize to Eaylish for whatever it was he'd done. The feeling of being rejected by Eaylish and chastised for something not his fault by Qoreen has put him in a foul mood.

Rather than talk to anyone about it, he's fallen to brooding. It was right around this time he was secretly contacted by a mysterious someone named Geofra. (The contact came through Sorino's ancillary mouth, which Geofra figured out how to temporarily hijack in order to pass messages across long distances.) She wants Sorino to help her acquire the Azure Skull. Sorino flatly refused. He continues to talk with Geofra in the privacy of his own tent because he is on the outs with the other two members of the Company of the Azure Skull.

Stats: level 5, cooking as level 6; health 22; Armor 1; two short-range energy tongue attacks inflict 5 points of damage each; can ask questions of the mouth and gain truthful insights; can communicate with other individuals who know how to interface with the mouth (such as Geofra)

CAMPFIRE TIME

The PCs can choose to interact with the following scene, or just watch it play out, as they choose. Options for how things play out if PCs get involved are provided.

Geofra, page 141

As the sun leaves the sky, Sorino breaks out his cooking supplies and begins to put together a scrumptious-smelling meal of mushroom handpies. Eaylish looks on, but seems to stiffen with surprise or anger when Sorino glances up and catches her eye. She mutters something under her breath.

Sorino responds by taking one of the handpies and tossing it into the flames, saying, "Well, maybe that will be more to your liking."

Qoreen emerges from her tent just in time to witness the handpie begin to char among the coals. She says, "Will you two stop it? I swear by the Avatar that you're both acting like children."

If any character cares to try to overhear what Eaylish said under her breath, a successful difficulty 4 perception task reveals it was, "Such lowbrow food, these handpies. I grow so tired of them."

If no PC cares to become involved in the situation, no further interpersonal hostilities occur. However, the three Company of the Azure Skull members proceed through the rest of the night in a sort of sullen silence.

Assuaging the Situation: However, if characters say something meant to calm the situation or otherwise draw attention to themselves to reduce tension (such as by telling a story, playing an instrument, and so on), they must succeed on a difficulty 5 persuasion task. On a success, the ice among the NPCs seems to thin a bit.

Qoreen will tell a story about how she once saw a star fall from the sky, which turned out to be a craft containing creatures who needed healing. She provided it, and once they made repairs to their craft, they flew back into the night like a star falling in reverse.

If a PC or two follows in kind with stories or revelations about themselves, Sorino joins in and talks about how he used to be a baker in his community before the lure of exploration pulled him into the world. (If PCs ask about his ancillary mouth, he is happy to demonstrate it; sometimes it sings, on its own or when asked to.)

A success here counts as decreasing the tension in the camp. Add this to wherever you're tracking the tension throughout the adventure.

CAN I TALK TO YOU?

An hour after the events of Campfire Time resolve, Eaylish approaches one or more of the PCs (especially if they have any air of nobility or status to them) and asks if she can confer with them on a sensitive topic. If PCs agree, she lays out the following.

⮞ READ ALOUD ⮜

Eaylish says, "Can I ask where you are from? I get the unmistakable sense that you are of noble lineage. Is that true? You don't know what it's like to be here out on the road with only riff-raff to keep one company."

The character or characters can choose to humor Eaylish, or challenge some of her assumptions. If PCs reassure her and/or allow

her to proceed, Eaylish tells a story about how she grew up and how things out in the wild are so different. She tells of trying to break out of the rules of high society, but how those same rules have a way of always pulling her back in.

Assuaging Eaylish: Merely listening is enough; Eaylish feels a bit less isolated, and the interaction counts towards lessening overall tension in the camp. However, characters might be emboldened to offer her advice about the need to follow the so-called rules of her previous station. If so, they must succeed on a difficulty 5 persuasion task. If they succeed, it actually takes Eaylish back a bit. She blinks and says that's not something she'd thought about before. She says it's something she'll have to think about, as she steals a glance at Sorino (or his tent).

If they were successful in making Eaylish think about things, this decreases the tension in the camp. Add this to wherever you're tracking the tension throughout the adventure. However, if PCs fail the therapeutic-persuasion task, they don't really get through to her, and the tension remains the same.

TESTED IN CRISIS

After the PCs have a few interactions with the NPCs of the company, the entire group comes under attack. If you're running this adventure as part of a larger campaign in which the PCs are exploring a ruin (and the Company of the Azure Skull is accompanying them), the attack should come from whatever threats are related to that. Alternatively, if during the course of the campaign the PCs have previously made any enemies with the ability to follow and attack them (or to send agents to do the same), those enemies attack.

If none of that is suitable, you can use the following.

Erynth Grask Ambush: Two multi-tentacled, wormlike erynth grask stalk and ambush the PCs and the Company of the Azure Skull. They set up the ambush by quietly burrowing underground, then simultaneously using their telekinetic attack abilities, each sending a tentacle to reach up out of the ground— one beneath a PC and another under a mercenary—that shorts out the victim's nervous system for one round.

◈ READ ALOUD ◈

A cloud of small loose stones and unsecured bits of equipment rise up into the air, released from the earth's grasp. The floating material becomes a hail of dangerous projectiles a moment later as it implodes—with you at the center. At the same time, the earth shudders beneath you, then splits open to reveal a tentacled horror.

Handling the Erynth Grask Combat:
The erynth grask can make multiple attacks each round, as described in their creature entry. They are higher level than the NPCs, so when one is attacked, the NPC is usually affected. One of the creatures usually keeps the NPCs busy while the other attacks the PCs.

Ideally, this attack gives the PCs and NPCs a chance to help each other. For instance, if a PC is stunned, one of the NPCs uses an ability or cypher to return the character to normal. If a PC is hurt, an NPC uses a cypher or ability to heal them. The PCs may, of course, choose to help the NPCs in the same way.

Use GM intrusions (even the appearance of another attacker if necessary) to keep the fight desperate if it isn't already. Ideally, the combat should make the PCs at least a little afraid for their lives.

Ending the Fight: Finally, Qoreen decides that the only thing for it is to reveal her secret. She pulls the Azure Skull of the Avatar out of its wrappings, screaming, *"Is this what you're looking for? Then behold!"* As she yells, she triggers the artifact's psychic blast ability to inflict 17 points of damage, directing it against a surviving erynth grask. This either kills it or causes it (and any of its surviving fellows) to attempt to flee the field by burrowing away.

Combat Aftermath: Ideally, Qoreen used the skull to end the fight, which, of course, reveals the existence of the skull to the PCs. Presumably, PCs have questions, though Qoreen can't answer for about a minute if she used the psychic blast. Once she recovers, she sighs and promises to explain, once everyone's wounds are tended to, and it's certain that all the attacking entities are either dead or gone and unlikely to return.

TROUBLED RELATIONS

Relationships among the three principals of the Company of the Azure Skull—Eaylish the Shimmer, Qoreen the Crasher, and Sorino—remain strained even after the erynth grask attack. PCs have a few more opportunities to interact with the NPCs and reduce tensions. How they interact in these situations affects the final encounter described in Treachery or Redemption.

HEAVY IS THE HEAD THAT WEARS THE CROWN

Not long after the erynth grask attack, Qoreen approaches the PCs (or they approach her, wanting to know more about the situation). She comes clean, summarizing the situation as follows.

◈ READ ALOUD ◈

Qoreen says, "The Azure Skull of the Avatar is the real reason I and my band of 'mercenaries' travel to and fro across the Steadfast and the Beyond. We do take the odd commission now and then from those we meet along the way, but it's to fill gaps in time and help finance the trips we would have made anyway. You see, the Azure Skull of the Avatar is the focus for a transdimensional intelligence, and it prompts me to move around the world so it can witness strange locations and events. Somehow, it seems to know ahead of time where momentous things will happen."

Qoreen will continue to describe her relationship with the skull, as noted under her description, if PCs are interested. She says that, from time to time, various transdimensional horrors melt out of this reality's fabric, apparently drawn by the skull's power. Also, using the skull's abilities has a debilitating effect on the user, as the PCs may have witnessed. It's obvious to PCs that an edge of sorrow seems to underlie all she says.

Assuaging Qoreen: If the PCs inquire and succeed on a difficulty 2 persuasion task to get her to open up, she reveals how the strain between her two fellow Company members is wearing her down, reminding her how tired she actually is of a life lived almost entirely on the road. She is afraid that tiredness is making her testy with the other two, reducing her effectiveness as a leader. And, instead of seeking ways to heal the growing rift between

Eaylish the Shimmer, page 134

Qoreen the Crasher, page 135

Sorino, page 136

GM intrusion:
The erynth grask tunnels up directly beneath the PC, giving it an automatic hit with its bite and tentacles and knocking the character prone.

Eaylish and Sorino, she is probably only forcing the gap between them wider.

Merely listening to Qoreen eases her distress. It counts toward decreasing the overall tension among the travelers. Add this to wherever you're tracking the tension throughout the adventure.

Giving Qoreen Advice: If characters decide to take on the role of advice-givers to Qoreen, they must then make a difficulty 5 persuasion task. If they succeed (and actually have good advice), Qoreen seems to take it to heart and, if applicable, acts on the advice later.

TALKING TO HIMSELF

One evening (possibly even the same evening after the erynth grask fight, if the period when the PCs and mercenaries will be traveling together will soon draw to a close), one of the characters notices something that seems a little bit out of the ordinary.

The hushed sound of an argument emanates from Sorino's tent. A bluish glow from within illuminates Sorino's silhouette. It almost looks like he is arguing with his hand.

If PCs draw close enough to eavesdrop, they overhear the following.

◦ READ ALOUD ◦

Sorino says, "I already told you, Geofra, that's not the way I want to do it!"

A different voice, definitely not Sorino's, replies, "You said you'd think about it. Well, have you? Because I doubt your so-called friends have seen the light. Or apologized to you? Or even talked to you?"

"No, not really," Sorino mumbles. "Maybe you're right. Maybe—"

"Quiet," the strange voice hisses. "Someone's listening."

If PCs stick around, they see the light flicker out and, a round later, Sorino emerges from his tent to look around for listeners. The PCs can elude detection if they slip away, or remain and ask Sorino who he was talking to—possibly even inquire who Geofra might be. If they succeed on a difficulty 3 persuasion task, Sorino will be halfway truthful, and tell the PCs that he's been feeling a bit ostracized by the other two members of the company, and that he's taken to talking to the ancillary mouth to make himself feel better. For no particular reason, he says, he calls the ancillary mouth "Geofra."

Convergence, page 216

Assuaging Sorino: If the characters try to make Sorino feel better by assuring him things aren't really that bad, that they're happy to talk, or similar, that's sufficient to help decrease the overall tension among the company; even just listening to his troubles counts. Add this to wherever you're tracking the tension throughout the adventure.

Confronting Sorino: However, if the PCs press, demanding to know who Geofra is, the outcome is less certain. If one of the PCs actually healed or otherwise directly helped Sorino during the fight with the erynth grask, and that character succeeds on a difficulty 4 persuasion task, Sorino finally comes clean. He says that some entity called Geofra started speaking to him *through* the mouth, but is not *of* the mouth. Geofra wants Sorino's help in obtaining the Azure Skull of the Avatar.

Sorino tells the characters that—of course—he won't be helping Geofra. He even half-believes that himself. However, what he actually does isn't revealed until the events described in Treachery or Redemption occur. Unbeknownst to Sorino, Geofra is monitoring events near him through his ancillary mouth, and she could launch her ambush within just a few rounds if the PCs believe they have stumbled onto something sinister and demand an explanation. If they do, the events described in Treachery or Redemption occur immediately, instead of at some point later in the overall journey.

OTHER INTERACTIONS

Other interactions between the PCs and the members of the Company of the Azure Skull occur organically if this adventure is part of a larger campaign. They can also be layered into a regular adventure where they are all involved in a secondary task, like exploring a ruin or, as earlier suggested, investigating the scarred monoliths in Ghan.

But sooner or later, the events described under Treachery or Redemption occur.

TREACHERY OR REDEMPTION

A Convergence magister tries to take the Azure Skull by force. The only question is whether the company named after the artifact is working as a cohesive team or a splintered crew of self-doubting failures.

GEOFRA'S PLAN

A magistrix named Geofra uses the fix she has on Sorino's ancillary mouth to locate the Company of the Azure Skull (whether she has Sorino's cooperation or not). She takes some time to assemble what she hopes is an overwhelming force (limited only by the number of allies she can teleport to the company's location in order to launch an attack).

Which is why, in addition to gathering allies, Geofra has been working on turning Sorino away from the company and into her ally instead. She has been doing this through a combination of listening to Sorino's laments and applying various gaslighting techniques. Has she succeeded? The PCs' interactions over the preceding days or weeks (if any) help decide.

GEOFRA'S ATTACK

Geofra and several allies appear within a short distance of the Company of the Azure Skull and the PCs. Allied NPCs (and probably the PCs themselves) are too surprised to do anything other than let the brief interaction, described in the read-aloud text hereafter, play out.

If PCs succeed in initiating combat before the interaction plays out completely, Geofra—holding a long staff (an artifact called a terrorizer)—still uses her first turn to demand the skull from Qoreen, who provides her answer in the same round. Enemy NPCs defend themselves from PC attacks, if any, and use their actions to protect Geofra from any direct PC attacks against her. Allied NPCs are still too surprised to act.

On round two, Geofra puts her question to Sorino instead. Sorino makes his decision during the same round. After that, round-to-round combat continues normally.

☙ READ ALOUD ❧

A polygon of light smashes down from the sky, pounding the ground. The structure instantly evaporates, revealing two humans and several creatures standing unharmed in the small crater. The creatures include a human-sized insect, a shambling automaton, and a few hound-like lizards that crackle with electricity.

One of the humans carries a long staff and is accompanied by a floating device. The staff-wielder points the staff at Qoreen. "Hand over the skull, or have it taken from you."

Qoreen guffaws. "The skull stays with me."

The stranger fixes her gaze on Sorino and says, "Well?"

Sorino's Decision: Even if the PCs don't understand the backstory as to why this stranger is talking to Sorino, the PCs' earlier interactions help determine Sorino's answer.

If the PCs previously decreased the tension in the group three or more times, Sorino laughs at Geofra's question, saying, *"There is no world in which I would betray my friends."* (The PCs' activity in the camp have turned the group dynamics around, which means "convincing" Sorino to rebuff Geofra's offer is a routine action on the part of the PCs and the other NPCs. Therefore, he rebuffs it without anyone having to make him think twice about making a bad decision.)

However, if the PCs decreased tension only once or twice, then more convincing is required to bolster Sorino's inclination to rebuff Geofra in the moment, despite all her gaslighting. In this case, any attempt by the PCs to defuse the situation, or to remind Sorino of who his true comrades are, is eased by one or two steps, respectively, against a difficulty of 5. (One step for each time the PCs successfully decreased the tension in the camp.)

If the PC fails at the persuasion task, Sorino joins Geofra. He makes an instant surprise attack against Qoreen, reducing her to 1 health and knocking her unconscious. Then the combat proceeds normally.

If the PC succeeds, Sorino stays loyal. He says, *"There is no world in which I would betray my friends,"* and then the combat proceeds normally.

The Combat With Geofra: The PCs and the Company of the Azure Skull stand off against Geofra and her allies.

The Company of the Azure Skull includes the allied PCs, Eaylish, and maybe Qoreen and Sorino, unless Sorino joins Geofra and knocks out Qoreen.

Geofra's forces include herself, Kaylara (a spy), and several servitor creatures under Geofra's control, including a human-sized insectile oniscid, a mech shambler, and three babirasa.

Allied NPCs among the company choose enemy NPCs who are not already engaged by at least one PC. For NPC vs. NPC battles, it's not necessary to figure out exactly what's happening each round; just compare levels and decide how things will probably end up within two or three rounds. By then, PCs may be in a position to offer some aid to flagging NPCs.

Generally, the enemy NPCs approach the combat as follows.

Sorino (if radicalized by Geofra): After his surprise betrayal attack on Qoreen, Sorino focuses on Eaylish with his ancillary mouth attacks.

Geofra: Geofra focuses on taking out the PCs with terrorizer attacks, setting up her babirasa to attack the now-defenseless PCs.

Kaylara: The spy tries to find cover and fires poisoned ranged attacks at her foes.

Oniscid: The creature uses its subsonic abilities to cause foes to hallucinate and/or flee in terror.

Mech shambler: The automaton takes control of any device used against it; otherwise, it fires three energy beams per round at foes.

Babirasa: The creatures initially target foes stunned by Geofra, but otherwise just attack opportunistically.

Geofra: *level 6, mental defense and deception as level 7; Armor 4 (lasts ten minutes via esotery); two long-range pain attacks from staff inflict 4 points of damage each and, on a subsequent failed Might defense roll, targets lose their next turn; accompanied by a crashdown transporter artifact*

Crashdown transporter, page 37

Eaylish the Shimmer, page 134

Qoreen the Crasher, page 135

Sorino, page 136

Kaylara (spy), page 286

Oniscid, page 269

Mech shambler, page 266

Babirasa, page 254

GM intrusion: *A PC must succeed on a difficulty 5 Speed defense roll, or the teleportation effect used by Geofra "lands" on them, inflicting 5 points of damage and knocking them down.*

Concluding the Fight: If Qoreen wasn't ambushed by Sorino, she should still be part of the combat as things begin to wind toward a conclusion. If it looks like Geofra's side is about to win, Qoreen produces the Azure Skull of the Avatar and uses its ability to eliminate Geofra (either through damage or by teleporting her). Using the skull causes Qoreen severe psychic pain, but she finally sees there is no other choice.

However, if Sorino laid Qoreen low, the fight just plays out normally. How well the PCs fight determines the outcome of the combat. If given a reasonable opportunity, Geofra steals the skull from the unconscious Qoreen (or even takes her whole body) and teleports away in the same way she arrived (via the crashdown transporter).

WRAPPING UP THE ADVENTURE

Among the many ways this adventure can end are the following two starkly different endpoints.

Geofra Steals the Skull: This scenario probably only plays out if Sorino joined Geofra, and thus effectively took Qoreen out of the fight (in turn preventing Qoreen from using the skull's extreme abilities to turn the fight around). In this case, Geofra takes the skull and teleports away in the same way she appeared, possibly leaving one or more of the PCs alive.

This outcome could serve to instigate one or more additional adventures if surviving PCs wish to exact vengeance on Geofra, and/or regain the skull, but that's something for you to decide for your own game or campaign.

Geofra Rebuffed: If Geofra is rebuffed *and* the PCs helped Sorino recognize who his actual friends are, then the PCs see Eaylish and Sorino embrace after the conflict concludes (assuming they both survive). Eaylish promises to get over her status issues, and Sorino promises, in turn, to stop doubting himself.

However, the event also leads Qoreen to question whether she remains the best bearer of the skull. If at least one of the PCs is on good terms with Qoreen, she may approach them soon after and offer up the burden of bearing the Azure Skull of the Avatar. She explains how it works, and further, how the pressure to travel never lets up. But, seeing as how the PC seems to enjoy that sort of life already and how they rebuffed the Convergence member who tried to steal it, they might just make an ideal carrier. It's up to the PC (or PCs) whether they want to take on a companion that is essentially a disembodied extradimensional alien intelligence driven by raw curiosity about the Ninth World.

XP Award: The PCs each earn 1 XP each time they lowered tension in the camp. In addition, they earn 1 XP if they help the Company of the Azure Skull repel Geofra's attempt to steal the skull.

Azure Skull of the Avatar, page 136

INDEX

air travel, equipment 16
airfins (cypher) 44
anywhere door (artifact) 45
armor, underwater 18
augmech crown (cypher) 44
augmech handset (cypher) 44
augmech throne (artifact) 45
autarch actuator (artifact) 45
basic travel equipment 13
book of doors (artifact) 45
bridge builder (cypher) 44
bubble flyer (cypher) 44
burrowing boots (artifact) 45
carapace component, wings (artifact) 45
cloudskimmer (cypher) 44
Codex of Travel 40
conveyance supremacy
(optional rule) 80
crashdown transporter (artifact) 45
crossroads vestibule (artifact) 45
Croxton (NPC) 73
customization, by numenera device 32
customizations, other types for
vehicles and mounts 34–36
customizations, weapons for
vehicles and mounts 33–34
Darli Kos (NPC) 73
datademon 57
Dimensional Survey (ability) 54
divers' disease, effects of 17
Divine Nex (NPC) 73
dreamtooth 58
Duchess Aranda (NPC) 74
Electrical Flight (ability) 54
Encounters and Hazards Table 79
Flight (ability) 54
flight armor (artifact) 45
flight pack (artifact) 45
flux suit (artifact) 45
flying cap (cypher) 44
flying harness (artifact) 45
foldable coach (artifact) 45
glow skates (artifact) 45

GM intrusions, flying vehicle 31
GM intrusions, land vehicle 29
GM intrusions, travel-themed 110–112
GM intrusions, void vehicle 32
GM intrusions, watercraft 30
gnath 59
gray singer 60
grindral 61
Homeworld Bridge (ability) 54
horticuller 62
hover square (artifact) 45
howler 63
hypoxia, effects of 16
instant vehicle (artifact) 45
instant wings (cypher) 44
Into the Outside (ability) 54
Jas the Eye Eater (NPC) 74
jet gloves (artifact) 45
Kresithan (NPC) 75
lacewing shirt (artifact) 45
light flyer (cypher) 44
light steed (cypher) 44
liminal sail (artifact) 45
mazocacoth 64
Mental Projection (ability) 54
Merthon (NPC) 75
mind slime 65
mirrored beast 66
mounts 19–21, 41–42
Nightwalker 64
node interface (artifact) 45
overland travel, equipment 12
overland travel, special equipment 14–15
photon transporter (artifact) 45
pico wheel (artifact) 45
portable steed (cypher) 44
powered boots (artifact) 45
reality eater 67
retenan 68
Return to the Obelisk (ability) 54
road builder (cypher) 44
road imposter 69
Safe Wayfarer Travel Guide 29

Encountering Creatures 56
Meeting Strangers 72
Packing 12
Selecting a Proper Mount 22
Trip Planning 10
Sarrank (NPC) 75
seiskin 70
Storyteller (NPC) 76
Teleportation (ability) 54
teleportation and interdimensional
portals 51–52
teleporter, mass (cypher) 44
teleporter, traveler (cypher) 44
temporary wing (artifact) 45
The Safe Wayfarer Travel Guide to
Selecting the Proper Mount 22
time skipper (cypher) 44
Time Travel (ability) 54
trail blazer (cypher) 44
transdimensional gate (cypher) 44
travel bubble (cypher) 44
travel devices (artifacts) 37–39
travel options, abilities 54
travel options, other 53
traveling shield (artifact) 45
Traverse the Worlds (ability) 54
underwater travel, equipment 17
underwater travel, special equipment 18
vehicles, commonplace air 25, 43
vehicles, commonplace land 23, 43
vehicles, commonplace water 23–24, 43
vehicles, numenera air 30–32, 49
vehicles, numenera land 27–28, 46–47
vehicles, numenera void 30–32, 50–51
vehicles, numenera water 30, 48
vestige 71
void ring (artifact) 45
weapons, underwater 18
Wind Chariot (ability) 54
Windwracked Traveler (ability) 54
wings of the Liminal Shore (artifact) 45
Xeobrencus stone (artifact) 45
Zin the Wanderer (NPC) 76

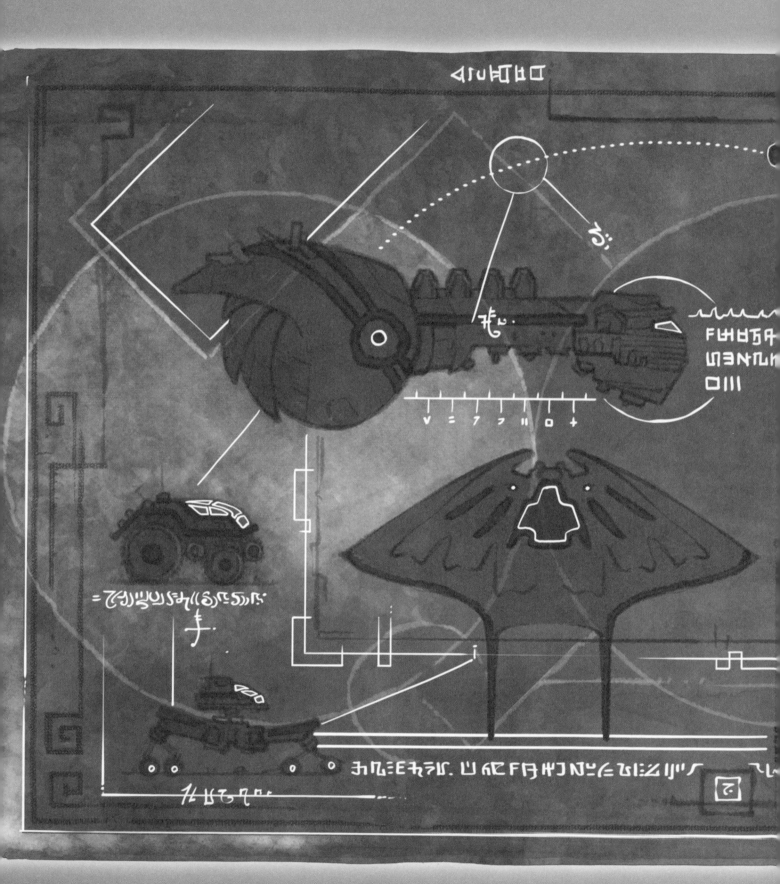